# The Colour of Radio

*The Peter Redgrove Library*

Other Peter Redgrove books available from Stride:

The Peter Redgrove Library:
1. *In the Country of the Skin*
2. *The Terrors of Dr. Treviles* ⋆
3. *The Glass Cottage* ⋆
4. *The God of Glass*
5. *The Sleep of the Great Hypnotist*
6. *The Beekeepers*
7. *The Facilitators*
8. *The Colour of Radio: Essays and Interviews*
[⋆with Penelope Shuttle]

*The Laborators*
*Abyssophone*
*Orchard End*
*What the Black Mirror Saw*
*Sheen*
*A Singer for the Silver Goddess*

*A Curious Architecture* [contributor]
*Earth Ascending* [contributor]

i.m. Peter Redgrove:
*Full of Star's Dreaming: Peter Redgrove 1932-2003*

# The Colour of Radio

*Essays and Interviews*

## Peter Redgrove

edited by Neil Roberts

*To D.M. Thomas with Thanks and best wishes*

*Neil Roberts*

ISBN 1-905024-15-0

Cover design by Neil Annat
Cover photos © Alistair Fitchett
Used with kind permission of the artist

*The Peter Redgrove Library*
*is published by*
Stride Publications
4b Tremayne Close
Devoran
Cornwall TR3 6QE
England

www.stridebooks.co.uk

# Thanks

*The Peter Redgrove Library* is grateful to the following subscribers who have helped make the publication of these titles possible:

Cliff Ashcroft
Andrew Bailey
Martin Bax
Hazel Carruthers
Philip Fried
Mark Goodwin & Nikki Clayton
David Grubb
Michael Longley
Adrian & Celia Mitchell
Brian Louis Pearce
Malcolm Ritchie
Geoff Sutton & Bernard Gilhooly
Leonie Whitton & David Westby

to the following for help, encouragement and support in other ways:

Tony Frazer
Neil Roberts
Penelope Shuttle
the late Philip Hobsbaum

*and to Arts Council England, South West for financial support.*

# Acknowledgements

The interview with Mike Erwin and Jed Rasula is reprinted by permission from *The Hudson Review*, Volume XXVIII, No.3 (Autumn 1975). Copyright 1975 by The Hudson Review, Inc. 'Scientist of the Strange', from *Manhattan Review*, Vol.3 no.1 (Summer 1983) is reprinted by permission of Philip Fried. 'Lazarus and the Visionary Truth' from *Arrows*, University of Sheffield (1984) is reprinted by permission of Cliff Ashcroft.

For reprinting essays and interviews, acknowledgements are also due to the following publishers:

'A Poet in Teaching', *New Universities Quarterly*, Spring 1980; 'The Other Funeral', *Poetry Wales*, 1994; 'The Alchemical Marriage of Redgrove and Shuttle', *We Two: Couples Talk About Living, Loving and Working Partnerships for the '90s*, ed. Chloe Goodchild and Roger Housden, Harpercollins, 1991; 'Work and Incubation: A Sketch of My Method of Writing' (as 'Redgrove's Incubator'), *Poetry Review*, Vol. 85 no.1, Spring 1995; 'The God-Trap', Turret Books, 1966; 'The Science of the Subjective', *Poetry Review*, Vol.77 no.3 , June 1987; 'Rimbaud My Virgil', *Sulfur 30*, Spring 1992; 'Mapping the Great Mind', *Times Literary Supplement*, 30 November 1984; 'The Moods of God', *The Powys Newsletter*, November 2002; 'Windings and Conchings', *Times Literary Supplement*, 11 November 1983; 'Why the Bomb is Real but not True', *Unholy Warfare*, ed. David Martin and Peter Mullen, Blackwell, 1983; 'Mesmer's Vision', *The Ley Hunter*, no.123, 1995; 'Pagan Survivals' from interview in *About Time*, ed. Christopher Rawlence, Jonathan Cape, 1985; 'Am I a Pagan?' from interview in *Pagan Voice*, 6, May 1992.

# CONTENTS

To Penelope Shuttle


'What colour is radio?'
Peter Redgrove, 'Raven at Goonhillie'

# Introduction

Peter Redgrove was not only a prolific poet but an indefatigable writer of prose. He liked to categorise his writing in terms of its relative 'heat': the hottest, at the centre, was his poetry; then progressively cooler, his prose fiction and plays, and his expository prose. He rightly recognised that his unique genius was in his poetry, but he was far from dismissive of his prose. He rarely let slip an opportunity to promote *The Wise Wound*, especially, which he considered an epoch-making contribution to gender study and to modern culture generally.

In his lifetime he published seven novels, a collection of versions of Grimm's tales, two volumes of prose poetry and three books of expository prose: *The Wise Wound*, *The Black Goddess* and *Alchemy for Women*, the first and last of these co-written with Penelope Shuttle. Several other projects of this kind failed to find a publisher. The pieces collected in this volume are very much at the expository end of the spectrum, though 'The Other Funeral' has some of the qualities of Redgrove's prose poetry.

I have not divided the book into parts, but the contents fall informally into four groups, with much overlap, since Redgrove was a writer to whom boundaries were anathema. To begin with the emphasis falls primarily on Redgrove's personal experiences as a son, husband, student, teacher and writer. Through the first three chapters a narrative of his life can be traced. He was born in a middle-class family, to parents who were both stereotypes of gender and vivid eccentrics: his mother was drawn to the occult, and his father excelled in the extravert masculine accomplishments of sport, gambling and confidence trickery. A deep discomfort about masculinity, and lifelong attachment to the feminine, flowed from this childhood. Awkward in personal relationships as a child, he was drawn to the physical sciences, which he studied at Cambridge. Before this, however, he suffered a breakdown on entering compulsory military service, at the age of eighteen. Exaggeratedly diagnosed with 'incipient schizophrenia', he was given insulin shock therapy, consisting of repeated induced comas. This experience of invasive psychiatric treatment seems to have been as traumatic and formative as the electro-convulsive therapy to which Sylvia Plath was subjected at about the same age.

Redgrove's hope that studying science would be an imaginative exploration of the natural world was disappointed at Cambridge, and his most important experiences there were not to do with his formal studies, but with his discovery of poetry. He met Ted Hughes, who remained a friend and not uncritically-regarded example throughout his life, and was welcomed into the 'Group' of poets led by Philip Hobsbaum: an early and very successful poetry workshop.

Leaving Cambridge without a degree, Redgrove married the sculptor Barbara Sherlock and embarked on family life and the life of a breadwinner, working in advertising and scientific journalism. He represents this as a period in which his real needs were buried by conformity to 'tribal' pressures. He published his first collection of poetry in 1959, but it was the award of a three-year Gregory Fellowship at Leeds University in 1963 that broke the mould of his life, leading to the end of his first marriage and whole-hearted dedication to poetry. He moved to Cornwall, where he became Lecturer in Complementary Studies at Falmouth Art College. He met the Jungian analyst John Layard, to whose influence he partly attributed his psychological rebirth at this time. He also, more importantly, met the poet and novelist Penelope Shuttle, who became the inseparable partner of every aspect of his subsequent life. Redgrove reflects profoundly and informatively on all these personal matters in the first three sections of this book.

The next five sections are focussed primarily on Redgrove's own writing. In a short essay he describes his unique method of composition, which can be studied in detail in his archive at Sheffield University; in another he outlines the background to one of his most important poems; and he discusses his work and its context in a series of interviews published between 1975 and 1987. I was initially concerned about including so many interviews: I worried that the effect might be too loose and repetitive. In fact Redgrove is an outstanding interviewee. His answers are almost invariably full, articulate, allusive, and barely distinguishable from discursive prose. I cut some material from the interviews because of repetition, but much less than I expected to. Although Redgrove's discourse invariably revolves around certain central and pressing themes, his was such an enquiring mind that there were always new points of reference, often to recent scientific speculation of a more or less orthodox kind. Redgrove behaved as an interviewee very much the way he did as a correspondent. He always gave generously, and uninhibitedly, what he had in mind, and never seemed uninterested in what his interlocutor had to say, but found every question a way into his own imaginative world. This is perhaps an aspect of what he meant when he referred, approvingly, to the 'egotistical sublime', and lamented its absence in modern poetry.

Although he read very widely in literature as well as in science and religion, Redgrove was not a poet-critic. When I asked him to contribute an essay on Wallace Stevens to a book I was editing, he modestly replied that he felt unqualified to do so. However, he did comment on the work of writers who were particularly important to him, and with whom he felt a special affinity, as well as on his own work. In the third group of pieces in this collection, he writes about Rimbaud, Yeats, Ted Hughes and T.F. Powys. These essays are not, strictly speaking, literary criticism, but explorations of the meeting points between other imaginations and his own. I would dearly have liked to see similar pieces on other writers who were equally important to Redgrove, such as Langland, Blake, Coleridge, St John Perse and Wallace Stevens.

The last informal grouping is of essays and interviews that are directly about aspects of Redgrove's world-view. The lecture, 'Healing, Creativity and the Black Goddess' is his most complete statement of his beliefs about humanity's place in the world, outside his full-length books. It is indeed a precursor to *The Black Goddess* itself. Redgrove's use of the lecture format to invoke the powers and influences present to the unconscious senses in the very room in which he is speaking, is a particularly effective piece of exposition. At the heart of his vision is this awareness of consciousness being linked to everything within and without, of being flooded by messages and influences that consciousness itself does not register: of the dominance of the 'conscious senses', and above all the eye, producing a blindness to most of the sensory information we are receiving. When, in the poem 'Raven at Goonhillie' (*In the Hall of the Saurians*), he asks, 'What colour is radio?' he is not indulging in surrealistic provocation, but literally alluding to the continuum of colour and radio waves on the electromagnetic spectrum. This is why, according to the system of the thinker who meant most to him, he considered sensation to be, in our culture, the 'inferior' one of Jung's four functions.

Redgrove truly believed that there is no division between science and religion, but that they are complementary approaches to the unknown. At their orthodox extremes, where they flatly contradict each other, he judged them both to be wrong-headed and destructive. But he was deeply sympathetic to religion as a symbolic representation of the 'unseen real' (to cite the American subtitle of *The Black Goddess*) and to scientific investigation that did not cut itself off from this unseen reality by rejecting subjectivity. In 'Why the Bomb is Real but not True' he recommends one such model of scientific thought in opposition to Einstein, while in 'Mesmer's Vision' he laments the failure of British Romanticism, and especially of Coleridge, to embrace a true union of science and poetry. Perhaps the closest he came to finding a shared religious practice was the Obby Oss festival in Padstow, about which he speaks movingly as a genuine survival of the pagan past. But, characteristically, when asked if he is a pagan, he responds indirectly by defining his position and throwing the question back. He was chary of labels such as 'pagan', 'occult' or even 'genius': words that implicitly assigned the things that were most important to him to a special category. He was always at pains to cite everyday experiences as examples of the life of vision: daydreaming, taking a walk, drinking, and above all making love. He was profoundly opposed to Eliot's division between the 'poet' and the 'ordinary' man. It is typical of him that his favoured example of shamanism was a local spirit medium: he was prepared to find genuine powers in the world that Auden snobbishly derided as 'lower middle class'. Redgrove was not a snob in the social, intellectual or spiritual sense, even though he was well aware, and rightly so, of the value and importance of his own work.

# 1. A Poet in Teaching

I was never really convinced by the idea that there were two distinct cultures, art and science. This may be because I have come to poetry after some training and professional experience as a scientist. I certainly think there are two extremes of temperament, one of which prefers to consider the inner universe, and the other the outer. I think there are those who prefer deep subjectivity to deep objectivity, and vice versa; and I also think that one temperament may transform to another. But these are two extremes of a continuum, to my mind. Nor are there two kinds of creativity, scientific and artistic. Precisely the same operations favour and disfavour both. There is the imagination, and that best operates across the whole human spectrum.

I have been asked to write of this autobiographically, as a kind of illustration of this point of view. I was, I think, rather a chilling kind of child, being, from the age of kindergarten, interested in none of the usual childhood things. I remember — it must have been about the age of five — clutching a vividly-illustrated book about dinosaurs on my first day at the Misses Williams dayschool at Norbiton, Surrey. These vigorous and fiftyish women must be dust, as this was forty years ago. Perhaps they are still alive, and my child's eye made them old. I clutched my dinosaur book to me because I was scared, and its strange pictures comforted me. I am sure there was some sense of keeping myself separate by having unusual interests, but what I remember about that sense of comfort was that the book was strong, because it knew facts. It knew of strange worlds into which one could imagine oneself because they had been 'discovered by science' and the ground was firmer under one's feet than in that curious shifting world of persons, their conflicts and temperaments. I was always far too much impressed by people: in the presence of teachers or schoolfellows I immediately became writhing embarrassment or a blank sheet. Dinosaurs, with their serpent-heads and swan-like bodies and their shiny skins and immense innocent confidence, one could trust, especially as their skeletons were on show at South Kensington. They were as big as churches, but did not demand so much. They were more ancient than the other book I had to take with me to kindergarten, the Bible, and because their images and the landscapes in which they trod were vivid and simple, they comforted. I have never been so pleased with a recent scientific hypothesis as the one that tells us now that birds are the descendants of the dinosaurs which were really hot-blooded. I never much saw the point of birds until that moment. We live among multitudes of unnoticed dinosaurs.

The Bible frightened me. I wanted to read it through, because I felt sure I should learn something, that I would change by doing so and become more acceptable and less scared. But I hated the piles of foreskins (not that I knew what they were, since it was the fashion then to circumcise children) and the sudden bloody deaths, the people struck by fire, and the electrocution if you touched the Ark. I remember dropping my Bible in the hall of the Misses Williams house when I was late for school, and creasing the pages, and how I got on my knees among the thickets of hats and coats to apologise to the book for marking it.

On the wall of the classroom was a panoramic picture of Jesus presiding over a peaceable kingdom of animals. The blues and the greens and the creams of this picture seemed to me the most beautiful thing I had ever seen. The picture went with a hymn '. . . all creatures great and small, the Lord God made them all,' and I used to look at the lush grass and the sunny sky of this picture with delighted amazement. It was the world I saw myself, but simplified and abstracted, and in it were no spiders or worms, creatures that disturbed my own garden-of-paradise feelings in common life when I was playing. I didn't like worms because I felt cruel towards them, and wanted to squash them; they aroused feelings I did not understand, and as they were weaker than me I could stamp on them. Spiders were as black as the Bible and had almost as many legs as that had pages, but they moved unexpectedly, or would be revealed like a splash of ink on the wall above my bed. If you squashed these they were full of unpleasant juices and custards. And one mustn't be cruel to the little animals because in the peaceable kingdom Jesus was kind to all of them — except you, if you were naughty. It was at the Misses Williams that I first heard the name 'Jesus Christ'. I must have heard it in church, but it was at school that I first consciously heard one of the Misses Williams pronouncing these rather sickly syllables —

or that is how they struck me then. I was amazed at these words, they were like no others in English, and they meant somebody whom it was better to keep on the right side of, otherwise one might be stamped on, cruelly. I got the impression that the Misses Williams knew this, and had made their dispositions, which they were uncertain about, and this accounted for the way they spoke the name 'Jesus Christ', very carefully, in case they did it wrong.

Like many children, then, I was highly imaginative — and very scared, particularly of school. After the security of home, I was forced to make demarcations, to draw lines, to understand new feelings. I got comfort from the shared realities of science, rather than the individual realities of religion: I remember how in church everybody seemed to be quite separate in themselves, even though they were supposed to be together in a congregation. Even when they were singing hymns, nobody I knew as a child was good at singing, so everybody sang their own version. In the statements and responses, the lessons and the sermon, each person seemed to be grappling with private fear and guilt, and no wonder, if they felt about the Bible as I did.

The effect of this and surely many other factors, was to turn me into a kind of small Faust. I pursued my scientific interests. There was one Christmas when I took what seemed an indicative choice. I was offered a ventriloquist's doll, or a microscope, and I chose the microscope. It was really a toy, but it was still just powerful enough for me to see another world. It was like the world of the dinosaurs in that it seemed remote (though in reality it was all about us), vivid, strange, and there were in existence people who seemed to know a lot about its actualities (I have always been disappointed in theologians and clergymen because they never seemed to know much about their world). It was the world in the water-drop, the drop of dirty water that was crammed with vibrating beings of complex patterned structure. In every drop of water there was the bright green Euglena, the little jumping creature like a twist of lime-peel; the stubbly Paramecium, like slippers of glass, just visible to the naked eye; once seen, the majestically-rolling Volvox; the Desmids, looking like roman quinqueremes, all in green; the Diatoms like the plans of cities. I took my earthworms and insects and woodlice to pieces now not from cruelty, but to investigate their structures in the name of science, though it was really to marvel at what they were in this other world. I cultivated tubes of murky water on my windowsill, assured of marvels and magic therein. I crystallised photographer's hypo, and watched the steely needles shoot across the illuminated field of my microscope; I moved my little microscope about on the table-top and watched the rainbows form within the needles, shifting like the aurora borealis. I think in doing this I lost my image of myself: I drew blood from my finger and watched the rouleaux of incredibly multiplex round corpuscles stream like a population in the rush hour across the slide, and I was made up of such things just inside the skin; and just outside it were all the germs that would have a good try at taking me apart if I were ill, and would inevitably do so when I was dead. I developed unhealthy and inconvenient obsessions about these germs and how I could avoid infection. This was the dark side of my development as a juvenile scientist, and now these studies were beginning to show in my school work, where I had a better grasp of scientific matters than of arts subjects. I wonder if I had chosen the ventriloquist's doll I would have made for myself an interlocutor to comment on people and affairs rather than, as happened, gaining possession of a cyclopean eye that gave me images of swarming, bustling life beyond the accustomed appearances of human life. Did Jesus of the kindergarten scare me away from subjective life? Eventually something that was not that kind of religion lured me back again.

I think this was the right course for me at the time, though it came out of quite evident faults of character: excessive fear and shyness, a desire to hold myself apart. I think that these kind of studies trained my imagination to expect wonder from the world, and I think I was trained by the precise images of science and those seen in the microscope to particular and strong visualisation. I am often bothered by people describing my poetry as 'surrealistic' when it is attempting to be quite objective and observational. It is that nature is so surprising that one grows accustomed to move among astonishments and to delight in them. I think too that the scientific habit of forming hypotheses which one then checks with further data bothers readers of poetry who do not have this habit of mind. My poems tend to springboard off a wonderment at some observation — into a sea of similar observations that qualify or extend the original one. This is different from the 'egotistical sublime': the eye of a fully-formed personality that advances through the world reducing all to its likeness. That is perhaps like having a ventriloquist's doll. As a small scientist, my personality was late forming, because it was dissolved in wonders. Languages like Spanish and German seem more accustomed to this kind of poetry, where the poets have not lost the capacity for surprise. Perhaps the egotistical sublime in English poetry has declined into mumbling gentility, as A. Alvarez long ago suggested. The Jesus of the Misses Williams was perhaps an apparition intended to produce genteel children whose mentors' lips writhed on those syllables in distaste at any untoward behaviour, which genteel Jesus, meek and mild, would punish; and as Faust I became unutterably damned in these enclaves; and also at my later school, where I was a barbarian scientist, and stranger to the refinements and poises of the arts sixth.

One might as well be hung for a real scientist, so I worked. I was fortunate to have excellent teachers (among them E. G. Neal, the naturalist), and I got scholarships to Cambridge. Arriving there was like coming to an enormously magnified Misses Williams. I expected to find a real explosion of encouragement, energy, scientific wisdom. Instead I found a machine geared to conformity and show. Well, it was a large place, there was room for every kind of person — yet people seemed anxious to form stereotypes of themselves, and not to explore. I use this word 'stereotypes' because it is current, and describes a real phenomenon, but I think at the time (the fifties) the idea was to 'cut a figure' in the university, if one was on the arts side; and to 'get a good degree' on the science side. The scientist was a sort of mole, to the arts man, and the latter a wastrel and a spendthrift to the scientists: ('spendthrift' was unjust, it was possible to cut a figure even if one was poor merely by the purchase of the right kind of hat, second hand, or an elaborate cane, or by adopting an unusual mannerism). Cambridge seemed a place for extraverts, and I was not one of these. The science departments which I had joined were not places where one explored with a sense of wonder, but rather machines for producing limited knowledge in identical formats, which were known as degrees. Introspection was represented by the religious men — quiet handsome dark secretive catholics for the main part, who simply spoke politely and communicated nothing. I could not enter anywhere: not among the science or the arts people, since I was not so extraverted; not among the religious, because of what I feared about Jesus; but there was one new force abroad that did take me in and changed my life, very inconveniently, because it took me away from the sound professional living that a 'good degree' in science would have brought, and showed me that course of life to which my feelings and experiences had been leading me was to try to become a poet.

II

Many confluent events determine an event like this, few of them entirely conscious, many of them symbolic. For me, a direction is often pointed by a strong, almost sexual feeling about some material thing. A strict morality would discard such a feeling; I have preferred to follow it. Here it was the smell of books. I was in one of the Cambridge bookshops — Deighton Bell, possibly, looking for a scientific textbook. All the science books were too fat and too formal, containing equal wedges of grey type with strict diagrams and equations: I did not believe that much in equality. There was a case of poetry books, anthologies that felt better between the fingers, contained more irregular and exciting structures of type, and whose ink smelt better. I took up the Auden and Pearson anthology: *Poets of the English Language.* I read the first lines: 'In a somer seson when softe was the sonne . . .' and my hair stood on end, my skin felt sunny inside my clothes. I bought first the one volume (being short of money) and then could not resist the whole five.

That was the sensuous aspect. My mind also tells me that the new force abroad that meant personal salvation for me, isolated as I was between the two opposites of scientific moles and *jeunesse dorée*, was Downing English. The presence of F. R. Leavis and the example of the work of I. A. Richards seemed to show that there was a new world in literature, and that poetry was a thing that could be grasped by objective honesty and not by joining a club. Looking back, I see that there was a club there, but it wasn't an exclusive one, since a barbarous scientist like me was allowed to hear Leavis lecture and to go to H. A. Mason's home to join a tutorial group. I was welcomed into Philip Hobsbaum's group. Hobsbaum had (and has, from all accounts) that genius as a teacher that welcomes people on their own terms. I had begun writing poetry out of the feelings I have described, of a young scientist travelling into a new side of his imagination. Hobsbaum and his group discussed seriously what I and others like me did among the more accomplished work of other members, and this was an inestimable boon to one trying to find his way in an unfamiliar world of self-expression.

The point was that a poem was a phenomenon, like any other phenomenon. In science, you make a controlled experiment, and restrict the number of variables. I. A. Richards showed how the prejudices of the readers altered their perception of what was actually in the poem. Hobsbaum cut down the variables by insisting that texts were circulated beforehand so that people's reactions had settled down by the time the meeting came round; and he insisted that the author read and then take no part in the general discussion until it came naturally to an end. Then it was his turn to say what he meant. This ensured that the author — the experiment — could not influence the scientist — the group; and it also meant that the author found whether what he meant the words to say actually produced the results and images he intended, so in this sense he also was a scientist; and also that he sometimes had written better than he knew, that is, his work produced by consensus of the group a certain effect that was in the words, but that the author had not realised. This made his work a phenomenon that had arisen from him, rather than a merely personal communication, and he too could take an objective and workmanlike attitude to it.

This interesting manipulation of a 'communication gap' between author and readers, combined with Hobsbaum's inspired chairmanship, made an extraordinarily powerful group. After Cambridge, it continued in London for some years. Philip Hobsbaum moved to the Queen's University, Belfast, and the groups he set up there helped many of the now well-known Northern Ireland poets. I used Philip's methods in American universities and when I came to teach at Falmouth School of Art;

and I think many people have: there must be many cuttings of this plant husbanded by Philip Hobsbaum in a lot of places by now.

For myself, I have said that discussion like this was a boon. The poem — once written down — was as objective an object as a painting or a piece of sculpture. One could walk round it, author or reader, and comment on it like any other member of the public, and learn from it. Parturition had occurred; one's baby had to take its first steps without one's assistance. The poem was not merely a personal utterance; it was a hypothesis with certain data attached that could be discussed. Something in it that was bad was usually something that people visibly had to make up their own poems about; some image that meant entirely disparate things to several people was usually acting as a kind of do-it-yourself kit, so it wasn't really 'made'. If one's poem was taken as one had intended by several people seeing the same thing in it, there was a reasonable supposition that in some sense that poem was alive. Then again, the better things that happened could be something that had sprung into the poem beyond the author's intention. This too he had to recognise equally with the ill-made things. It is important in poetry too, that things should happen beyond the author's apparent ability. If he realises this, then he will be humble, as a good artist or a good scientist should be in front of phenomena, and he will grow. In a sense this was a group for studying phenomenology, since trying to answer the questions that come up when you are reading and writing poems is a way to self-knowledge. Thoughts change perceptions, and vice versa, so what is objectivity? Is there any such thing? Can there be objective truth, and if there can, in what manner can the subjective experience of the percipient be included in this truth. As I have indicated, not only were the readers studying the poem, and the author, but the author was studying the readers with the aid of the device he had made for studying himself and his own world, the poem. The procedure was simple, but the implications and advantages were enormous, and I think most of the people who attended these meetings over the years gained great advantage. I certainly did.

I began to find my feet as a writer by these means, and this was needed as I was most unhappy about what else Cambridge offered.

So unhappy that I took the quite serious risk of changing over entirely to these studies: lectures in the English school were open to all the university, and many tutors would accept 'outsiders' from the 'other culture'. I tried to change my degree course, but the authorities said that this was impossible, so I simply did what I felt right anyway. Whatever my poems of this time might have been to others, for me they were the best way I had yet found to use my mind and senses. In this they were equivalent to, and were accompanied by, discovery of sexuality. Neither the discipline of science alone nor of letters alone could match up to the feeling of the objective and the subjective world fusing and becoming another mode of experience. In parallel, there was my discovery of sex. The first time I slept with a woman, which was about this time, such a peace and a silence came into my conflicting head! Then into that peace came of itself a measured statement, and this was my first poem.

This 'third thing' made of two opposites — man and woman, science and art — gave me enough energy and confidence to make the professional difficulties about coming down without a degree seem unimportant. I didn't want to be a scientist anyway — and I was sure that if I kept writing my poetry that would give me enough ability to master any job in advertising or journalism, since this was now the obvious way to earn my living. Of course this was an arrogant view in that it underestimated the real skills of these professions — but it worked, for a time. The poems enabled me to reach a kind of reality that the awful little jobs I did in the publicity departments of various publishers and the like couldn't touch — not to begin with, anyway. I found my stance wearing down eventually, though I never let my occupation stop me doing what I considered to be my real writing; and I got a new lease of interest in them when Edward Lucie-Smith, who was chairing the Group in London at that time, said that I should present myself as a 'specialist' copywriter, and combine in a monetarily profitable way such writing skills as I had developed with my scientific know-how. This idea worked, and the jobs became more interesting — one in particular at Glaxo Laboratories — but I then sailed into ethically dangerous waters when I found myself engaged to write advertising copy for Thalidomide, which everybody at that time thought completely safe. My first book of poems was published at this time by Routledge, by the kind intercession of Bonamy Dobrée and Herbert Read. It was reasonably well-received, and I was able to get my first teaching job — in America. When I returned the first Thalidomide babies were being born. I was glad that my advertisements had not been used nor had contributed to this disaster, in which I might have shared in a direct way, since the copywriter, myself, true to his duty to the product, had given Thalidomide to his pregnant wife when she was unable to sleep. We were lucky.

I could have stayed in America, but I was offered the Gregory Fellowship in Poetry at Leeds University. This was the only Fellowship in the country at this time which allowed an artist a living wage to do his own work, in return only for his presence on the campus. There was also a Gregory painter and a Gregory sculptor, and we formed a true Fellowship. I believe we all felt a responsibility to do our work, since that was what we were paid for, and a responsibility also to the University that paid us, to make it available to as many students or staff who were interested, and to try and communicate our sense of dedication to this kind of work which was, after all, very different from what most members of that community were engaged in, since practical art as opposed to criticism at that time took no account of degrees. It was a valuable time for me as I was able to see in action the unity of these three arts, painting, sculpture and poetry. We all spent our daily hours in our studios, and met to discuss what we had been about, and to explore our common ground. I think we took strength from this sense of common ground, and of being in a community that paid us for doing this work: I certainly did.

Thus it seemed a lucky development when I applied for a job to a West Country school of art, and was appointed. At the interview I used my argument that since they had painters to teach painting, and sculptors to teach sculpture, why not have a poet to teach an imaginative approach to the written word, since that was what 'complementary studies' seemed to be about. The panel considered my arguments and accepted them — must have, since they appointed me — but I remember they thought me a little brash, since when I was called in again one of the lady governors interviewing told me that she thought that I had been interviewing them, and was that right? I replied that I thought that it was something to do with the nature of interview proceedings — I was certainly strained because as soon as I saw the palm trees of this semi-tropical seaside resort I badly wanted the job — and said, quite sincerely, that I expected to learn as much as I taught. I think this perfectly sincere remark got me the job.

I wasn't really sure what 'complementary studies' for art students was, as I had been guessing at my interview, but I began in an experimental mood to put those ideas into practice. I had a free hand, since the department was minute. There was the lecturer in charge — to this day one of the kindest and most affable men I have ever met — and he was concerned most with art history, which was taught in lectures copiously illustrated by slides. There was also an art historian, who gave more specialised teaching. Complementary studies clearly was not art history, otherwise they would not have needed me, and it was 'complementary', that is, it 'completed' a student's studies which were, I assumed, in some manner thought incomplete if he confined himself to studio work and the history of his art. At that time the qualification awarded was the Diploma in Art and Design, later to become the B.A. (Fine Art).

I decided that since both students and staff must be interested — and indeed dedicated — to making things, that is, creativity, then my job should be to attempt to show as tellingly as I could how that creativity spread into other realms of life besides their specialist activities. I would try to show how so many matters confined within the covers of books cried aloud to be interpreted in visual form, I would show how the poets and the scientists too used their imaginations as well as their individual crafts and skills to bring their works to life, and I would try to open up as many areas of life in my students as I could for the creative imagination to operate in. In doing so, I would be opening my own work to the influence of other ways of seeing, and to the influence of much younger imaginations (I was then 34, and this all began in the summer of 1966).

All this worked reasonably well. My head of department was enthusiastic about the duplicated lecture-notes I passed on to him, and the other staff seemed reasonably impressed, though I was — regarded with a little suspicion as a 'poet from London' — even though I had not lived in the Metropolis for nearly ten years. Students seemed interested, for the main part, and read the books I lectured to them about, many of which I lent from my own library. Here I must pause for a tribute to the honesty of the English art student. In thirteen years in this school I have lost only one book though I must have lent hundreds, and that was to a pre-diploma student, not really on the course!

What I was concerned to teach were those matters that helped me in my own creative search. I had found the images of science very potent indeed for my poetry, and I think at that time artists were beginning to take cognisance of the interpretations of science and its formative influence on our ways of life. I remember that later on I found Jonathan Benthall's *Science and Technology in Art Today* very helpful, but in the earlier days few such books were available and I relied, with reservations, on what I call 'emotional' science: the more respectable ones were Jeans and Eddington, but there was also wonderful Theodore Swenck on *Sensitive Chaos*, the forms and transmutations of Water, based on the Steiner school; and Ouspensky and his associates too. Mythology was a study that had meant a great deal to me, and I used to lecture on this with Joseph Campbell's *Hero with a Thousand Faces* as a back-up book. It was apposite, since Campbell showed how the ancient images telling a constant story of the withdrawal of the hero and his return with creative riches were recapitulated in the life-story of each individual person. Mythology was the dreams of the race, and dreams were the mythology of the individual. I had been interested in dreams too from my early twenties, and had worked hard at understanding the various theories available, particularly Jung's, and how they were involved in the writing of poetry.

The teaching conditions were exceptional. In 1966 there were only fifty-five students or so; even now as I write in 1979 we have only a little over 100. One could do a great deal of one-to-one teaching, and I was a sort of one-man band, a kind of rag-bag or seedsman of all the things I thought were useful that had been left out of strict art education.

To my pleasure I found that these matters began to spread not only in the students but among the staff: not entirely my own influence of course, but due to the changing scene in the art world. Art was spreading its boundaries, and many methods of working besides the conventional ones of easel and model were beginning to bear fruit. In our school, performance and theatrical matters were beginning to arouse interest, and I did my best to contribute to this, as I had written a fair amount for performance. My head of department, a painter by training, sat down and wrote a novel, and became interested in psychology. He invited into his home a celebrated psychologist and anthropologist who lectured in the school. I found myself a further role in that there were certain students whose talents did not fit easily into the painting or sculpture schools, and at that time such students were sometimes asked to leave the course. I found that I was able to discern talents in them which belonged to the areas of study in which I had experience, and was able to mount 'rescue' operations for students who otherwise might have had difficulty in finding a home.

I remember well the first of these. It was my custom to ask students to record their thoughts, activities, events, grouses, dreams and anything at all in a notebook, since I had found over the years that if I did this myself instead of using scraps of paper, I could often see a sequent idea developing, like mice running through tunnels under all the rubbish. This student's notebook was perhaps worse than most, long-winded grousing about lodging conditions and the inadequacy of the grant. But as I turned over the pages, I couldn't help noticing in the margin a 'doodle' in the manner of Leonardo (an artist that interested this student) of a crucifixion: perhaps as this young man saw himself, nailed down by the conditions of college life, unable to fit in anywhere. This doodle was repeated on each page, and I saw it was developing in an interesting way. At the foot of the Cross was a puddle of water, in which the shaft was settling. With each 'doodle' therefore the shaft grew shorter. The remarkable thing was that as this happened, a reflection of the body nailed to the cross became visible, in fragments at first, but then full length, and of course upside-down and reversed. The reflection was a woman, nailed to the cross. At the same moment of the notebook, so to speak, the dreary prose broke into life about a new process that the student had discovered, called 'solarisation', in which if an object were photographed in colour, the intensity of a given colour would *cause its reversal* into its complementary.

One often sees this done in cinema and TV now, but then it was a new technique, and it was one that burst in on the earth-bound notebook like the sun itself. So when a senior sculpture tutor called in on me to collect my opinion among all the others of the merits of this student I was able to say that he was brilliant (which he was, from that moment, in his book) and he should at all costs be kept in the school.

What happened then was that this student pretty-well created a film department for himself. Using the rather skimpy resources of photography, and the materials of my lectures that had worked on him more deeply than I could have hoped, he made a superb film (using solarisation) in colour about his own feelings of transformation. It was full of magnificent images of fire and change, semi-tropical Cornwall and its atmospheric landscapes inhabited by saints and ghostly apostles speaking with visible fiery words (this was the solarisation in colour-negative of the red inner speaking mouths and tongues!). All teachers will understand the gratification when I saw the film and its transformations introduced by the image of a great full moon that dissolved into my white bald head lecturing! This film is still remarkable, and has quite a following from being shown at Festivals. The student after graduation went on to the British Film School.

As a result of all this, I began to wonder whether I could introduce more practical work into my courses, and whether I could harness more of the benefits of written literature to my students' creative impulses. I had experience in teaching 'creative writing' in America, but the way I taught it derived more from my experience in that long-lived seminar called 'The Group' than it did from the more gymnastic American methods of exercise and improvisation. Now I wondered whether if I introduced some of these tried and tested exercises into a 'creative writing course' I could assist the students to develop their verbal as well as their visual imaginations, and whether the two would not react together in a beneficial way.

Accordingly I worked out a little art-course of my own. I reasoned that most of us, since we have been using language from the age of one year, have superb technical equipment in that skill. This is different from the visual arts, where the technical skills have to be acquired. On the contrary, much of one's initial progress in the written arts is to throw off prejudices and bad habits about language, and to make the product new and exciting in one's own and one's readers' eyes again. Accordingly I would not at first set exercises in verse technique and suchlike, but rather teach my students to surprise themselves with what they could write. I had the added difficulty that many art students have dropped out of the verbal aspect of our culture: this was counterbalanced by the fact that they have developed their visual imaginations so that they can respond well to simple sensuous writing. When they wrote too, they wrote with impressive visual authority. I had to show them how this could naturally or even by accident come about.

So I began my course with jokes. I tried to show them how humorous things and surprising things were the stuff of poetry, which was never except by mistake a solemn affair. I showed them that simply by letting the words have their way, beautiful oddities could be produced, which might be suggestive enough to be the seeds for further work. I remember one exercise which brought inevitable gales of laughter was called 'The Exquisite Corpse' which I learned from Robin Skelton's excellent *The Practice of Poetry*. All you do is to write down a simple sentence at the head of a page, such as 'The Green Knight Slew the Crimson Dragon'. You then fold the paper in vertical columns and pass it along to the next person, like 'consequences'. The paper is folded to conceal all but one part of speech. Your column has 'The Green' at the head of it, and you simply fill the column with an article and an adjective, fold the paper to conceal your adjectives and to expose the following noun, and pass it along. You then fill the column passed to you with nouns, following 'Knight', and so on. Eventually the paper is filled, and when it is opened out you find it is filled with very peculiar sentences, all of them surprising, some hauntingly beautiful, like drunkenness, or convalescence.

> The uncreased wine apologises to the candlebright corpse
> The orphaned drops drench the blissful directors
> The long-eared skull whistles in the salt breeze
> The second serpent whitens the unwinding fire
> Her natural body-incision confuses the rhythmic lace
> The devoted shit disturbs the tattered confectionary
> Her ginger hair shocks my buxom green pillow

We did newspaper collage work — visually beautiful as well as verbally startling once you begin to juxtapose headlines (especially *Guardian* headlines!) — and at some stage or other I would pace round solemnly with my fountain-pen depositing a drop of ink into the centre of each student's fresh white page, which they must crease and rub to make a suggestive ink-blot against which they would write phrases that it inspired by its insectile, hooded, winged appearances. I felt that if I could help them to overcome their inhibitions about writing, then after that was the time to teach them control and special expressive techniques. I followed Robin Skelton's saying about beginning to write 'Invent a jungle — then explore it'.

The courses were, I'm glad to say, successful. In general students did lose their inhibitions about writing, and this, according to my colleague the art historian, improved their English all round, particularly in their art history essays. I also had reports from the painting department that certain students seemed to be able to work out creative problems in their writing that would have occupied them an unnecessarily great time if they had had to work them out in paint and canvas: in writing they could survey themselves, as it were, rapidly, and overcome blocks and obstacles, or change direction. Indeed, the head of painting sent me several students for short intensive courses in writing when he felt that images that didn't belong to painting needed to be worked out in another medium.

But there was a third result that perhaps I should have expected, but which surprised me when it came, and also pleased me very much. Two students in that first improvisation course showed me work that had come out of it that was by any standards excellent writing. They were also students, as I learnt, who had shown so little talent in their main courses that their future in the school was in serious question.

I myself had no doubt what their future in the school should be. They should not be sacked and exiled from their natural development, but they should be allowed to develop the talent that they had shown by every means possible. My head of department was in sympathy with the problems of the writer (his novel had been published, and well received) and our Principal was also a man of ideals and wide sympathies who made no separation between the arts. I suppose we bent the rules a little, but we believed that students' artistic work, in whatever medium it showed accomplishment, should be allowed to contribute towards the assessment of that student's qualification at the end of his three years. Our Principal believed, quite rightly, that the quality of the work should be judged by a specialist adviser to the external assessor in painting, so that the award had proper validation. It was an exciting day when the distinguished writer we had called in as external adviser agreed that one of the writing students deserved a 2:1 and the other First Class Honours! In the latter case, the student had illustrated her writing with visual metaphors taken from poetry and had produced a stunning visual show as well as a book of amazing poetry. She had returned, as it were, to her life in painting from poetry and had enriched both. I felt that the idea of an art school had extended its meaning, and this (if it spread) could be a most powerful influence and reassessment of the scope of art education.

The next year a similar thing happened. A student who had not got on well visually, with encouragement and tuition produced notable poetry, and graduated with First Class Honours, even though his visual show was rather weak and mostly photographs. He made history in a small way too, since he was accepted for the M.A. in creative writing course at East Anglia University, and duly graduated there, the first time that an art student (to my knowledge) had done such a thing. I should explain that part of the excitement was that this East Anglia postgraduate course was the only course resulting in a qualification in this country for people who wished to write, and live as students on a grant while doing so. I felt, and feel, that it is a great anomaly that thousands of art students learn their craft as undergraduates at the very many art schools in this country, while anybody who is a writer and not a visual artist has nowhere to go as a student to learn his or her craft. This is why I thought that our results in this little art school had some importance as a kind of pilot scheme. Perhaps it would point the way. Also, why should my job be the only job where a writer teaches his art on terms of equality with the other teacher-artists, the painters and sculptors? Where was the job-market for teachers who were writers? Sculptors and painters seemed seldom short of at least an interesting part-time job in education if they wanted it.

At this time (during 1970) I happened to be serving on the Literature Panel of the Arts Council, and I put these arguments forward to the Panel, and wondered whether if we could demonstrate that the writer had his place in education as much as the painter or sculptor did, then there might not be possible a scheme that would be of benefit to writers and students alike. Accordingly I wrote to 100 writers of note asking for their opinion of what they felt they contributed to English education *by virtue of their being writers* rather than of some other qualification. I compiled the replies into a report to the Panel which was adopted with enthusiasm, since my correspondents had been so articulate and circumstantial about their experiences as educators that there could be little doubt about the strength of their case. I am glad to say that this was the seed of the excellent Arts Council Scheme whereby an institution of learning can apply for a 'Creative Writing Fellow' subsidised by the Arts Council (at little cost to that institution beyond the interview expenses), to live on the campus much as I did as Gregory Fellow in Poetry at Leeds University ten years or so before. There are now many of these Fellowships. In 1977 our Art School applied for one, and we were fortunate to have Philip Callow as our Fellow. In the meanwhile a third art student got a First with her creative writing; she was also admitted to the East Anglia M.A. course. It was marvellous to have Callow during 1977-8, as I no longer felt like a one-man band. That year also 'my' fourth writing student won the highest marks in the whole school for his degree work, which was mostly writing, and has gone on to postgraduate work at Sussex University. I feel that the point is proved: students can gain from the melting-away of the old categories between art and literature. Our degree-validating body, the CNAA, however maintains that art schools were founded in order to teach the visual arts, and it will therefore require a change of mind by the DES before a course in practical literary arts can be validated for a Fine Art degree, though there may be some elasticity under the existing arrangements towards creative writing in a few students that show the talent. I am content with this; I have done my experiment under controlled conditions, and it worked. Now, as is proper in science, I am hereby publishing my results in a Journal, and I hope others will verify the work and establish a natural law.

## 2. The Other Funeral
Towards a Lecture on Love and Death

Loving the loved ones after they have died — what resentment!
— when one is angry with them for getting old and nearly
unrecognisable — and then on top of that, they become
inaccessible — beyond the door — of what? the best-kept secret.

My mother's funeral was in May. It was a springtime funeral,
but the gender seemed to matter more than the season. It was as
though all the doors were opened to let her spirit out — where
to? The doors in the mind that had been fearful of her going –
the doors of the springtime flowers; the floral tributes; opened
in welcome to her as she as ashes was put in the earth. And it
seemed that as she went, she left the door open — perhaps for me
to follow one day, and a message. I reported all this in a poem,
and people seemed to believe my unlikely but true tale.

It was the ritual of the funeral I think brought about the
visions. First of all, since the doors were all open, anybody could
attend. And the whole of creation wished to. This was brought
about by one of the other mourners remarking, as an intrusive
bee dipped into the sunlight of a Victorian gothic window, that

> Ninety-two percent of what we eat is from direct
> Pollination by the bees, he tells me this
> To cheer me and if true ninety-two percent
> Of what he says with his mouth is said by bees . . .

So everything had become creaturely, because of that funeral.
I remembered too — for all funerals take place in the same
time-warp in which the dead and the living meet — the obsequies
of my soldier-brother, dead a few days off twenty. I remembered
feeling nothing until I saw one of the 'floral tributes'. It was in
the shape of a sword — David was in the Household Cavalry and
the sword was the emblem of his soldier-hood — and it was as
though the sword had relaxed and transmuted into a glory of
flowers. To return to my mother's funeral.

> The other thing the funeral showed me, unpromising
> seance,

My mother, subject of it, at the door ajar
On the field of light, looking back over her shoulder,
Smiling happiness and blessing me, the coherent veil
Of the radiant field humming with bees that lapped the water,
      and she bent
And washed her tired face away with dew and became a
      spirit
      'The Funeral' from *The Man Named East*

How is love to flow again, is the puzzle, after either parent suddenly disappears and terminates their time-stream, and becomes one of the dead. We mourn — and we must not be too quick about it, as it is a long process — perhaps five years, perhaps longer. This sudden estoppal is not often likely to be open and flowing like my mother's was. It is more often like a door slammed in one's face. Completion of the death may then be long delayed. Some completion there has to be. They say the father holds the gates of heaven.

One can instead become like that dead person, try and fill up their place, becoming Mr. Redgrove Snr. and denying their absence. This is obsession by a ghost, not recommended. 'Hades bobbin bound in mummy-cloth' will anyway unreel its life of pictures, but if one has become the dead one, marmoreal and unchanging in grief, one cannot see the pictures, which are like the confession process, that two people recite to one another, in the afterlife, for an indefinite period. For certainly the mourner has to go into the underworld, and reform his relations with his dead parent there. If the grieving works as it should, then both of you love each other in a new way.

Poets are said to have trained their imaginations, and that is not to keep things out. They are always descending somewhere to find things out. This is not as easy as it sounds. I had to eat my sins towards my father; I had to eat the food of the dead to be in communion with him. This meant that I not only had to re-feel all the relationships I had ever had with my fellow males, now I was seeing my father's masculinity as it was and not as one subject to it; as a consequence I was presented with certain irrational tasks. One of these was to read the Bible through, because that was the book that the masculine world to which he belonged used to enforce its sanctions. I did this, using one of those day by day reading Bibles, so it took me a year. I read both the King James and a modem translation. The second was to complete B. K. S. Iyengar's 4-year-course in pranayama — yogic breathing. I think this task was set me because of the wholly wild unacceptable craziness of doing such a thing, the stubborn persistence of it. My father did many things with such a persistence, in his games and sports, which he was very good at, and often for the benefit of others, as he saw it I also hope that these practices might keep me younger longer than he. But that is in the lap of Shiva, patron of yoga. The course took me five years, as did the main stage of my mourning.

An alternative to the marmoreal mourner, the Commendatore Manoeuvre, is to become dissolved in the family as a consequence of that potent instrument, the funeral. One makes treaties with the family face, which is sometimes like a mirror image, at others like a caricature by a political cartoonist. A death in the family loosens all the faces.

> For many weeks after the funeral he was without wishing it
> All the dead people who had composed him without his
> permission;
> He thought he had no affinity at all with his father's mother
> But there she was in his place reflected in a shop window
> Dressed in a man's jersey and without her jabot of lace;
> A reality photograph of his father, bulky and upright
> And wearing dark glasses made to his prescription
> Came and sat down in his body; that was more than a face,
> That was the whole being of the dead person in a stolid
> mood.
> These faces flew about the crematorium like putti
> And alighted where they would; the people made fluid
> By their flux of grief only had to gaze into the eyes
> Of one closely-related and charged with weeping
> To turn into that person, even setting into a deathmask.

'Loose Faces' from My *Father's Trapdoors*

\* \* \*

Dream recalled: My father was reading to me out of a printed book — I saw the columns of type clearly, and it was a poem he was reading aloud. I became alarmed that the poem was going to say 'Here lies the poet, priest and prophet, Peter/Who broke the laws of God and man and metre', and I wanted to stop him saying this, and I think he stopped reading, but I suspect that these were not the words he was going to read, or that were in the book! I invented at least part of this accusatory father.

* * *

Is this my earliest memory? The complex of soft touch and sweet smells I knew was my mother was steering me into a brightly-lighted room. I paused at the threshold. I did not like the atmosphere, but I was safely enfolded in the aura of my mother's dress. There was a big lumpish armchair on the other side of the room and in the armchair was a man. It was difficult to put the parts of him together: the round head, the smile, the spectacles, the armchair. I pointed. My question was as firm as an adult's speech. 'Who is that man?' 'That's your father, dear.' 'I don't like that, Mummy.' Then from the armchair came over-loud laughter, and I was handed over, before I knew what was happening, transferred to the lap of this amplified presence. He uttered a gargling sound and pointed to me. 'What's that?' 'Your name. Redgrove.' That name of my father was too harsh, it sounded like the tread of a tyre on a red car. I still cannot believe that this is my name.

What shame! To deny one's father while a mere toddler. Yet it seems to me now that I knew what I was doing, and that it would hurt if not kill. Or as if my spirit in those long-ago days was fully-grown and ready to enter an adult conflict. In this atmosphere, as it was, of rejection (for clearly I was a mother's boy) how could my father get at me or me at him for purposes of repair? Why, by ghostly methods of course, similar to the methods my mother used. A spirit-voice from a tooth — a pain striking like a cymbal, and after it an imagination of what my father would have said. And with this little event of interior concentration, I finding that the doors were opening, of my less used, less conscious senses. Everyone knows how a smell will

34

bring back an event or a person in vivid memory. I discovered that the smell of the skin of my father was my own smell, 'olfactory pedigree'. As for smoking, I did at one time, and he did always. I think I wanted to fill the house with this plasm, wall-to-wall exhalation, to assert myself, for smoking to his generation was the say-so of manhood.


## A Passing Cloud

I

They tell of thunder picked up on the teeth,
Or radio decoded on a filling, one's mouth
Buffeted with Sousa; but this was a dull ache
Pouring from a black cloud, I could get
No message from this broadcast, I must have
This radio pulled. 'No,' said my father,
'Keep your tooth, this is but a passing cloud.' I knew
It was him, because that was the brand
Of cigarettes he smoked, 'Passing Cloud' by Wills, and
'Yes,' he said abruptly, 'It's me,' and turned white;
By this token I knew he was dead,
Knew it again.

2

When I had flu I always sweated his smell; his two
        wardrobes
Were exhaling it from hanging woollen shoulders like a last
        breath,
This ancient eighty-four-year-old sandalwood was his
        presence now,
It soaked into me and travelled home and stayed some days,
Grief like flu; but I could close my eyes and use it as an Inn
To meet up with this wayfarer and imagine him . . .
His presence fills the house when he is smoking,
His nature reaches into every cranny,
Into the carpets and eiderdowns and squads of suits;
The chain is broken now, finis,
And though I can smoke in his house now without consent

The smell of cigarettes does not bring him back,
As he is ashes and has been smoked and stubbed out
'A passing cloud . . .' so that time
For him never forges chains again.


5
Except I notice that being under the weather
I sniff my hand-back and his scent appears; my whole skin
And atmosphere remembers him, the rain falls
And my toothache turns to tears, while the world fills
With reflecting mirror-water fathered out of rain-smells.

from *My Father's Trapdoors*


I think I have an earlier memory, from my pram. I call it

### REVERSE POLICE

Looking up out of my pram at the notice of letters on their
bracket POLICE and passing under them ECILOP and then the
traffic light. Some eight years later I set foot in that police
station. 'Take your cap off, boy. You are in the Queen's house.'

Does this belong to my father's process, or my mother's? Of
course each parent is involved in the process which is essentially
mine. After all, I am the one who still breathes and eats. How shall
I become the master in my own house, while still surrounded
by these influences. For example, there were influential female
aphorisms.

*Mother said father was a kind of genius, and geniuses are
destructive. She averred a genius would project qualities in himself
which were unconscious on another person, and blame them f they
did not match up to those qualities in himself he denied consciously
he possessed. Also this process would prevent or delay the evolution in
that person receiving the projection of his own qualities. There would
be a stunned area round him.*

Mother may have been right. My father's actual death was a
masterpiece, guaranteed to stun.

'He had paid his newspaper and Access bill, had laid out on

the dining-room table all the documents in their clearly-labelled folders that would be of use to his executors; then it seems he went upstairs to his bedroom, sat down in front of his seven-years-dead wife's dressing-table with the three mirrors, and in full sight of his threefold mirror-image, died.'

But this leads to the question, how many people were involved in this process or trial. I count eight, leaving myself out, as mere heir of their conflicts.


Eight Parents

1

At the climax of the illuminated
Book of Hours the Trinity is seen in truth to be
Three self-same white-clad bearded figures
Of Jesus on three identical thrones.
It makes the eyes go funny, like trifocals.


2

This devotional picture resembles
My mother's triptych dressing-table mirror;
When she sat there, three other mothers appeared.


3

The fourth turned round to me and smiled;
The three simultaneously looked back over their shoulders
At somebody out of sight down the glass corridors.
Then she got up, and the thrones were empty.


4

Nearly a decade after she had emptied her throne, my father
Sat himself down in front of the same mirror and died.
He paid his Access- and paper-bill, laid out
Like hands of cards folders on the dining-room table
For his executors, climbed the stairs to his widower
        bedroom,
Sat down at my mother's mirror and saw there were three
        more of him,
Then his heart burst and shot him into mirror-land.

5

Where is that mirror now? You may be reasonably sure
If you buy a second-hand house or bed, then
Somebody has died in it.


6

But a dressing-table triple mirror? Can you
Enquire of the vendor, expecting nothing but the truth,
'Who died in this mirror?' Death
Leaves no mark on the glass.

From *My Father's Trapdoors*

There were of course other stunned areas around the house,
symbols or doorways.

*All human teaching is accompanied by an emotion, pleasant or*
*unpleasant. The scientist gets his rocks off by imagining his probity*
*and puritan scepticism; the English teacher wants to catch you like a*
*squashed fly in the books, or live through you; and these feelings the child*
*will detect by their perfumes.* Father's urine carries his mysterious
male passion in the loo used by all, the stag's convening power. So
that is a stunned area, as all will allow. I will not pursue this now,
but consider two further stunned areas at which my father was
exceptionally good, even striking my childhood senses with the
force of genius. There is the wardrobe, and there is the Christmas
tree. The wardrobe is as religious with its inner regions as the
tree, but darker.

The clothes hang, worn by the smells of saffron and
sandalwood like ghosts. They tune up as I stand in the wardrobe's
entrance thinking of the dead. Headless and handless jackets.
The smells expand like a room in the past rebuilding. I hear him
laugh in the smells of his wardrobe. I enter their ghost-lands by
putting their clothes on. I am a ghost in blazing white sleeves
and a check waistcoat. I pick up his slender wand and chalk his
cue. I don his jockstrap, I slip his cricketing box into its pouch
creating a codpiece, surely this word is a corruption of 'God's
Peace'. I pick up my cue and look at my father's Grandpiece in his
self-approving, self-improving mirrors. The mirrors are restless
and the clothes restless and I can smell the starch of my father's

stiff shirt, a boiled shirt, for wide-chested evening wear ironed by
my mother hissing among its folds with her flat-iron.

Tree

I stand by the bridge
Of the ship-white tablecloth and toast the Yule:
'Your excellencies and your admirable ghost-ship!'
And drink. The ghost ship is sailing there,
Full of lights.

We put the lights there ourselves
Which are souls nevertheless,
Glass caves with souls lodge in them,
Glass spires with blazing chambers,
Now launched like a green ship's wake
Sparkling with souls from under the skirt
Of the crowning star-lady, sailing invisibly
In the air around us too
In the perfume of pine and newly-open presents.
We decorate the tree to make the soul of it visible.
The lighted tree smells of children, a full freight.

From *Abyssophone*

★ ★ ★

Father's ghost as Trickster: I remember foxy tricks by Dad,
getting free into restaurants and cinemas — a comedy-idiom of
the time in films: the black beetle kept in the waistcoat pocket
to be 'discovered' in the food, the gatecrasher confusing the
footman with his hat, coat, gloves, stick — but the invitation, sir
— the Foxy actor in Pinocchio — it seemed he could do anything
that way but did not look foxy but rather a person of massive
probity (which he also was) — except in his early photographs,
and here the Fox declared himself. I remember how solicitously
he hovered about my mother as she was ushered into the best
seats of a cinema showing a film she didn't particularly want

to see — he had talked his way in by pretending she was very pregnant, though with half an eye you could see she wasn't. This was one of his trapdoors — rather than stunned areas — trapdoors — more of them later.

Perhaps I can contrast the stunned areas and trapdoors left or operated by my father with the open doors sustained by my mother's spirit. In the first extract I am dissatisfied with her photograph as a memorial:

> A piece of paper opening into a house, the snapshot
> Through an open door, and at the table sitting still
>
> Somebody; the house
> With one room and no kitchen
> The house with the card door;
> The disposable house.

and as an alternative I conjure her spirit into a quartz stone on a ring, that with its facets gives her many doors for her spirit-travels:

> So, with her death
> I will baptise this small
> Quartz; it shall stand for death
>
> Like a glass room
> Of which only a spirit knows the door,
>
> Which only a spirit can enter
> Turning and showing itself in the walls
> Lined with warm mirror
> Knowing its form in floor and ceiling,
> Able to say 'I am here!'

'Warm Stone for N' from *The Man Named East*

In return my mother, now being raised to seniority, is called by the name of honour, grandmother, or at any rate the one who wrote the poem accommodates her shining secrets, which appear

in return for something that hopefully seems to have gone right
in mourning for her.

*When Grandmother*

The looking-glass the vast yoni of the grandmother
In which she conducts the strictest self-examinations;

We know when grandmother is looking into her yoni:
Not only do all the other mirrors in the house deepen

And grow more silent and inner-voluminous, but
So do all polished surfaces, the dining-room table,

The picture-glass, a splash of water in the kitchen sink,
All the rain-puddles linking in the garden. After long
       scrutiny

The whole house and garden of mirrors is her yoni,
And we stand in it, nodding, like a knowledgeable

Marvelling penis. I hold a lamp in my hand,
Its light is multiplied endlessly in my grandmother's yoni
       where

Her nectar is like a reflecting glass.

From *The Laborators*

Freud asserted that the death of one's father was the most
important event in a man's life, presumably so that the Oedipal
child no longer has to wonder how he is going to kill the father,
which is his instinct (and which I wanted to in my early memory)
so as to turn him into a ghost from whom he can gain knowledge.
He becomes this ghost, without his heir having to lift a finger.
My mother in contrast illustrates that other Freudian belief that
'the play of the penis in the vagina is only one example of the
play of the body in its environment'. What this means in terms
of fulfilment of the mourning process, is that the mother can

41

turn into the World (think of the Tarot trump) while the father, a deuteragonist if not actual assailant, when he was alive, becomes a conversible ghost by the processes of poetry, thus allowing the psychic streams to flow again in new channels. The Emperor, with his sceptre.

As ghost, or ancestor, he becomes a kind of tribal spirit, whom all may consult, but not everybody does. This is how I consult my Storydad.

*Storydad*

1
We did not know we were on the ships
That throbbed grandly between the endless
Horned islands until the professional
Story-teller told us just that, and we saw them
All around, jungle-islands sliding past the ports,
The triple pulse of the ship, the foam-crescent islands;

We were in fact at home and he was our picture-daddy.
He was the place that was always healing
In happy endings, breaking out and healing.
He was a hobbling cottager, his roof leaked
In the great rains during story-telling, and he recruited
The water-voices to reconstruct the South Seas,
But the dampness hobbled him - why should he care
When he had these stories for speaking furniture?

2
I came in while he was talking
To no one, for he was blind, and had no idea
Once the stories started if there were listeners near.
Upright in his rush-bottomed chair,
The tales continued day and night, with a short repose,
And when asleep he dreamed in silence until one
Came up to him and laid fingers on his eyes
Which during dream-time throbbed
Grandly; and the tale proceeded.

Then once I touched his penis and he fell
Silent. I gripped it in my hand
And it seemed as though he were reading
Though silent, many tales aloud to me through it.
Eventually he will retire to Iron Mountain, to a hermitage
Of slate, haematite and vine. I will visit
My picture-daddy there, and he
Will tell me until he dies stories through his penis,
And after that, resounding through the whole iron
       mountain.

From *My Father's Trapdoors*

        ★ ★ ★

The two together, Mother and Father, were an explosive mixture, stunning many areas of all our lives.

In the lounge there was a thirties poster-style print in a light oak frame of a lake streaming with colours, both formidable and friendly, and across the water, standing by a cave in a white cliff, were the forms of a man and woman, the man with his arms protectively over the woman's shoulders, in sharp silhouette. This is how I felt my mother and father ought to be. I wanted them to be like this, and in the pause of and after a vehement row I tried to move them together, physically manoeuvring to make them a couple in the attitude of the people on the shore. They moved to my wishes, but I could tell by their body tension which seemed to produce a stunned kind of light in the air that as soon as they were able they would begin hammering at each other again, stepping out of the silhouette I had made of them.

        ★ ★ ★

*'The oedipal crisis is normally resolved when boys stop identifying with their mothers and begin to develop empathy with their fathers. The problem is that for years little Tommy will have been identifying with Mum: he can hardly transfer his psychological loyalty without paying*

*a price.' And, say Hudson and Jacot, 'that price is the male wound'.*
*This empathy will occur willy nilly when the father dies, it also happens*
*when the man becomes a father, with his own willy.*

The most stunned areas I have called MY FATHER'S
TRAPDOORS. These vampires — the old name for stage
trapdoors — open underfoot and on every hand. There is nothing
which may not be a trapdoor if too many tricks have been played
on you, often with the best intentions. My father both nurtured
me with constant astonishings and bound me with them. They
were his poetry, his need to display this imagery to his son. What
trapdoors did I open for him, in those days before the war when a
splinter in a baby's tender finger could in a flash burn up the whole
baby with its septicaemia (days now returning, with the immune
system weakened with radiation fall-out and pollution).

One very big trapdoor into which one was supposed to fall and
then climb out, changed profoundly, was boarding school. Such
schools are devices for tearing the child away from the mother to
give him magnified images of his father instead, which operate
by ventriloquism. I recoiled from all this. My father needed to
display his passion for his son, and one way of doing that was
to send him away, but he could not help his more immediate
emotions, all dressed up in his city clothes, and got into my space
and face on Paddington Station. I was on the brink of tears, my
natural reaction, but like a little man I would not cry, no, I would
not show how I felt.

*My Father's Trapdoors*

I
Father led me behind some mailbags
On Paddington Station, my grief was intense.
I was a vase of flowing tears with mirror-walls,

He wore a hard white collar and a tight school tie
And a bristly moustache which is now ashes
And he took me behind the newsprint to kiss me hard,

The travelling schoolboy,
And his kiss was hungry and a total surprise.
Was it the son? Was it the uniform?

It was not the person, who did not belong
Not to father, no.

Such a father, testing himself all the time, had become immensely good at all sports. I once stood on the putting green and watched him drive off from an immense distance and drop the ball exactly in the hole. I was so happy for him - but with a deprecating smile he turned my too-effusive enthusiasm aside. He told us he paid for our holidays by sitting in the Casino a certain length of time, and allowing himself to win just enough money. He took me to the old magic shows on stage at Maskelyne and Devant's — Jasper Maskelyne — what a name! — the grandson, was still flourishing at that time, immensely posh and lean in full evening dress, Kuda Bux, the man with the X-ray eyes, Dante — not Alighieri — but a South African Wizard — this was my introduction to male magic which is usually phoney or at least contrived — and led to my interest in science. For me, a woman on stage as a conjuress would have presented the whole glory, but alas that was seldom seen. Schoolmasters were a variety of magicians in their black gowns and canes for wands — it was many years before I found a true teaching once again from a woman as I had from my mother. But I have to say there was no phoniness about my father's skill in turning his body to useless sports, that glittered in cups on the sideboard.

2
He drove a hole-in-one. It flew
Magnetised into its socket. He'd rummy out
While all the rest shuffled clubs from hearts.
He won always a certain sum on holiday

At any casino; called it his 'commission'.
He could palm cards like a professional.
He had a sideboard of cups for everything

From golf and tennis to public speaking.
He took me to magic shows where people
Disappeared and reappeared through star-studded

Cabinets with dark doors, and magicians
Chased each other through disappearance after
                disappearance.
He sat down in front of my dead mother's mirror

And disappeared himself, leaving
Only material for a funeral.

Then he disappeared himself, like the master-magician he
was. The Japanese in their language do not say that a person
does something or suffers something, but rather that they play at
doing something, or play at suffering. It is to maintain a kind of
aristocratic balance, or Zen state, so that the meditation of life
shall not be troubled. Thus: 'How's your father?' 'Oh, he has just
started to play at being dead.' I used to believe that everyone did
indeed play at what they were doing, and only looked that way
because it was a game. Now my father has gone, I cannot any
longer believe that he has played at going.

3
I looked behind the dressing-table
Among the clooties of fluff and the dust,
I looked under the bed and in the wardrobe

Where the suits hung like emptied mourners,
I looked through the shoes and the ironed handkerchiefs
And through a cardboard box full of obsolete sixpences,

I looked in the bathroom and opened the mirror,
Behind it was aspirin and dental fixative,
I looked through the drinks cabinet full of spirits,

And I found on top of the chest-of-drawers
Where there was a photograph of my dead mother,
My living self and my accident-killed brother,

A neat plump wallet and a corroded bracelet watch
And a plate with one tooth which was hardly dry,
And I looked down the toilet and I turned

All the lights on and I turned them off
But nowhere in the bedroom where he sat down
And fell sideways in a mysterious manner

Could I find how he did it, the conjurer
Had disappeared the trapdoor.

He who gives presents binds the receiver of them. On the other
hand, it is said to be more blessed to give than receive. Blessing
or trapdoor. The presents at Christmas appeared like the grand
finale of a magic show. I look out of my window and I see the
cranes of Falmouth Docks. I first saw them at Christmas when I
was about four, but then they were toys and not, motionless, the
symbol of a declining economy. Some presents last a long time.
I was overwhelmed by my father's Christmas generosity. How
could I return it? Would kisses do? Not likely!


4
It was easy to disappear me.
He was doing it all the time.
I did not return that bristly kiss.

On my fourth Christmas there were so many toys
I disappeared into them thoroughly,
There was a silver crane on my mother's counterpane

It was faulty but I did not want it returned,
I have reappeared and so has it,
Nearby and grown-up in the Falmouth Docks,

And there was a conjurer's set
With ping-pong balls that shucked their shells
From red to amber, amber to green,

With a black-white wand that would float,
And half-cards and split rings as tawdry
As going up on the stage among the trapdoors

And meeting Maskelyne close-up, his cuffs were soiled —
White tie and tails should be spanking clean,
My father's would have been, and I hoped

The conjurer would not kiss me,
It would disappear me.

I do not think my mother's love was a conjuring trick. Like the funeral, it had a very different quality. It was unconditional. I suppose I was ten when my mother would still take me in bed in the mornings for a cuddle. The deep pulse that came from her body and filled the bed like wings beating was her femininity and caring and the natural bliss of her body, and I suppose you could also call it non-genital karezza. If one can know this once and find it again more than once with other women, this subtle carnal spirit, it is a singular fortune, and gives one faith in sex.

Wolfgang Lederer wrote in his *The Fear of Women*: 'Any love after that first one is, after all, at least a partial transference; and thus with any woman we love we commit incest by proxy. In last analysis, our actual mother was, herself, only a stand-in — a proxy for nature, for the mother-archetype, for the Unconscious, for the whole dark realm of the emotions, for the Goddess — put it any way you will. Through her, as by a bridge or a pipeline, or a navel cord, we are in touch (with reality).' And Norman Brown, in *Love's Body:* 'The mother would, properly, be the symbol of and partial substitute for the sea, and not the other way round'.

Yes, all very well, if you are 'in her touch' you are in the thing itself. Sexuality is one of our greatest spiritual resources. The trouble is that we have borrowed most of our guiding models of spiritual experience from the patriarchy. I believe Freud is usually right about men: you should have seen the instinctual fury on my father's face as he brought in the tea and saw in his ten-year-old son's face the glow of carnal understanding. 'Get out of there my lad,' he rasped, 'get out of there.' And I got — but on wings, I believe the wings of Ishtar.

5

He could wave his wand casually
And I would reappear elsewhere;
Once in bed at ten cuddly with mother

He waved a wand in his voice
And I got out of the silken double-cabinet
For ever.

Having children myself made me feel like my father. This is
how it is said that the Oedipus complex resolves itself — having
children oneself, becoming a father. But supposing you don't
like that feeling, as I didn't like that man in the armchair. And
supposing one finds in the cut and thrust of married life that one
can make one's partner disappear, temporarily or permanently. I
did not ask for this power-brotherhood, this bearded sexual equipage which secretes that notorious poison, testosterone. I too can
create stunned areas, abrupt trapdoors, like any other grown-up.

6

The rough kisses come round the door.
I give rough kisses myself, I am as bristly.
I am not a woman or a little boy.

And I can frighten her or make her disappear
Temporarily so she has to go to find herself
Again in the mirror somewhere;

But having learned this I am careful not to do it.
I do it less than I did.
I did not ask for this bearded equipage.

Though testosterone has other properties, and with careful
study one may take full advantage of its glitter. The wedding
tackle may with its magic wand assist children into the world, and
the spiritual children too that are made as a kind of field between
people who enjoy sex and relish its creativity. Then again, instead
of disappearing entirely, one may become the Other, and the
Other you. It is the deepest reverie we have, next to death.

7

It has taken me a long while
To appreciate this wedding-tackle at its worth.
My father gave it to me like a conjuring-set.

I do not use my wand to disappear you,
I am rather too fond of disappearing it myself,
But I also use it to empower us both,

It is the key to a wonderment openness
Like turning inside-out harmlessly
Among lights, turning

Over in bed into someone else.

According to Freud the son fears castration from the father.
He fears being dropped down a trapdoor, stunned by a father's
skilled territory, completely disappeared. On the occasion when
I saw my father's penis as a child, I didn't like the look of that
either. But when he died, he as much as my mother became a
spirit, and was everywhere, that is everything I saw became a
trapdoor and reminded me of him. Everything. That meant that
not only was his moustache ashes, so was his penis. And that was
everywhere too, just like my mother's yoni. Again the adage 'the
play of the penis in the vagina is only one example of the play of
the body in its environment'. So at last the doors swing open. I
see my father is enjoying his all-penis, and I am enjoying mine
because I have one just the same as his. It is our companionship
and our kinship. All clothes disappear in the magic cabinet and
out he comes in the buff laughing and happy, and that turns me
on properly.

8

The conjurer in his soup-and-fish
Vanishes into his cabinets,
His rival reappears, they cannot bear

To be together on the stage
Not while they're dressed in their power
Of black whiteness with starched bows

And cuffs that make the hands flash
While explaining here's a new trick:
The Chinese Cabinet.

It is a silk tent with a front door
As black and tall as Downing Street.
This must be a special trick, shall I expect

Mr. Major to ride out on a white horse?
Three people with slant eyeliner have erected it,
They are dressed as spirits who seem

Of the one sex which is both sexes
And this cabinet is not coffin-like,
No, not at all, what coffin

Would be painted with sun, moon and stars?
A Grand Mandarin with a little drum comes in,
And throws an explosive down as conjurers will

So that the tent shivers and collapses ——
Yes, it is a wardrobe that has disappeared all the clothes,
The white tie and tails, the sponge-bag trousers, the
        soup-and-fish,

For someone is coming through stark naked
And it feels good to him
For he is laughing and the mandarin bows as if proud of him,

He who touches everywhere for all clothes are gone,
Why he's in the buff and happy as Jesus save that
His lean rod is floating out just as it should,

Floating like my own, pleased to be like him.

# 3. The Alchemical Marriage of Redgrove and Shuttle

There was this young woman over by the window in the house at Zennor. She was reading a book, but not as I had seen others reading books. There was a quality of attention, of *listening* as she read, as though the book was all that was visible of another person, whom she could see entire. I learnt that this was Penelope Shuttle, and that she was a novelist. One of her books was on the table.[1] I opened it and read. I had seen nothing like it before: it was the story of three people in a sexual triangle and though they were almost entirely caught up in their jealousies they moved through a clairvoyant world that sparkled and hummed with awareness that the characters only intermittently shared. As in Wallace Stevens, they were unhappy people in a happy world. Shuttle's sentences slid over each other, chatoyant, exposing layers of texture, sound, scent, abrasion, silkiness, sentences of every kind that explored the spaces they created like fighting ants and bejewelled leopards establishing domiciles. I was reminded of Rimbaud, extended. I have since heard celebrated by the French feminists of the 1980s 'the feminine sentence' and the quality of *jouissance* in writing, and the notion that language may be as much a vital plasm as a personality is, and that writing is the plasm of the world, and the two may interact to find a transcendent completion. This was in summer, 1969. I also learnt from Shuttle's blurb that she had 'itinerant boyfriends' and lived in Frome, near Bristol. I tucked this useful item of information away.

My first marriage was in disarray. I had fled to Ireland, where I sought oblivion in the dark and velvety world of Dublin and Guinness, in and on which I lived for three weeks. My turds resembled the graphite of pencils. A kind lady put me on the plane to Bristol. It was time to renew my acquaintance with the novelist Shuttle. I rang, and agreed to meet in the George, at Frome. Her mother (who lived far away) had remarkable skills as a dressmaker, and Shuttle stepped into my life with a wardrobe full of 'the long series of wonder-awakening dresses'[2] which were the sartorial equivalent of the feminine sentences the daughter constructed: 'her wonder-awakening dresses, star-rays combed into a shaggy dress, bone-flounce skirt, turbinal blouse

. . .' — quite an eyeful. I could not wear the dresses, but I could do my best to allow the feminine sentence to write through me, and for a while I became the novelist, and she the poet. My first novel was called *In the Country of the Skin* and it was a record of the passionate multi-media show of our first months of living together, and it was not a patch on Shuttle's work. Two sentences in a piece of her work in progress had altered me and brought me through to my own novel: 'in the distance I see a bridge of white granite. Whistling its tune, night ends . . .' [3]

★ ★ ★

During those first months together the personal equivalent of the dark rhythms of the prose books manifested itself in intense depressions late in Shuttle's menstrual cycle with intense cramps when the period came. The atmosphere at these times crackled with unaccountable electricities and screaming nightmares. I had studied analytical psychology and dream analysis for many years and had recently spent some 18 months as a pupil of Dr John Layard, who himself had studied with Homer Lane, C.G. Jung and had published many seminal contributions to psychology and anthropology. With the help of Layard's methods I helped Shuttle draw a picture of the depressions — she could not write them — and then to dream vividly as a consequence. She dreamed every night for five months, and we analysed the dreams every day, in sessions often lasting many hours. There was great concern at one point when some astronauts appeared with their machine and penetrated an eye-like Earth right through its axis — this was a 'great dream' which portended either disaster like a brain tumour or a penetration to new levels. When she woke, Shuttle had begun a series of intense headaches. When she went to the ophthalmologist he looked at her heavy spectacles after his examination and said 'You don't need these.' So the dream was a healing dream after all. With the dreams so vividly and physically present, the premenstrual time now became intensely creative and the cramping bleeding uncramped itself and became an extraordinary vagina-time. Her vagina is the one thing we did not share with our daughter, as medical technology resulted in a caesarian. That was seven years ahead.

We did not look up any books on menstrual psychology as we did not want to pre-empt the dream story that was unfolding round the cycle of descent and return, of the restoration of the Goddess Persephone, the Fallen Daughter. Eventually, though, it seemed sensible to seek illumination from other people's work and advisable to consult the literature. There must be a lot, we thought, as 50 per cent of the human world menstruates. WE FOUND THAT THERE WERE NO BOOKS ON THIS SUBJECT. This is why we wrote *The Wise Wound,* and published it in 1978, since when it has remained in print.

*Horasis* was centrally important to us. This is Barbara Walker's word for mutual illumination during sex. As everybody knows, sex can take you to the deepest creative depths, and its energy can enthuse with their actual natures person and world. Two things stand in its way: one is when the man will not train himself to withhold his ejaculation long enough for the woman to expound her whole orgasmic capacity; the other is when the menstrual cycle is not sufficiently studied by the woman to find those days which are best for sex — orgasmic windows, you might call them, in the cycle. It is also the best thing to choose a position — such as the 'scissors' — in which one can not only make love effectively in mounting peaks but, without uncoupling, relish the deep relaxation moving into dreams and out again to waking. Games of all sorts can be welcomed as aspects of this *jouissance,* part of the novel.

* * *

We were perfectly happy unmarried, until we discovered that you can't put half a house in another's name without being mulcted of taxes, nor has a common law partner any rights or control over their partner's estate, nor has the partner's child any. I couldn't bear the thought of the way the law could victimize either of us if anything happened to the other, so we agreed to get married. Of course we were already married and sacramentally too in an alchymical wedding: or, to put it another way, John Layard maintained that the illegitimate relationship was the strong one.

In sexual alchemy — which is to say an artists' relationship that is erotic—you cannot hop from partner to sexual partner. The Work is a long process, and the Soror and Frater Alchymica work on each other and the work works on them for as long as it takes, which may be a lifetime. When you make love with a person, you interchange essences. This is why promiscuity fragments; now AIDS seems to reinforce this message. Concentration is needed, an accustomed temenos or laboratory, Minnebett or esplumeor charged with these conscious essences that distil and redistill . . . One life must be as open as that to the other, and only then do the partners symbolize the universe to one another. This must not be mistaken for current ideas of 'romantic love'. It is hard chemistry.

No man seems to understand this first principle: when the child arrives the lover is no longer the lover, the child has become the lover. This is nature's provision and there is a set of female instincts that puts the child at the centre, for otherwise it might not be adequately cared for. In my first marriage I felt betrayed by the relationship so radically altering — nobody teaches men that this will inevitably occur. It is why so many men start affairs just at the time when the lover should have changed at least temporarily into the father, as the nest needs protection. I was guilty of ignorance. Which didn't make it much easier when our daughter arrived in my second marriage, but it did prevent me blowing it, and I gave what I could, even though it sometimes seemed to me that I had lost the best thing in the world, our alchymical work. Which, as it happened, we hadn't.

Better than 'romantic' . . . it is best to say that we live a 'poetic' life together and as we are freelance writers this also means hard graft, as the first thing that suffers in a recession is trifles like authorship . . . All our writing is so closely shared and formed between us that there is not (so far in 20 years and some 30 books written together) this conflict. Love-making often leads to a creative clarity, and creative work often leads to a deeper love-making: we both rejoice in each other's small worldly successes though I cannot say what would happen if either one of us became lop-sidedly successful; I think in that event one must take the money and run and hide, for the media pull people's images about in distorted ways. We are happy if we can make a living within which we can continue the Work. I think I have moved further towards the feminine than Penelope has towards the masculine; this is because society is ill-balanced towards the latter.

Undoubtedly our work on menstruation together formed the deepest of bonds. During our study of Penelope's dreams and my own, it would often happen in the early months that I bled (from my anus) on the morning of the day when her period was due. This was the outer sign of a deep mental resonance, which has persisted. I will almost every month experience the distress of the late luteal phase (about day 20, when the corpus luteum in the ovary is working at its peak, yet the egg itself if not impregnated is breaking up) at the same time as Penelope, and many of its physical troubles, especially in the skin. I dream at this time, or she does, the dreams of the great paradox of the female cycle: that the death of a potential child brings spiritual renewal by its sacrifice when the blood comes: one of the world's great tragic themes, now restored to us in its actuality of the feminine after centuries of taboo. This renewal happens for both of us, and is accompanied with an especial sexual high, which is alchemical and transforms the perceptions, so that everything that falsely appeared dull and 'ordinary' is transformed to the extra-ordinary, and makes poems that testify to the joy and strangeness of descent and return. In sharing her cycle I have moved towards the feminine: 'I found God in myself and I loved her fiercely' (Ntozake Shange).

Of course I have blotted my copybook irretrievably red for danger by collaborating in a book on menstruation, and have received many insults from the masculinist establishment as a result. In France this would not happen, as feminism is advanced there sufficiently to include sexual man into feminine gender, and physical, body transforming *jouissance* into poetry. (I have been scorned by several reviewers for writing as though suffused with 'the beatific vision' when I have simply been describing what the language allows me to say of what sex shows me; just as Penelope's superb erotic poem 'Act of Love' in *The Lion From Rio* has been called 'a brave effort' as though she were not describing actualities.) But, as they say, 'No sex, please, we're British.' I expect the literati will learn to fake their orgasms as we move culturally into Europe.

I am far from being a perfect lover, even though I am 60. I have many hang-ups. I have been very lucky. The first time I had adult sex with a woman, my first real poem slid into my head. My mother on the other hand was an unhappy and imaginative woman who confided in me distresses that I now know are inflicted by patriarchy. I took harm from my parents' deeply divided marriage, and good where it might be least expected. I suppose I was 10 when my mother would still take me in bed in the mornings for a cuddle. The deep pulse that came from her body and filled the bed like wings beating was her femininity and caring and the natural bliss of her body, and I suppose you could also call it non-genital karezza.

*References*

1 Penelope Shuttle, *All the Usual Hours of Sleeping* (Marion Boyars, 1969).

2 Peter Redgrove, *In the Country of the Skin* (Routledge, 1973)

3 Penelope Shuttle, *Rainsplitter in the Zodiac Garden* (Marion Boyars. 1977).

## 4. Work and Incubation
*A Sketch of my Method of Writing*

I

The creative process has been well charted — but is still mysterious. There are basic procedures the artist can use to open to the possibilities inherent in himself and the situation; yet the process can't be forced. Berlioz called it 'careful luck'. 'Inspiration' is thus a composite.

There is always an important unconscious component. Hard work is essential — and it is hard work — but the 'germ' of a piece may seem to come from nowhere, is plucked out of the air. Henry James described the operations of this unpredictable grace in his Prefaces. Creators also agree that work at certain stages has to be *incubated*: that is, it must be allowed to 'cook' out of view somewhere in the psyche. Next time one looks at least part of the work may be finished, as though it had created itself.

There is, then, the germ to be caught, which infects one with the fever of the work, the active drafting, the conscious experimentation with words and phrases right down to the last comma and vowel; then follows as deliberate a decision to be patient, to lose the work for a time in unknown regions to see how it fares there; and afterwards, to fish it out again, like Dylan Thomas's Long-legged Bait, and find in one's nets — what? a pile of bones or a new-born child . . .

More soberly, two components are clear: the tension of conscious work, and the relaxation that allows the work to speak for itself. It is best to cultivate a balance and pliability between these two in order to make the best use of one's creative powers; the artist must be adept at both phases of this two-way process of willing, and receiving, of work, and incubation.

I evolved my own system of work because I consider the creative process the most valuable of mental events, and I wanted to make the fullest use of whatever gifts I have. I believe that the process is evolutionary, whether it occurs in art, science or in human relations. Thus, it is 'Faust' which creates Goethe. It is in this way that I believe the creative process can be lived; for example, in answer to the old question 'When is the analysis finished?', that is, when is a person functioning properly, Von Franz gave her answer 'When that person lives in a continual state of active imagination.' And to the other old question, put to Rodin by younger artists, 'What do I do when I can't work?' the answer was 'Work at something else.' I wanted a method whereby there would always be creative work to do, always work-in-progress to be taken up. What I evolved is very simple, and like a 'cascade' process in chemical engineering. I have used it for about twenty years, and thus there is in existence, for that time, a complete record in this detail and moving towards this form, of every stage of creative process in all my work: poetry, prose fiction, drama and psychology. For the purposes of this sketch, I will speak only of poetic composition.


## II.

The 'germs' of a work are all about us. The world is full of creative suggestions: it is composed of them. Most of us are too busy in other ways to take up these ideas; the professional creator must be very open to them. They are found in chance observations, words overheard, sudden headlines, fragments of dreams, the colour of a dress glimpsed through a window. The artist who wants to make the most of his world must set down these hints and guesses, sudden clarifications, brief mysteries, unexpected openings. They are the basis for his sketch-books or Journal, found objects for his studio. They are live things, he must catch them on the wing. He must at this stage not worry them to death. He must allow them to reside in his Journal, which is the lobby of his studio, so they can find their own space there, and establish their own presence. In my own Journal — the first stage of the process (though at any time a complete poem may strike) — I set down everything I would like to remember, everything I would like to become part of me or my world, both friends and enemies, from life or book or newspaper or companion. I record there also that spontaneous cinema of poetry that comes from within in dreams and reveries.

I let my Journal grow over the months. Currently I use large foolscap notebooks. When the Journal is full I begin reading it again: three or four months will have elapsed. As everybody who keeps any kind of diary knows, it is astonishing how such a practice widens one's awareness. One is astonished at what one loses in the ordinary processes of recollection without benefit of diary. Themes, thoughts and feelings become visible which the ordinary jerky occasions of daily amnesia would have fragmented and blown away. One discovers continuities of observation which would otherwise have been lost for ever, messages to oneself which would otherwise have been ignored, perhaps something terrifying claiming notice before it decides to emphasise its message with a toothache or migraine, perhaps some subliminal daemon murmuring endearments. The Journal becomes a jungle, inhabited by a whole natural history. Since I have created this jungle, now I must explore it. As I am a writer, I will do this by writing.

My next act, then, will be carefully to corral this fauna and flora in a second-stage 'imagery' notebook. I will copy out from the Journal the most sinewy images, the most voracious metaphors, the strange centipedes of thought walking with more legs than I could have predicted. I may have seen, and can now contemplate, because the occasion has been fixed in a phrase, 'a young man holding in on leashes a pair of Alsatians like holstered and loaded pistols' and as I contemplate him, his whole past history may rise up before me, and why he brings these perilous beasts to a quiet wedding. 'Why' is his poem. I may think of how a person could lead another 'into her own secret wine-cellars'; I could establish in my mind the sheer 'legginess of a young cat drinking the dew off the cold window-glass, his eyes as he drinks yellow as the yolks of two eggs'; I may *notice that I have noticed* 'how the fresh smell comes off the lawn just *before* the first drops of rain fall' or how the swan flies overhead with booming wings that rustle too as they thunder. Simply opening my eyes to some of these fragments and germs which would otherwise have been swept away on the currents of daily living may create a poem. I notice for example in an 'imagery' notebook of 1981 (71B I) that seeing how a clown's eyelids in makeup were 'cancelled with a cross' suddenly broke into twenty-eight lines on the antics of a circus as an allegory of death. These lines survived many drafts almost unchanged until the Secker volume of 1987 (*In the Hall of the Saurians*).

These are instantaneous moments of creation at an early stage; normally poems will need more incubation and more assembly than this. It is only after an interval of time that the second-stage 'imagery' notebooks are studied for the third-stage 'prose-episode-first-rhythm' notebooks. I have found that at this part of the cascade the revealed themes of the solid imagery set themselves quite naturally into short prose pieces (which are pasted on to the left hand pages). Why a prose draft for each of these many poems? Maybe it just happened; maybe I was following the great example of Yeats; maybe the prose rhythm is the first *sound* the fragments take up, their first intuition of connected voice, cry or howl. However it may be, this third stage notebook continues to capture its stories until the last left-hand page is reached, then it is put aside. After an interval it is opened again, and, with 'careful luck' the diary magic has happened again, and the prose episodes have learnt further speech. Some of course will have succumbed, and say nothing; others crowd forward to the next stage (though it is not unknown for a sequence of poems to take full form at the prose stage, thus being seen as prose-poems: there is, for instance, an 'Alchemical Journal' composed during the last 2-3 years which is about to be published).

This stage or platform in the cascade then is to reopen the same 'prose-episode-first rhythm' notebook after the interval for the diary magic to work, when the prose episodes will be found to have taken voice (as described in the last paragraph). In this voice will be (with luck and attention) a tighter rhythm, more dramatic and declaratory than the prose, in which certain words and syllables must be omitted and others brought forward. At this stage the poem begins to sing, to require phrasing and lineation, which I give it, to the best of my capacity. The resulting 'first-rhythm' draft is pasted on the right hand side of the third-stage notebook (3) opposite its prose counterpart. When I have drafted and altered this first-rhythm version and taken its song or recitative as far as I can, then, again, I close this book and allow it to incubate.

When I open this book for the fourth stage, the poem must step up out of its pages of its own accord, for the next book is for *final drafts and fair copies*, the latter to be sent for publication, and the printed versions to be pasted at the back also: these will provide the material for the very final stage of all, the publication in volume-form.

I notice that the young cat belonging to my daughter, last seen in an image-fragment in 7lB II (1 June 1986) has arrived with his legginess intact on p. 325 of a 'final draft and fair copy' notebook (79: begun 3 Feb 87) ready for consideration for a new Secker volume: 'A cluster of drops scuds down the glass/And shatters on the sill, his paw darts out/And inquisitorially turns the meagre/Water over and over — and then his tongue/ Darts out and swiftly laps it up,/The innocent water which squeals with light.' The swans, however, of 1981 (71B I) go on booming, and the fresh smell of the grass just before the rain rising to the nostrils, in a poem called 'Word' in the 1985 RKP volume *The Man Named East and Other New Poems* (pp.89-91).

# 5. The God-Trap

('The God-Trap' was the original title of 'The Case', Redgrove's longest continuous poem, and one of his most difficult, collected in *The Force*, 1966. The poem was also published in a limited edition with this preface.)

'The God-Trap' started with my hearing Verdi's *Requiem*. I don't know whether my view of this marvellous music is an orthodox one, it had a very violent effect on me. I seemed to hear a plea for the eternal rest or punishment of all sinners and it was, naturally, sung in the confident words of orthodox religion. The singers on the other hand were not the high calm voices of much church music, but rather the full blooded singers of opera, seemingly fully aware both of their sensuality and their mortality — and they were scared stiff by what they were singing, although they put a bold face on it. Such people could not help making love as they sang, I felt, whatever words they were singing.

And I too was very disturbed by this, because I saw for the first time how you could believe in a God separate from his creation, frowning down upon it. Loving both God and the creation, one's being would be split in two.

Later I came across Hermann Hesse's *Steppenwolf* and when I encountered the following passage, I felt again as if I were living in the two worlds simultaneously: 'Man is not by any means of fixed and enduring form . . . He is much more an experiment and a transition. He is nothing else than the narrow and perilous bridge between nature and spirit. His innermost destiny drives him on to spirit and to God. His innermost being draws him back to nature, the mother. Between the two forces his life hangs tremulous and irresolute . . . bourgeois "man" is a transient agreement . . . a compromise . . . an experiment with the aim of cheating both the angry primal Mother Nature and the troublesome Father Spirit of their pressing claims, and of living in a temperate zone between the two of them.'

I happened too to be reading a little about Manichaeism, which as I understood it meant exactly this dualistic split between the glory of created things, which were evil, and the glory of

God the Creator, who was good, and during my reading I was surprised to learn that Mani, the founder of this 'heresy', was often known as 'The Son of the Widow'. I was surprised because I had already begun to write 'The God-Trap', and my cast was settled. It comprised a Widow and her son, and the Son was searching for a Father.

The clinching thing, though, as far as this poem was concerned, was an actual happening. We were visiting one of the great national trust houses near Harrogate. It has a wonderful walled garden. It was in this garden that I saw an elderly woman — she was about sixty — wearing a cotton dress with a floral pattern that spread great flower-blooms over her motherly figure. She was standing by a great bank of flowers, her eyes half-closed, leaning back slightly, and saying, quite softly: 'Oh, this is life . . . what a shame we have to die . . .'

The figure of this woman haunted me and I had to work it out. She seemed so in love with the gardened earth I wondered what God she could have and whether he were apart from it, and if he were God in heaven, up there, how she could possess both him and the flowering earth. What could there be in the death of this woman, for others or herself, but terror and absence, the spirit and the flowering body taken apart, the white from the yolk.

And I thought of the son of such a woman, she perhaps pious and widowed, he sent almost by hints, misunderstanding of her piety on a mythic quest for God, the missing father, and how his inherited senses and his inherited piety would be as great as hers, and how he might court his destruction in his search, and where he would find his equilibrium, his compromise, Hesse's 'temperate zone', and the poem seemed to give its answer; that his fate would be a modern fate, a Faustian fate, in his striving to command absolute experience, but the outcome would be the same as that of King Oedipus in the old story.

And lastly I wondered if I had ever met an actual person such as this, and where he would be found if I had not. For I saw that I was trying to write an elegy for him, a requiem, and one for a split in Man's consciousness, and then I found that I had noted, as if by chance, this paragraph from some journal:

Clinic Director: 'This is schizophrenia. The boy was close to his mother: a widow after a very unsatisfactory marriage. His illness, which must always have been latent, accelerated when she died . . . He suffers also from hysterical blindness, and cannot open his eyes. They have remained closed for the ten years of his illness . . . He likes to spend his time in the garden and likes also to be called "Father". He never replies when he is so called, but only smiles a little, and turns away . . . I have noticed that such cases, which are nowadays very widespread, often seem unwilling to be cured.'

## 6. Interview with *The Hudson Review*
(Mike Erwin and Jed Rasula)

**Mike Erwin:** In many of your poems, I suppose in your more automatic surreal poems in *The Hermaphrodite Album,* there are very rapid shifts of image and metaphor and something verging through the poem; and I wonder if you have a sort of built-in sense of limitation about the repetitions and mutations of your energies and the metaphors you work with? What are the bounds of surrealism in your poetry?

**Peter Redgrove:** Well, there isn't any surrealistic content. I mean, I don't understand what you mean by surrealistic content anyway. None of those poems are, in the sense of arbitrariness or of desire to shock, surrealistic. They're surrealistic in the sense that they explore a world whose boundaries shift and change and transform. And they're surrealistic in the sense that they draw on this kind of dream-like life, or a world in which the limitations *are* only subjective. But I think we need another word than surrealistic for this. I myself would prefer some word which had a notion of eroticism in it. Because those poems are really quite straightforward if you take the notion that in an erotic state of mind you are living in a state somewhere between dream and waking, where the imagination becomes literally true. This is the theme of *In the Country of the Skin,* too. Obviously within this world certain personages and events recur. In *In the Country of the Skin* this black woman and the death and the recovery of a child who is the man himself, this kind of process is an archetypal one. This is Isis re-growing her child, or the child of the black Sophia. These things, however, were discovered post-facto. This is an experience. The poems are supposed to be experienced, I would say, as in a light trance. That is to say in a trance of concentration. I like to use the Chinese or Japanese notion of mirror-mind for this. Or the Zen notion, though I got it from judo where one is supposed to have mirror-mind as well. Nothing is held onto; things change. 'Surrealistic' is the wrong notion, I think. I would say 'pentecostal' if it didn't seem to recommend the worst. But perhaps in the existing categories 'symbolist' is a better one.

ME: In that world of symbolism do you have a sense of limitation as to where you would stop the suggestiveness or something like it in your poem?

PR: This would depend on my audience. *The Hermaphrodite Album* itself is written between us, to each other, in the attempt to recreate an erotic atmosphere which is also an intellectual one. The sense of limitation in that is I discovered that many people do not live in an erotic way. So many people seem to live in their heads. That's why the book is called *In the Country of the Skin* because it's living in the skin. Limitation — no. The kind of activity in this world leads toward a transformation, a change and new vistas of consciousness. There is the point where one falls back from this kind of state of mind, this incredibly capacious and sensitive state of mind. One falls back from this from time to time. And this is subject matter of course. So in that sense limitation. There's also limitation in the sense of formal boundaries — well, yes, the vessel changes. The vessel changes. For instance, in *The Hermaphrodite Album* I think of the way it's become more formal and incantatory later on in the book, more patterned. Why this should be I don't know, except for increasing confidence, since the poems are more or less arranged in chronological order. What happens in that book is that the two kinds of poems, which are our own, Penelope's poems and my sorts of poems — at the beginning you can tell them apart, you know, each of our work. As you go on in the book it's not so easy to tell because they fuse and change, and then people make mistakes about who did what, you see. This is the point of the book, really. It's to say we have our own particular talents, and we're interchanging them and learning them. And I would hope in reading the book one gets this sensation. Few of the poems are overtly love poems. But the book itself, as one reads it, is about mingling and the exchange of abilities. Which is, you know, love in practice rather than love stated and depicted. So the word limitation is manifold, isn't it; there are four or five implications there. I think it's quite true to say we are intent on becoming each other. I'm quite sure I'd rather be her than myself. And I think she'd rather be me than herself. So we exchange in this way. But this is quite normal, isn't it, in any love affair. And it looks surrealistic because I suppose the surrealists were highly erotic men.

ME: What about the shift in your work in the last few books, more markedly from *The Force*, into this more pentecostal, if you like, world, this more exploratory world of the unconscious. Was this fairly deliberate on your part, or was it gradual?

PR: Obviously it was a delightful gift. My first marriage wasn't very happy. Neither were the jobs I had to do for a living. I was in an office and so on and I believed that one *should* go to an office and earn one's living in this way and wear suits, etcetera. And I was lucky enough to get a three-year fellowship at Leeds, which required of me nothing except that I should do my own writing. And a great deal of unnecessary and obsessional formalism began to disappear at this point. Because, you know, I'd been taken on my own abilities, as it were, or my own interests, rather than doing somebody else's job for them in an office hierarchy. And I think this produced in *The Force* a relaxation in subject-matter, because it allowed me more time for contemplation. I mean, I could work all day if I wanted to, instead of working as I did in office jobs: I used to get up at five-thirty in the morning in order to work, you see, before going to the office. Spent some time on benzedrine doing that. This was about fifteen or so years ago. And then recently my marriage broke up. This is an English middle-class story. English middle-class men of my generation are rather liable to marry the first women they sleep with, do you see. I was born in 1932 and I would have come to sexual awareness just shortly after the war. Very austere time, when tribal values were paramount, really, because you couldn't allow the healing energies which were trying to put England together to leak at all. So there was no question of any kind of permissiveness. So the influences brought to bear on the young people were really very very strong, particularly in this English middle-class sort of thing. So if you slept with a woman you would probably want to marry her, and I did. I was faithful to her for thirteen years. When I got out of the office jobs and the nine to twelve sort of thing, which was part of the tribal values (one's woman expected one to work in this fashion, whatever it did to one), with the Leeds thing all sorts of other powers and interests started to arrive. Including the inevitable love-affair, which separated me from those tribal values, since they represented — this love affair — the things which my marriage had left out. My wife was quite forgiving about this, do you see, but she really wanted to return to the old state. And so did I, I think. But this was impossible and the thing got wilder and wilder and I started being seventeen instead of whatever I was — thirty-six, something like that-and slept with a great many people, which she got fed up with so she went off. On the other hand, you see, this liberated very many perceptions which had been trained into these middle-class shapes. So it's a little piece of social history which, I'm very interested to discover, is matched for instance by a lot of the lives of my colleagues here at the art school, who are artists, who made similar kinds of marriages, had similar kinds of trouble about the same age. I think you find this generally among middle-class people, who have become artists in England.

ME: Also I'd like to ask you what kind of lasting effects you feel were made on your work by the insulin-shock comas?

PR: Well, this is a very strange business. It's entirely double. As Empson says, 'ambiguous gifts as what the gods give must be'. Well, the exact equivalent is an acid trip, I think. You see, we didn't have LSD at that time, there was no LSD at all. There was no hash, no pot either, for that I had to go to Spain later on. I used to get a great deal of psychedelic adventure on liquor. Then I went into the army, I had this experience, and I was a very obsessionally tidy sort of person. The army was obviously too much, so I said I'd lost my memory, in order to get out of it. But I started telling the psychiatrist some of the things that had happened to me, which were no more than the distortions of ingrown virginity. And a doctor said, 'I can't quite understand you, you must be schizophrenic or you must have incipient schizophrenia. Therefore we'll try on you this new treatment, insulin shock.' I said, oh I don't care, if I get out. It was only very much later I realized how barbarous it was. Because they draw all the sugar out of your blood till you go into convulsions and then into a coma; then they bring you back again. Nobody knows why this works for schizophrenics, whoever they are. There's no diagnostic category of incipient schizophrenia. Nowadays they give you drugs instead, which is much more beastly, I think, really. It was quite unnecessary in my case. I mean, I meet students every day who suffered from little obsessional fears like I had. And they gave me this thing. And the myth of it is that you die and are reborn. And that's exactly what happened. I remember being taken to pieces and put together again. And subsequently I've learned that some such experience, when it happens to people, often liberates great tracts of their lives. When I started writing poetry, for what reason I don't know . . . Oh yes, that was erotic too! The first time it happened was the first time I slept with the girl who became my wife. There was a great peace in my head and into it came the lines of a poem. So that was the first poem. When I was doing this, starting to write poetry, I thought to myself, 'Who am I, with my middle-class background and no experience of life or anything, to be writing poetry?' And then I said to myself, 'But I've been dead fifty times. I have something to say.' And, of course, later on one learns that many kinds of artists, adventurers of the mind, have had this sort of experience. Up there's the book on Shamanism by Eliade: the shaman always suffers an initiation of this kind. Graham Greene talks about his Russian roulette. I'm not comparing myself to these people. Herman Melville had this experience of falling on the deck, but the ship keeled over and he went in the water instead; but he saw the grain of the wood. And it was a reprieve made Dostoyevsky go out 'queer and clear' I think Empson says. And younger people nowadays, if they don't find a death and rebirth out of their family situation or out of their adolescence threshold (society doesn't provide thresholds for us), they cut their wrists or go on an acid trip or many acid trips. They will have a time of such exploration. And this happened to me quite inadvertently, you know, without my seeking. And it gave me a root in a kind of experience which was both of death and erotic in nature. So it had, I think, an important effect. But I still think it was a barbarous thing to do to a young man of eighteen.

Jed Rasula: There's an interesting level of anthropomorphism, I think, in *In the Country of the Skin*, which is suggestive to me of the organic nature of poetry and language. One of the passages is a description of crabs:

They mate, with the sound of typewriters. The tide is

returning, they retreat to their caves. They have written their page on the sand, as a pack of cards writes its game on the baize table. The tide is coming like hands to gather up the writing.

And in another passage a description of a tree, where you say:

A tree throws down its library of books every autumn,
it throws out all these books, and it grows new ones.
A tree takes off its brain, throws it to the ground. It
shatters. A new brain grows.

And in both cases there is an element of ritual, possibly, which I think is related to human activity. And I wonder if I'd be correct in thinking that you see poetry as having an actual organic relation to other creative forces and cycles?

PR: Certainly. You're absolutely right. I do. It's the signature of all things, isn't it? I mean, this is God's handwriting or nature's handwriting that you read. What you write in a book is only one variety of organic growth, organic life. Poetry, insofar as it has to do with visionary matters as opposed to (well, I don't think it *can* be opposed to social matters), but directly in visionary matters, the visions are visions of matter. I'm a materialist, you see, but I'm a materialist in the Hindu tradition, which regards matter as a song. This is not so far from contemporary physics of course. What we're made of is a complex vibration. Poetry does vibrate, it is a pattern of vibrations. I say I'm a materialist: for instance, I have great sympathy with the French neurophysiologists who maintain that dreams are a replay of the genetic code. I find the conceptual link between mind and matter a very easy one. I find no division between mind and body; I am not a Cartesian man. I find that it is very easy to think of matter as being conscious on a molecular level. All sorts of things come from this. It's to do with being originally trained as a scientist, I think. It's this notion that, for instance, you hold a golf ball in your hand: now, the relation in size between this golf ball and the earth is the same as that between the ball and a molecule in your body. In other words, your body is a world. How do the inhabitants of this world communicate with the *anima mundi* which you call your personality? Of course, they communicate by means of dreams and visions. There's a very strange experiment which I've written about in the new novel, *The Terrors of Doctor Treviles,* and which is completely authenticated and absolutely respectable. And it has to do with warts. Warts are a variety of benign cancer, of course, and probably a combination of allergic and viral disease, and there have always been legends about warts that they could be charmed away. You know, you could go to the chemist and have your name put in the wart book and they would disappear, you would pay a penny. And there are wart charmers here in Cornwall. My colleague here, Lionel Miskin, has taken his family to a wart charmer and the warts went — mind you, they came back again, but they went. And there is this man, this doctor, called Stephen Black; and I read this, many years ago when I used to work in the offices, in *The Lancet.* It was part of my job to read the medical journals. And what he did was to get a considerable number of very warty patients in one hospital, and experiments properly supervised by doctors and nurses and so on. And some people have warts so badly that they're in agony from it, they can't move in their clothes without these things turning over on their skin. And he got a good deep-trance hypnotist there, and in full view of all these doctors and nurses he had the hypnotist say to the patients (perfectly controlled experiment), 'The warts on the left hand side of your body will disappear and the ones on the right will remain.' Lo and behold it happened. Properly supervised; it was written up in *The Lancet,* and there is nothing more respectable. The implications of this experiment are enormous. Later on he wrote a book called *Mind and Body* in which he explored these implications. What it amounts to is that the voice changes molecular structure, the voice, in trance, communicates down to the molecular level Thus, the shapes of the proteins, which have to do with the antigen manufacture, which fit together like keys and locks, were altered by the voice of the hypnotist. Or by the body of the subject responding to the voice of the hypnotist. Therefore there is in certain states of mind — visionary states of mind — a communication between what you call the mesocosm, the size-scale of things we inhabit, and the scale of the very very small. This links up in a gratifying manner with Ouspensky's notion that when we look for God we look for Him in the wrong place. We look for him in the heavens — well, he's there as everywhere else. But where we should look for him is in the very small. It's in one of his discussions about further dimensions, one of his fourth dimension/fifth dimension discussions. He says that the freedom of other dimensions is at the level of the very very small. There is a paper by J.B.S. Haldane which I had the pleasure of bringing to the attention of Arthur Koestler (after reading his book *Roots of Coincidence*) in which Haldane maintains that the brain has its ability for apparent decision of free will as sub-atomic particles seem to in a sense, because it is a magnifier of quantal events. We've got a very marvellous continuum here. Koestler's own book *The Roots of Coincidence*, of course, was about the strange similarity between the science of ESP and psychic research and the science of sub-atomic physics. He didn't make the conceptual connection between the two, that in fact the scientists and the investigators were talking about the same worlds. But he might very well have done. I wrote to him about it and he said yes. Do you see how this means that when we are in a visionary state we are seeing the world? The shaman is not a man who doubts (this is a mistake made in later Greek thought), is not a man who separates his mind from his body and goes into the universe and flies away like an angel, as Blake knew very well. He's not that sort of man at all. He's a man that goes *into* the universe of his body, and in the universe of the body all the forces that make us are compiled. That is, we are a focus of many many forces in the world. So if we investigate ourselves, we investigate the world. So I'm a materialist. I can't remember your question *(laughing)*.

JR: Well, that comes around to it in an interesting way. Do you think that poetry is a necessary focussing on the life of bodies and the components, the forces, that are centered there?

PR: Poetry is life talking to itself in its own language. Said Novalis.

JR: Yes, that's in *In the Country of the Skin*.

73

PR: I think Novalis originally said it. But I certainly said it in *In the Country of the Skin*. This notion, incidentally, is in a very respectable tradition. You can read Wordsworth, you can read Shakespeare *(Midsummer Night's Dream)*, you can read Rilke, you can read Novalis, I think Hölderlin, all in this tradition. There's a book which was a revelation to me when I read it after writing *In the Country of the Skin*, called *The Orphic Voice*, by Elizabeth Sewell. She talks about a line of poets, inherent in whose beliefs is that poetry is not mere ornamentation but is actually *about* something which is important to us and actually can affect not only the way we think, the way we feel, but the way we grow, and the way that things grow around us. Magic, in other words. For some reason Christianity doesn't like this sort of thing. Of course, Christianity *has* to separate itself from the world in order to bring about the rise of technology, for whatever purpose that was; personally I think it was to invent organic chemistry and thereby contrive the birth pill, which renders women independent creatures and their own mistresses instead of chattels of men. I could be wrong about this *(laughing)*. Christianity, which is a male-oriented religion with a triple male in the sky, was perhaps invented by women in order that the birth pill might be discovered. And now, if that's true, we've got the birth pill: we don't need Christianity.

JR: On the dust-jacket of *In the Country of the Skin* there's mention of a hope that your work might lead other people as well as yourself into what you call 'a neurosis-free world.' Do you feel this as a driving impulse behind the writing of your work or more as a hope for what you've already finished?

PR: Well, I think poetry ought to have a healing function. I can't really hope that mine could do what I want in this respect, but it looks in this direction. I would think that somebody who had gone through the experience of *In the Country of the Skin* would have gone through what I went through in writing it, which was a very healing process. It's as simple as that. One goes through these things and one doesn't see them at a distance, one participates in them if it's a good book — if it's a strange book and a good book as well, which really draws you into it, it should have something of the same effect as the events it describes.

Which for me were a transforming experience. I have, you see, through the years — partly through the practice of poetry and partly by the study of psychology — lost a lot of neuroses, I mean, lost a lot of quite gross clinical troubles. I had these two years of study with this old gentleman John Layard, which were extraordinarily revealing to me and liberating. And I believe that a lot of the baggage and hangups that people carry around with them *are* in fact dispensable. It's simply a matter of inhibition: there's something which is standing between them and their proper natures. I'm reminded of Eliot's remark in this respect. He said inspiration is not something which descends on you, he says it is more like an inhibition to inspiration being taken away; it's more like something being taken away which interferes with the proper state of your mind which is inspiration. The proper state of mind is inspiration And having lived in a state of ecstasy in writing that book — not by writing it, but living in a state of ecstasy and being a writer writing about it for this quite extended time — in a state of continued inspiration which, in my case, may be of a fairly archaic kind, but is open-ended — I believe that this state is available to people. It's a state in which the mind is *not* separated from the body, it's a state in fact of being in love with the world without ignoring anything about it. Many of the psychedelics give accounts of this sort of world. I think it's one's birthright, I think this is mankind's birthright. And what we call neurosis is the impediment to existence in this state. And of course neuroses can be external as well as internal — they can be social neuroses. They can be social habits which are unexplored abuses, doors in the mind which shut off avenues of exploration, because growth is painful.

JR: There's something quite related to that from *In the Country of the Skin* that I'd like to read and ask you about. You say there that:

> Poetry is the calculus of growth, and intuition is how we articulated ourselves through all those dangers, and the final shock-gate of growth, the birth, where most of us forget ourselves, forever. No one can deceive themselves, or be mad themselves, or become insane.

They can be out of contact with it, shocked back into life which is too much for the grey shocked core called brain.

And a few pages later you say:

Not sex only, not magick only, not poetry only, not madness at all, but womb-talk, the first conversations of the growing spirit with the life that lives it and the death it will die into life with its bride the earth.

And I'd like to explore a bit more this notion of poetry as the calculus of growth. And whether you think that is the way in which poetry has its most effective healing properties.

PR: Of course, that passage has specifically to do with the sort of materialism I was talking about. There is something that must be here, and that is pre-natal experience. You see, I think poetry, the calculus of growth, art generally, is the reflection or the top end, as it were, of the processes that grew us. This is why I say that dreams or poetry are a replay of the genetic code. Something happens to us. We went through nine million years of evolution in nine months in our mothers' wombs, but we've forgotten it for the main part. It seems that in art quite often, particularly when the times are such that nothing seems to be declaring it outside, and people have to go within, that there is a capacity for remembering back into pre-natal experience, or into very fine physical detail. I think one of the first times I noticed this was when I was looking at the paintings of a student here, and he was drawing a cellular structure, a muscular structure, at photo-micrographic enlargement. And I happened to recognize this because I did a histology course at Cambridge. And I saw this thing and I said, 'That's very interesting, where did you get this?' He was quite offended, he said, 'It's an abstract.' I said, 'That's fine, but can I show you the book?' So I came up here and got the book of histology off the shelf and took it down to show him. He said, 'My God, yes!' And this actually helped his drawing, you see, because we've got a microscope here and he looked at the tissues. What was amazing about this was that shortly afterwards he started suffering pains in his leg and his leg muscles started to wither for an unexplained reason. He couldn't get any treatment for this. It was shortly after painting this. Now, I think (there's other evidence for this too) I think that what he was drawing or painting was his leg going wrong, because those were the tissues that were affected. Now, this ability to see within in specific and exact ways, I mean, it's almost medical, isn't it! What a diagnostic instrument! I'm quite serious about this. Now Waddington, the embryologist, has written a book on modern art in which he gives a parallel (I don't think he goes quite as far as I just did), but he says that the organic forms that painters discover in much modern art *may* have to do with an ability to look into cellular structures. He's an embryologist. Why is he writing on modern art? Perhaps even further. We forget what happens in the womb, and yet because of this recapitulation of evolution, because of our own growth from molecular structures, because of the bringing together of the world in food and focussed in this womb we're grown in, there's a most extraordinary extent of magical knowledge possible. What we *call* magical knowledge, but it's only natural. This is lost at the birth trauma, only remembered by such explorations as art and poetry provide into the unconscious. You *cannot* understand people's dreams, you *cannot* go through a psychoanalytic session, without realizing that pre-natal experiences are being depicted in dreams, without realizing a change of scale which has to do with experience at a different level of size and intensity. And what is more, without understanding or allowing yourself to be open to the notion of telepathic and precognitive experience also (which seems to happen at this womb-level, this molecular level). Now, what poetry does as a meditation instrument is to accustom one's mind to the mutations which are natural on these levels of being which our ordinary mental constructs do not allow ourselves to consider. Many people, for instance the psychologist Otto Rank, believe that a hero was a person for whom the birth-trauma had not been amnesic, a person who had not forgotten his womb-life. I remember also reading a suggestion by one commentator about circumcision. He maintained (it was only a suggestion, he said) that the reason why God insisted so much on circumcision was because it was a trauma. The Jews are great poets and prophets. The beginning of their history started with God stamping his feet and shouting at Abraham, didn't he, that the sign of his covenant was circumcision. Why? Desert hygiene? The Arabs don't circumcise until puberty. The Jews are the only people who circumcise the baby at eight days. The only people. So, why was God so insistent about it? The suggestion here is that it sets up a trauma. If you cut the penis, you (as all wounds do) energize the nervous system appertaining to those organs before, of course, the reproductive organs are mature. So what you do is to set up an ego-structure. By means of this wound you awake very early. You set it up against the birth-trauma, which is a terrible nightmare we try to forget. But the circumcision sets up a memory, an ego, shortly after that time, only eight days. This commentator's suggestion was that people who were not circumcised were more susceptible to mob effects, you see, collective effects, than the Jews, who are individualists. The effect of circumcision is to set up an ego structure, so that you stand as an individual in relation to the birth trauma, rather than there being an undifferentiated force in your psyche.

JR: In *In the Country of the Skin* everything is alive, to my perception of it, *everything*. And as you say, even on a molecular level. In fact, human life only seems to be finding itself in terms of the other life it's near to and often is. In your poetry also the sense of life isn't tied to the human orientation or human interpretation, by any means. Most of the work in *Dr Faust Sea-Spiral Spirit* is like this, and even some poems in *The Force* ('The Young Forester Protests,' 'Really Gone,' and 'A Testament' are poems which I see in this way). And this really vigorous vitalistic approach to the world is very interesting in relation to a point made by Marie Peel in writing about your work, in which she notes a lack of social reference, and I'd like to ask what you feel about that? With regard to your work, what sorts of responsibilities do you feel, or pressures, to introduce a kind of articulated social awareness?

PR: Well, I mean I'm only forty-one; you can't do everything at once, can you? My attitude to that, really, is that you should get yourself right, before getting the rest right. Though, of course, you may have to sacrifice yourself in the interest of the revolution, but as an artist I don't think this is the priority. You see, over the years I've had to work from inside out; like many artists I'm haunted by certain images which stand between me and my proper life. They contain the life, but they stand in front of it. These images have to be gone through. The only way out is *through* in these cases. This is what I mean by neurosis. With an artist, he's not a neurotic; the neurosis gives him images: they are doorways, they are thresholds. It's only fairly recently that I've been able to understand how these images that have haunted and obsessed my life have arisen not only from my own psychic structures (if there is such a thing, as I think there is) but have also been socially conditioned. We were talking about the war and the English middle-classes. I can see how my life, as is the case with many of my friends and colleagues, is an image of society *also*. I have a growing and forward-looking sense of responsibility about this. I believe, for instance, that if in writing poetry I discover or depict anything of value it is my business to relate this as far as possible to what people understand in their usual lives. This is the reason why I made the novel *The Terrors of Dr Treviles,* which I've written with Penelope Shuttle, almost an explanatory novel. It is not, I trust, a lecture. But it's like *In the Country of the Skin* with explanations. I don't know whether it's more or less effective because of the explanations. But it seemed to me that people who understood *In the Country of the Skin* understood it because of a sympathy of temperament. I would rather like people who do not have a sympathy of temperament to understand the matters that I was talking about and had experienced myself. So that's a responsibility. For example, Freud says the root of neurosis is the refusal to die. My image bearing on this is the idea of the Eleusinian Mysteries. Now what exactly happened in the Eleusinian Mysteries has been lost. It deteriorated and disappeared. But there was something in these rites that changed the people who went through them. This ceremony was at the heart of Greek culture, of Greek civilization, which is still with us. It was the thing that caused Greece to be the civilization that it was. People went through it: they learned something about death which removed anxiety. There are contemporary hymns which say that the person who has been through the Mysteries is fortunate because he doesn't evaporate like the other ghosts, but has learned something about death, about the other side. And what obviously happened is that anxiety was removed, to use contemporary terms. Therefore the people were free to grow into themselves. What was this thing that they learned? Something about death. Perhaps that death is more alive than what we call life. Something. Perhaps, I thought that *In the Country of the Skin* was a pale shadow of this, that it showed that everything *was* alive. This is what I mean, I think: that it is the poet's responsibility, perhaps, to discover and reproduce the kind of thing that was going on in the Eleusinian Mysteries.

ME: Do you think a relatively neurosis-free individual is possible?

PR: Yes. I've met them occasionally *(laughing)*.

ME: Are there destructive things attached to *not* being neurotic?

PR: Yes, because these people almost always involve others in their lives. I think they're people who give a great reflection. Omar Khayyam remarked (not, I think, in the *Rubaiyat*, but somewhere else) that, 'I am he who gives a perfect reflection of you,' and I think that neurosis-free people do tend to do this. And so if you see a reflection of yourself in this person, you want to follow it. You have a feeling that something can be changed. You have a feeling that they understand. Perhaps they don't. Perhaps it's only the reflection that you get. They can give this reflection because they have this mirror-mind, this ability to reflect without greed, without holding on. They seem to those of us who still have much attachment to ourselves and to usual things to be heartless, because wherever they are fills them, including you. But you need not necessarily be in their mind, as a portion of their being, if you're not there. In other words they don't hang on. Yes, I've met people like this. I think they're people clearly of a most extraordinary and rewarding kind to be with. The only thing is, they love, but you're not the only person they love. So they're inclined to produce jealousies. I mean, I'm describing something which is fairly rare among men but fairly common among women, I think. Mind you, this is a complex subject. The statement I think I'm properly making is that the mind, the psyche, is a very inventive place. It invents in the mode that we distinguish inappropriately as something apart, as poetry — it invents in this mode. If a person is damaged or if a person has been rendered too vulnerable or had too bright a light shone on his psyche, he will have a stasis there. And this we call a neurosis or an obsession. He is less likely to suffer from this if he is accustomed to the way his mind, his psyche, works. One way of investigating this is called poetry. The corollary of this is that a study of poetry will cure by making the reactions more fluid. Dissolving the scotoma, it will cure neurosis. It's a corollary. When I say poetry, it can be oral poetry, it can be a rite performed in some open place or in a church, or it can be the improvisation a gifted analyst gives on one's dreams. For instance, the man I've mentioned, John Layard, when he interpreted dreams it was spoken poetry: he improvised on the dream, do you see.

ME: In talking about the involvement of the voice in poetry, what effect do you think conscious effort at control has, in writing the poem?

PR: Well, I mean, the banal image is riding a bicycle, isn't it? I find, myself, that it's a condition that one mustn't ask too hard because that's pre-judging the question; one mustn't pull too hard on the strings, as they break; one mustn't assume anything; one must be receptive but not yet critical — no, one is both receptive and critical. It's like holding a very good conversation with another person, and in a conversation you have to behave with manners. I mean, if I keep on interrupting you, we'll have no conversation. And vice versa. It's very much like that, I find. I think there are also three very interesting things that happen, stages as it were. There's the stage when you write with exhilaration. Now, the results of that may be very good or very bad. One is improvising with exhilaration or feels very good — there may be incidental beauties among a whole nonsense. This is the jungle that one can invent before one explores, or it may be complete nonsense. One writes with exhilaration, and the result has no necessary relation to the exhilaration. That is one way. And another way is that one can write in depression, one can have something to write (perhaps something one has drafted) and one can feel very depressed about it. This is the control, you see, one can say, 'I will write this out. Maybe I'll not do anything with it. Let's see. Let's see what happens.' And it's very depressing, but you just have to do it. You do that. Now, the curious thing about that is that the results are usually better than you'd expect. The depression is in fact, I think, your truly critical abilities at work. Your mental energy is withdrawn into itself for the purposes of work, and one mustn't expect reward until the work is done. That's the second way. There is a third way, where all these processes of control and reception seem to be fused and become another person, and *that* person writes for you. The magicians call this (I think this is what they're talking about) the conversation of the holy guardian angel. This is the title for the experience. I think it's the same experience. But *there* questions of control and receptivity are quite irrelevant. There is somebody who is able to accomplish this work and does it. Now, these are mysteries of course, but what I'm saying about a neurosis-free state has something to do with what the magicians call conversations with the holy guardian angel. It's like supposing Rimbaud had decided not to turn his back on it, it's the 'I is another," of course. I think the artist experiences all three ways. You know, whatever stage they may be, in various degrees, I think it's valuable to know what's happening. A lot of people get terribly excited in the writing, and they say 'It must be all right because I'm excited about it' — and that's a very bad kind, I think. If you're depressed in the writing that is a slightly better guide that something may be going on. Can't explain this. But the third experience is what I think is one's birthright, really. And it happens to many people in many ways, but is a very remarkable and superb experience.

ME: What particular elements in a poem or poetry do you feel are important, say, like rhythm or visual imagery or assonance. Particular elements that you find are really essential for your poetry.

PR: It's something that John Castor calls the strength of the sentence. But this is begging the question, because the strength of a sentence may be rhythmical, it may be grammatical in for instance the way in which a sentence may be particularly

82

declarative because it's relatively simple, or because it's complex in a way in which the clauses run against each other; you know, the cross-ways. But it is something very sculptural, I think. When I read a good poem the first sensation of pleasure that I have is of strength in the sentences. That is the first sensation. This is a thing that one can see very quickly, of course, in looking at poetry. It's not the final pleasure, it's the doorway into the other pleasures for me. After this I distinguish. My pleasure expands and takes various forms within the poem. That's the first sensation, and it's the thing I want in my own poems. If I can see in my own poems that I have made sentences which are strong, then I feel I've done something. And when I look at a recent poem to see whether I've done it right, I don't look at whether I've got the thought right or whether I've got the rhythm right, I try to get that sensation of ah! it's there. So really, I'm substituting one terminology for another, but I can only say that: it's the strength of the sentences. And I don't quite know what that means. It's a position in space, it's as though the sentence is a space which is filled with dynamic energies which either hold still or interact. It's as though in the sentence there was a transaction which was taking place. As though there was in the poem an articulate energy (Donald Davie's words) transmitting itself from sentence to sentence and from one part of the sentence to another in various ways. Causing various pressures and lightenings and darkenings as it does so — It's a very material, physical thing. It has to do with structure. And that's the only answer I can give without faking up a lot of remarks about beat and rhythm. I used to think it was something to do with a four- or three-beat line which didn't fuss about how many syllables it had in it. Which is of course sprung rhythm — Hopkins and more loosely *Four Quartets,* going back to Langland and the pre-Chaucerian things like Gawayne and so on. These kinds of sounds. I think it's important to me that poetry not sound Chaucerian; I'm a non-Chaucerian in this sense.

JR: In the past few years you've branched out into a variety of forms that are developments beyond the short-poem form you used for your first three or four books. There's the novel, the pieces for voices, a radio-play, and *The Hermaphrodite Album* with Penelope Shuttle and now another novel with her. And I wonder if you see this development, this branching-out, as just occurring over a period of time out of the necessities of things that had to be said and were coming to be said in other than the short-poem form? Or whether this reflects an actual change in your thinking about what can be done in the various forms?

PR: Well, I always believed that the short-poem form could say everything. In a sense I still do. There's a double answer to this, really, because I've always been afraid of all sorts of things — all of us are. One of the things I was afraid of was writing prose. The reason for this is for ten years I earned my living in advertising and journalism. And in order to keep my poetry going I had to separate off the kind of writing I used to earn my living from the real things which, for me at that time, could only be short poems. This was partly due to my idea of prose writing being connected with educational things like examinations and economic things like earning one's living. But poetry has nothing to do with earning one's living, nor with purposes related to that, related to the corrupt capitalist structure that we live in. So I separated off the prose. Now, when I finally was able to bring to mind some things like the insulin shock thing, which of course you're made terribly ashamed of — this is another of the middle-class things. If you do something like that, if you go mad for a short time or pretend to go mad for a short time, you are of course ostracized — if you come out with it. If you're quiet about it they'll tolerate you. Though it's an awfully useful weapon for one's relatives to use. If they happen to disagree with you they can always say 'oh he's mad again' or something like this, you see. So I kept the insulin shock thing and various other preoccupations which occur in that book *In the Country of the Skin* very quietly to myself. And it was only as a result of meeting John Layard and meeting Penelope Shuttle that I ceased to be ashamed of these things. At the same time I ceased to be afraid of writing in prose. Thus writing in prose didn't seem to carry penalties and rewards of a monetary kind. So I was able to assimilate the prose thing to the poetry thing. So you see, once again my answer is rather than select one or two alternatives I have to give you both at once. Because both of your alternatives are true. It's both what I found it necessary to say and what I thought the poetry could talk about, or what my poetry could talk about. Both at once.

JR: Another characteristic of your later work, I think, is its more directive — possibly moralistic — quality, or its willingness to make statements, definitions and judgements. In the poem 'Directive' in *The Force* you say 'Attend to the outer world.' And in terms of the Jonas/Silas dichotomy, the mud-world/magic world dualism, there is a tendency to favor Silas because, to quote from that book, 'Jonas wanted to make maps of this, Silas wanted to live it.' Do you agree that you have become, say, more directive in your work? And does this reflect an increasing sense of responsibility as a poet, or stronger convictions about the world which are now being expressed in this way?

PR: Stronger convictions about the world, with which go some responsibilities as I tried to say earlier. This goes with the previous question also. One of the reasons for writing poetry is that, as I was saying about Dante last night — it doesn't matter if you're a Catholic when you read Dante. I mean, you may think it's a pack of lies, but still it's marvellous. It's as though if you write a good poem nobody can argue with it. It's as though opinions and the relativity of human opinion from one person to another doesn't matter. And in writing those shorter earlier poems, I was finding an area among all the disagreements of life where there was no disagreement. And at that time I used to think that I had no opinions, no declaration to make. I thought this might be related to what Keats calls negative capability. I realize now that this is partly true, but it's partly an evasion. Since the things about which I should have had strong opinions were the things on which I was turning my back, such as the irrelevance and horror of the tribal social structure. And the reason why I didn't have opinions, or a direction in a general sense, was because I refused to consider these matters. I refused to consider, for instance, that marriage to one person and bringing up a family were not necessarily centrally important things, and that one could change them. That one's masters and employers were not always right. See, I'm very stupid, for a long time I believed everything that everybody told me. And I found in poetry that there was no sense in which these things might be important, and that there might be an unbearable conflict; that in poetry, in making the poems which were of course about all of this obliquely, is where there was a reconciliation. But I could not intellectually face the consequences of being alive in this country at this time. As a result of these various events I've mentioned I'm now better able to face this, and to understand that much of what I was about before, though true within its own terms, was also something of an evasion. I think that's about it. But of course this happens to everybody as they grow. At first you're in the family home, and if you write poetry because your father is always arguing with you or always trying to put you down and this poetry is a place where there's no question of argument, this is your business for the time. If you stay there and things start to putrefy, well then you stink. I certainly began to stink (*laughing*), I probably stink a bit differently now. I have a view of life, or a hypothesis of life now, which the evidence doesn't seem to contradict. And at that time I had a partial view of life which, had I opened myself to other evidence, would have been full of contradictions. I suffered many severe neurotic symptoms because of this evasion. And writing poetry of course was one of the ways in which I came in relation to these things. I mustn't say understand them — to come into relation with them rather than to avoid them, as I believe many of my contemporaries do. I don't wish to make it seem as if I bring myself above them in this respect: I'm an infant taking steps. But I mean, some people just don't get born at all, really.

JR: I wonder what your sense of audience is, whether you write for a particular individual or a group of people or another aspect of yourself or what? Or how all these things revolve. Earlier you mentioned that in *The Hermaphrodite Album* you and Penelope were writing these poems to each other, each partially in a process of becoming the other. And I wonder what other sense of a reader you may have?

PR: I think my answer may once again appear to beg the question. I write for people who understand the language. I write for people who, in more banal terms perhaps, love the language and respond to it very profoundly. These are the people I write for, because writing for such people or such a person I learn myself. This is why feedback in relationship with the audience is important. Because you're learning all the time. I think in writing for such a person, if language is something that grows organically, one is writing for life itself. So one could say in that case that one is writing for the muse. This would be the direction that it takes; and this is true too, one way of putting it. But the simple one is for people who understand the language. Is it an educational purpose? I write to the best of my understanding. I think Graves puts this well — he says he writes for the muse, but he also says he sometimes writes for elder poets. He says that he writes for John Skelton. Now, you're perfectly sure John Skelton understands the language. That is, he won't — because he can't respond to a grammatical movement or an image — say the poem's no good. He will be able to see what the poem intends, because he loves and understands the language. And that's a good person to write for. I don't write for Bob Dylan, say, because I'm perfectly sure that Bob Dylan understands rather a narrow spectrum of the language. I don't write for people who don't read books or listen to each other but sit in a trance in front of television when they've finished their work at the office. I don't write for those people. I mean, I don't think I can write a television play, for instance. But I do write for people who listen to the radio, sometimes. I mean, it doesn't really beg the question, that answer. Have I a revolutionary notion of audience? A cultural unity in the world? Yes, but I find this a remote ideal, practically speaking. People I write for are also people from whom I can learn. Which is the feedback thing. Obviously some of the people I'm writing for are persons like yourself who are interested enough in my work to come and ask me about it. This is somebody I write for. I don't know them in advance. And how very excellent it is to discover that somebody is interested in what one has said! So it's a help. So I've been writing for you. I'd better write better. That's it, that's it, that's the answer — the question's like a dream *(laughing)*, it's like a dream: and somebody says, 'Who's your audience, who do you write for?' I should just roll in laughter and say you! *(laughing)*. I once had a dream in which my parents were in the kitchen, and they were saying, 'What's all this about the unconscious, then? What is the unconscious? Tell me what the unconscious is. Never heard of such a thing. What is it?' And I was very carefully explaining to them all the theories from Charcot onwards, because I'd been lecturing on psychology rather foolishly — one shouldn't lecture on psychology. And I told this dream to somebody and he said, 'That's nonsense, you should have rolled in laughter and pointed at them and said YOU, you're the unconscious!' You see, because one's mother and father were the people concerned. Now this is a different order of things: you are the conscious, I'm the unconscious *(laughter)*. But we turn and turn about here, this is the proper relationship.

JR: Insofar as you can be aware of what effect you have on a reader, are you more interested in provoking thought and awareness — widening perceptions of the reader — or in conveying and provoking a sense of responsibility? Or do you think this is a false division?

PR: I think it's a false division. I think awareness implies responsibility. To put it quite simply, I have experiences of wholeness and awareness which are brought about to me when I am in that area of things which has to do with my writing. It may be that I may achieve that in my writing, a sense that I am one and better than I usually am, more aware, more advanced, more able, a better person altogether. This is associated with my writing. When I read other people's poems it produces that state in me. So I think it's not unreasonable to suppose that if I write a good poem it will produce that state in other people. And I don't regard anything I've done as either final or my best work, because ... Who would? I'd much rather be Shakespeare, but Shakespeare is done, he's done Shakespeare. I haven't done mine yet.

ME: What about the overall effect of the arts on the world? What kind of conditioning effects do you think art has had on time and man, any?

PR: Yes. I think art-forms are responsible for the development of historical fact. I think societies take certain interior decisions — which may not appear to them to be decisions but rather insights — and the society develops accordingly. I hold an opposite belief not to Marx himself, who would allow this, but to many Marxists. For instance, what I was saying about the Jews conceiving a God who requires a certain circumcision. If this is true, if the psychological notion is true, and it would be very surprising if circumcision did not have a profound psychological effect on a child, and since they're the only race to do this circumcision so early, it would account for (not so much account for as explain) — but it would be a seeding point of their history. But to decide to intuit this necessity is an artistic decision. I don't mean an aesthetic decision: I mean, you don't decide that a penis looks better without a foreskin. I mean an artistic decision, a decision by image, by an image which conflates thought, feeling, sensation and intuition, all four faculties at once, and appears as a vision. When the Greeks 'invented' Zeus, who was originally the sound of the dawn arising, the sound of the dawn wind, the word 'zeus' meant first light. This was a moment between darkness and light where there was insight, where a world was entered in which many consequences were glimpsed which could not be known by ordinary methods of going about the world, which are linear methods. This moment between darkness and light was where many things were seen, many things that the Greeks saw in their own natures that were seen in advance. You can put it as un-metaphysically as that, if you like, though I think more is involved. And these events being seen at this moment so far into the future could only be told in the figure of a god called Zeus, whose attributes and figure and emblem guided the development of Greek history. I think this is how art works. Now, you can't there make a difference between prophetic religion and the emblems which express it, which will require artists for their making. And only if you make a distinction between Aaron and Moses can you say that the prophet is not an artist. I'm talking about the Schoenberg thing where Moses can hardly speak and hears the insights, so Aaron speaks for him. I think this is very much a later division, this is a contemporary division between a person who is a person of insight and the person who expresses the insight. I think this is not what we want, if we can avoid it, not what we're working towards.

ME: You don't agree with Auden's comment, then, that the history of man would have been the same if Shakespeare and Mozart had never lived?

89

PR: Well, it's a most arrogant remark, that. I mean, I don't know why he likes to shit on himself like this. how can he possibly know? And isn't it much more likely that it has altered as a result of these people seeing very deeply into the psyche? Isn't it much more likely that Goethe, discerning in his own psyche and the psyche of his culture the collective psyche, the myth of Faust, has enabled people to focus on their own desires and their own mistakes much more clearly than if he hadn't written? I think the evidence is all against Auden's remark. Certainly with the individual the processes of development and growth into oneself are related, I believe, to what happens in poetry. The books one reads, the experiences one has, the shocks of recognition one has in seeing likenesses between a person who's written a long time ago and oneself. All these things affect the individual. What prevents them from affecting the collective? Why should Auden make such a remark? I'm not aware that he justifies this view. I mean, a lot of writers on political history do attempt to maintain this, you know, that writers as individuals did not have much effect on the collective. But I don't think this is a view of history that can be maintained. One does have leaders and leaders who are poets.

ME: One last question. How does the idea of poetry as sacred activity accommodate you? Do you find it has often, say, surpassed or supplanted the role of traditional religion?

PR: Poetry's clearly a branch of religion. For myself, all the things that official religion ought to be about is in poetry. If we had a proper religion, that is, a psychologically useful religion in this country, it would be of course highly poetic. Once again I seem to be begging the question, don't I? What poetry is about is what is commonly called sacred. One can use any number of terms for this sense of the sacramental in existence, that everything that one does is very very real, that either within or without one there are personages who are full of knowledge and perhaps more than what we call human, or perhaps more truly human, personages in nature who suddenly appear and disappear. All these things poetry has to do with, which are not only true matters but absolutely necessary. I say 'psychologically useful.'

You see, we've forgotten that religion is for anything. What it's for — religion is only the name of becoming ourselves. But in this country at any rate our official religion doesn't have anything to do with anything actually going on, nothing to do with actual discoveries about yourself or other people. Only a rather stolid mode of conduct and moral prohibition. A religion, any religion worth its name, has to have women in it. Because half the world is. This is clear, and poetry's about women. One of the things it's about, of course. And the official religions leave sex out of it. I mean, it's all very well to have the four Gospels, but where are the sayings of Mary? Once again, to go back to earlier religions about that: the religions of Greece not only talked about the Zeus cult a little, but there was a Hera cult too. Now, the Hera cult (I mustn't confuse her with the goddess of the hearth) this was the goddess of womanhood, of I think they say matronhood. But at any rate what the Hera cult studied was the female menstrual cycle. That is, in this religion of Hera the woman was allowed, not discouraged, was allowed to contemplate the cyclical form of her own nature and her different abilities at various times of her monthly period, which was always related in the cults of Hera to the phases of the moon. Now, in antiquity it was held as a commonplace that a woman would menstruate with some relationship to the moon. This has been mocked by Joyce, who says if that's the case why don't all women bleed at once? Of course, if they live in community they do. He didn't seem to realize that, he was afraid of the subject, it's a taboo subject — there's nothing written on it. Jung, writing about the Miller phantasies (Miller was a woman). But you don't get any sense that a certain vision happened at a certain time of the month. In fact, over the month the dreams tell a certain story. Which has to do with these archetypal fears. Well, the statisticians can't decide whether a woman menstruates with the moon or against it or what relationships there are. Though there are varying accounts of this. The Swedish chemist Arrhenius did a survey on this, he said yes, the majority of women menstruated on the new moon. A recent German study confirms this; a North American study contradicts it. There is a Yugoslavian physician who claims 98% contraceptive technique — I think the scheme is that the woman ovulates at the phase of the moon that obtained when she was born. An empirical thing. But you see if you avoid sex then, and just have sex at other times of the moon's phases, there won't be conception. This is cheaper than the pill. This is one of the things that must have been taught in the Hera cult. These people did not contemplate the moon because it was irrelevant to them, but because it was profoundly important. Not only for mental knowledge, visionary knowledge of yourself in relation to the pulses of the universe, but practical household knowledge — that is, will you have sex, do you want a child at this time. Perhaps more, because there are legends that modern physicians are only just beginning to approach. That the two ovaries give (of course the modern idea is that the sperm determine the sex, but there's some doubt about that) — but the eggs come from alternative ovaries. And there is some suggestion that conception related to certain aspects of the moon's phases would give you a boy or a girl, depending on what you wanted. This is very important internal knowledge. And it's a kind of knowledge which no woman in our culture is provided with. In talking to students a woman says, 'Oh I can't work, what shall I do? I'm finished as an artist." I say, 'Well, I'm terribly sorry about this. What week are you in?' And she said 'oh." And I say, 'What do you like doing at this time?' She says she likes cooking. 'It's your time to cook. Simple, isn't it?' I've seen people have dreams in which the egg they are making appears in the dream. One very beautiful one was of an earring which was unused, put aside, a sparkling thing, very beautiful. But, you know, this is true knowledge which is hardly touched. Now, it's poetic knowledge. It's also what's right in front of one's nose. I had the librarian here check out what had been written on the subject — does a woman's psychology change according to her time and period? There's one paper in 1932, another a bit later on, the authorities on woman's psychology mention it hardly at all. But it's true. So that's an example of a practical religion which is poetic-useful and which is quite gone. It's one of the things Women's Lib is about, what Robert Graves calls the return of the goddess. He touches on the subject once in *The White Goddess*, he actually manages to mention menstruation. It's the taboo subject.

## 7. Scientist of the Strange

## Interview with *Manhattan Review* (Philip Fried)

MR: One concept I find today is that poetry deals with feelings, which are of secondary importance. I think this is an influence of positivism, which takes many forms, some of them quite attractive and sophisticated, like structuralism.

PR: Structuralist thinking, with its emphasis on the opposites, I find unsatisfactory because it strikes me as an intellectual shadow of Jung, who also, if you like, takes up a structuralist position, as far as the dialectic is concerned. But of course, it is one with feeling and symbology, colour. In fact, he insists on using the four functions, the idea that human nature is fourfold. This is, you know, a very ancient tradition. I mean the cross symbol is the oldest of all symbols. And he suggests that it points to the fourfold nature of human beings. And that if human beings are not composed, as it were, of the balance of these two sets of opposites, then they are not fully human. And that our purpose is to integrate ourselves.

The purpose of integration or of individuation rather, is to have these faculties in balance. The faculties or functions are thought, that is to say, intellect; feeling; sensation, that is, the senses; and intuition. If one is not operating with all these, and the quintessence of them which Jung calls the transcendent function and which is in fact the creative imagination, then one is not giving a complete description either of human experience or one's own experience. So that the structuralists, who are operating purely on the intellect, are only giving one . . . well, intellect and sensation — the common scientific combination — which is only one set of opposites. What is needed is an acknowledgment or differentiation or development of feeling and intuition, too, which are commonly given to that slave class, the women. Projected on them.

MR: I wonder what your response would be to something else Jung says. He says the function of poetry is to take what is being repressed in any particular time, the images that are being repressed, and to discover them.

PR: Oh, undoubtedly, but I wouldn't want to make, as Jung does, a discontinuity between the artist and the usual person. Jung tends to do this, for much the same reason that Freud concealed certain things in psychoanalysis. He wants to make it very, very respectable.

Jung didn't want to train his doctors as creative artists, because he knew how sensitive doctors are, that they want to be healing. Doctors want to be healing. So if they're told they're artists, they may get caught up by their anima and become artists and not doctors and not be healing because it was not the time to put the two together. So that Jung made a very deliberate attempt, I think, to conceal the fact that his chief therapeutic method, which he called active imagination, was in fact the creative process as it is known in art. He concealed this because he knew it would be unpopular in the medical profession. Now, of course, it comes out, as things have developed.

MR: Doesn't art emerge as a kind of siren call in his autobiography?

PR: Yes, indeed, it does.

MR: He looks at it as almost the last temptation.

PR: The talented female psychopath who tempts him with this . . . the anima image which tempts him with this notion that he is a great creative artist, and he says, No, I'm not, I'm a doctor! A healer. But he still went on with it, and he grounded himself in his sensation function, as far as he was able. That's an inferior function, because he was an intuitive intellectual type. And he grounded himself always in artistic work, mainly in sculpture and building, didn't he?

MR: That's right. I like the way these ideas work in specific poems. I like very much your 'Jabez in Cockaigne.' Is that related to the concept of the unconscious senses?

PR: Well, this is the image of the dog, the dog as psychopomp.

MR: It's very humorous poem.

PR: The ancient Egyptians had theriomorphic gods, they had gods that were beast-heads and so on. One of the reasons was because the beasts obviously had senses and perceptions that we don't. I mean, the dog can smell, is aware, the cat's aware of things happening, of psychic atmospheres and so on. So the image is given, in order to train one's own senses, of an animal head, a dog or a jackal head or something like this.

This is not Middle Eastern only but European. The idea of the little dogs on medieval church tombs was partly that the dog was said to be the creature who ushered the soul into the presence of the judge. This is what my Jabez dog does. He's got all sorts of senses, but he is very innocent, you see, so we don't give him the nastygod aspect, the superego aspect of the god. This is god as inquirer of the human, really, god as cooperator with the human, which is a Jungian notion or it's an ancient notion. You find it in Yeats, of course, that the immortals need us, need our emotions, as we need the immortals' perceptions. That is to say, the conscious needs the unconscious and vice versa.

MR: And that relationship comes out very clearly in the poem, the humorous aspect of the dog's relationship to the family. Just the humour of making a dog the speaker of a dramatic monologue, but at the same time creating a very powerful poem, like when he describes the sun, that image of it pouring out.

PR: He worships it.

MR: It comes across extremely powerfully, but the poem still retains the humour.

PR: It's very, very good that you see the humour in these poems. But England is so straight-laced. I mean, my novel, *The Facilitators*, I just had to write to the *Times Literary Supplement* about their reviewer, who took it perfectly straight as a sort of programme of psychological training. What I had to point out was that in an analytical situation, or, one should say, a therapeutic situation, you have what the psychoanalysts call 'moments of emotional insight.' The reaction is often astonished laughter, certainly wonder, it's philosophical wonder. Amazing, absolutely amazing, you see. This is often accompanied by laughter and humour and goodwill, which the therapist must contain so that there is no inflation. But it's funny! That kind of insight is funny. That's why the Zen masters laugh, I think. I don't know anything about Zen first-hand, but I think that's why the laughter.

MR: I find humour and good humour, which are overlapping but not the same, to be really important tonal aspects of your work.

PR: That's good. Glad of that.

MR: For instance, I find it in the poem 'The Famous Ghost of St. Ives.' I find that a really fascinating poem. One of the things that you seem to do is — and this relates to what we were just saying about Jabez — accommodate the earthly and the spiritual, without losing either. And the humour of that initial description. He thinks this drop of water is a constituent!

PR: (Laughter) He's looking for votes, isn't he? Wants to shake it by the hand, yes. Well, people are single-minded, particularly politicians.

I was thinking about some of these things because, well, it is a very interesting task, an interview, because one has to step back. I mean, I'm not the kind of writer who is able to work by programmes. These are experiences which I have to encounter. This is why writing poems takes such a long time. On an average, roughly three years from the first beginnings, what you could call the scintillae or openings, as I find them, which I collect, to the time when they join up to a statement, which may or may not work.

I have been trying to work out the pattern of themes in my work, in some of my work, and you pointed to the humour, and it's very very nice to know this is working on somebody else. As I say, it tends to be dry as dust in England. I was thinking that there are some themes here. There is the theme that the world is much more resourceful, has much more in it than we commonly allow ourselves to perceive. In other words, the psyche can expand, that our ordinary waking consciousness is insufficient to the material that is presented to it. The first poem in the book of *The Apple-Broadcast* is about that. It's called 'On the Patio' if you remember. The thunderstorm is pouring into a glass and he drinks it, so he's opening himself to something which is not a mere inconvenience because you get wet but a terrific event.

MR: In your work, the miraculous and the ordinary slip into each other so easily.

PR: But they do.

MR: Also, I was very curious about the arrangement of certain books, because they seem to be carefully put together. 'On the Patio,' of course, is a perfect initial poem, a wonderful overture, with the slamming down of the glass on the table —

PR: You're really encouraging.

MR: — asking for more, which of course we do, and we get.

PR: We do.

MR: Do you construct your books rather carefully?

PR: Oh, indeed, yes. I arrange them as far as I can as a sequence of expansions and scenes which, as you say, play off against each other. Sometimes there is a circumstance in one poem which can't be explicated in that poem without destroying the energy but becomes clear in the context of the poem that succeeds or precedes it. So it may be a process of increasing definition of some important theme. People say, you should do this in one poem. But I don't believe this. Nobody ever has. I mean, you can see the development of themes in any poet's work.

The various treatments at various times in one's life or of a poet's life is one of the pleasures in poetry because it is natural to the growth of the human psyche. And one of the reasons we read poetry is to participate in the growth of the psyche of somebody whose work we enjoy and admire. And this stimulates the growth process in ourselves. This is why we have art. Art is not a thing to be nailed on a shelf and valued by the auctioneer. This is not what it is for at all. The purpose of art is to inspire us with our own creative energies. And so if the author gives a record of the emergence of something which proves to be of significance, then he will be encouraging this process in the reader himself. It will be a paradigm of the creative process.

MR: Peter Porter, in a review of Carpenter's biography of Auden recently in *TLS*, said that he liked the book because it pointed out the extent to which Auden raided his own work. And then he said, to be against this one would be a prig and that it's quite usual in music. I just wondered if you agreed.

PR: Oh yes.

MR: Sometimes an image will appear in one poem and then the same image will be reworked slightly in the adjacent poem.

PR: And it becomes even more complicated in my case, because as you know, I work in close partnership with Penelope Shuttle. Because we offer these images to each other and we watch their transmutations in each other. And something may be, as it were, processed or developed in your partner's psyche which comes back to you transmuted for your use.

She's writing a novel at the moment which contains images from my work, and I'm writing poems at the moment which contain images from her novels. This is the process which is called in Jungian psychology the double pelican, in which the conscious mind of one person feeds to the unconscious mind of the other and the conscious mind of that person feeds the unconscious mind of the other. So there is a continual process of mutual distillation. This is the point, I think, in a two-gender partnership, that because of the difference between the genders and the different emphases of your Jungian functions, the genders become complementary, arid so work together. So it becomes very complicated, and I wonder how this will be . . . I'm sure it will keep scholars off, if scholars are ever interested, because it will be a fantastic process of extrication for them. Or, if they like our work, they might enjoy it.

MR: Does all this — I mean this way of working both alone and with Penelope Shuttle — imply a de-emphasis of the sanctity of the individual poem?

PR: Yes. I think a poem must work in itself. But I think a poem may work as, say, a scene in a play works. That is to say, it may be perfectly satisfactory on its own account, but it may be part of a greater whole. I think there's no point essentially in sealing off individual poems. I think in any large-scale work the poems always react. I mean obviously they do in Wordsworth or Shakespeare or anybody like this. I think the idea of a perfect poem is probably hubris. I remember that the Islamic carpet-makers left a deliberate flaw in their carpets, which they used to say was in case God was jealous. But actually that is not the reason. It is the place where God comes in.

I think in reading a poem there is a kind of dialectic with its imperfections. As Wallace Stevens says, a poem must resist the intelligence almost successfully. In other words, the reader has perhaps an uneasiness. A perfect poem, which sort of chimes down the ages like a silver bell — one thinks of some of Raleigh's poems — which becomes almost proverbial, has somehow been purged by time of its original conflicts, which took the reader to the edge of his own conflicts.

That doesn't happen in most, say, of George Herbert's poetry, which is always concerned with taking the reader into his own conscience, as it were, and producing a scintilla perhaps by conflict in the reader, a struggle. Hopkins, it's obvious with Hopkins, very obvious with Hopkins.

I think these things which are first seen as flaws or imperfections are secondly seen as generators of the poetic energy and perhaps thirdly, if the work becomes a classic, then they become resonant musical notes, having transformed the psyche of the collective. But I still like to think of those kind of imperfections as where God enters.

Now I'm not arguing for obscurity in poetry at all. Obscurity or not obscurity doesn't matter. What we're after is deepening language and deepening communication — I think he's quite right about this — by whatever means.

MR: Are your poems very often musically organized? Is music an important model for you?

PR: Yes it is, very important. I'm not learned in music as Peter Porter is, for instance. I can give very little technical account of this. But it is very important. I would say music and cinema, the two things. I mean poetry has always been like the cinema. It uses time, it's a time-based medium, I think, in a sense, though it's an interior time, and it plays very strangely — that is the purpose for having rhythm and verse in it. It uses flashbacks and cuttings and visual metaphors and all sorts of metaphors as the cinema does. And the cinema is almost all visual except where it strongly suggests tactile qualities. But you don't get smell-o-vision, do you?

MR: They tried it.

PR: I think some of the symbolist poets had a smell organ. Didn't Satie have one?

MR: I'm not sure, but going to this idea of the cinematic, I've noticed you have an interesting way of beginning a poem. Often, I've found it's with a nonverbal statement. There's no verb.

PR: One thinks of the apparently discordant beginnings of certain of Beethoven's last quartets. There are most discordant and difficult chords, you know what I mean. There is a sort of blare of noise which then is, as it were, rectified or demodulated into various harmonies, songs, themes of increasing sternness, which seem to recapitulate in a — how shall I say? — a rational fashion the attack with which the work began. That's the posh way of putting it, I think. Another way of putting it is tuning in a radio station. You are spinning the dial and you hear all sorts of fragments of interesting speech or music... and there is a sort of tone to it all which is the tone of your attention. And then you decide ah yes, that is near the station. Your first statement may be, the first line of the poem may be between a number of stations, you see, and then you tune it in, and there's the station you want.

It's like the religious use of a violent noise, the strepitous, the rattling of the sistrum, a noise on which the psyche improvises. So perhaps some of those first lines of mine are like affronts, you know a sudden signal: Wake up! Now use it, or improvise it. I can't explain that idea any better. Like the Anglo-Saxon poems beginning with Hwaet!

MR: The subtraction of the verb is part of the blare? A verb would make it easier for the reader, because that's what we look for. So the subtraction of the verb is partly what creates . . .

PR: That's right, yes. Because a verb would mean there was a transaction within the statement, and this is as yet an untransacted statement.

MR: By subtracting the verb, it's as if you're producing in front of yourself an object for meditation. It's like, there, it's produced, and then the movement begins.

PR: Yes, that's right, the poem itself would be actually the moving into or out of the deepest meditation, which is imageless. So that would be the two worlds intersecting, which is what I think a poem is.

MR: Do we have a philosophical paradox, I mean that poetry is really imperfect, poetry has to be grainy, sensuous, whereas the true meditation would be imageless? Is that a problem?

PR: I think that is a very mysterious business. The form of deep meditation which is sought is, indeed, imageless. But in descending from this state, or ascending to this state, there may be many, many images. Now, what I do in this respect and what I teach my students, who are art students, that is to say, people who are concerned with developing their imagination, I teach them a form of meditation which is with images. It is a relaxation response in which the image-making faculty is not transcended.

There is a philosophical tendency for practitioners of meditation to despise the senses or despise the body. Now, I think the wiser meditators, some of the Middle English mystics, or I think John of the Cross says this, but I think they talk about the interior senses being alerted and the exterior senses being dulled or ligatured or bound. So what one is doing is awakening the interior senses.

I was also going to say something about the progression of themes that I myself was discerning in some of the work. I said the resourcefulness of the world, but it is also the matter of correspondences. To a particular way of looking, objects in the universe, objects in the world resonate to many, many other objects. To describe this perception, we use metaphor. The beautiful image I think in Buddhism, in Mahayana Buddhism, is of the net of jewels. This is like a spider's web of dew in which every globe, every crystalline globe reflects in itself every other globe and is itself reflected in a complete — the image in modern science would be a holographic field or a field of interfering wave fronts or creative wave fronts. So this is the correspondences.

Well, this is a familiar idea, I mean we have this in Baudelaire, don't we, the temple of living pillars. And the correspondences can be horizontal, that is to say, across the world, like bells in a church resonating to those of the distant cathedral. Or they may be vertical, which is more metaphysical. That is to say, as in Blake, the world may be the vegetable mirror of the eternal verities, which are elsewhere. Or in Platonism. And that's the second phase of the correspondences which I found in my work.

Now, the third phase we've already touched on, which is what we called the Scientist of the Strange. That is to say, the poet as a kind of investigator, slightly batty maybe. I mean the image here becomes cinematic. In horror films, the mad doctor. The mad doctor is played by Boris Karloff, he's somebody who has found a truth. He's found out how to bring the dead back to life, for instance, and Boris Karloff is The Man They Couldn't Hang, which was just on television. He's going to use this grand thing, and so he kills the young student, with his consent, in order to bring him back to life. But unfortunately, the nurse has got frightened and calls the police. So the police come in and say this student is dead, he can't be brought to life. So they take the mad doctor off to be hanged. However, his other assistant, after Karloff's been hanged, brings him back to life. So he proves his point, you see. He can bring his murdered people back to life again, and he has his broken neck repaired. Unfortunately, the experience of not being understood so embitters him that now he wants to destroy everybody who caused him to be hanged in the first place.

But the figure is there, you see, the horror film figure, the mad scientist who has gone over into mysticism for the sake of science, or he can be a mad clergyman who begins taking his religion not as a metaphor but as a scientific reality. So that the Student of the Strange, the Student of Magic, the Student of Prague, the Faustian image is the third image, one of the personages that enters my work without my conscious participation, oh yes my conscious participation, indeed, but without my volition or my programming.

And there is another figure, the fourth phase, as it were, we have a Jungian four. The fourth phase is a personage that I call the Witch Who Loves Us, which relates to what I was saying earlier about gender resonance, resonance between genders, as with my partner and myself. This person, the Witch Who Loves Us, is a person who is human but is also of the other world, as people of the opposite gender are. I mean, they seem perfectly matter of fact to themselves, but to us they are very mysterious and very energetic and very strange and, of course, stimulate our unconscious minds as they stimulate our sexuality.

This Witch Who Loves Us, being a woman, is, of course, privy to what the Student of the Strange regards as magic, that's why she's a witch. And indeed, in rational terms, in accepted terms, if she is the mother of a child, she is the producer, the source of the original magic, which is the creation of persons, without which there will be no magic, science or anything else. So she is a magical object. She is partly the student's fellow student, studying the universe with him, and partly the thing which is studied, that is to say, closer to that mysterious universe than the Student of the Strange seems to be. This is like 'Delivery Hymn' in *The Apple-Broadcast* in which the mystery of the child is described. So in counterpart to what you were saying, those are four sorts of pulses in my poetry —— that I discern at any rate, and may be wrong about.

MR: In your poems, you ignore what people commonly regard as barriers. One of these is between 'pop' and 'high' culture. I know you use the Dracula story in *The Wise Wound*. But you use these things without condescension. You have found a way to tap a great source of energy.

PR: Well, this is good Jungian practice. The notion here is that there are four functions, and a person is commonly gifted with the operation of two of these, a main function and an auxiliary one, and then, if he's lucky, he'll have a subsidiary function. In middle life, the person who has differentiated, say, three functions will need to complete himself. One of the things that Jung believed is that there is an instinct for not merely Eros-Thanatos, as in Freud, but for completion, individuation, a creative self-evolutionary instinct.

The horror films, however contrived they may be commercially, have the energy of folk-tales. And this is because they deal with a matter which is left out and undifferentiated in our culture. Many of them are Faustian horror stories. The Scientist of the Strange is negotiating with the devil, or in Frankenstein, with the woman's womb. He is trying to become a mother, isn't he? He is negotiating with this inferior function as a scientist and trying to do what the poet's discipline is to do, which is to think and feel at once. And so, of course, the poet looks like a devil to the scientist.

In therapeutic work, what one looks for is the inferior function, in order that one may set up negotiations with it, you see. The question is what is the inferior function in the modern psyche. Now it's often said to be feeling. But I think the inferior function is sensation. I think we do not live in our bodies. I think we do not live in our senses. And that's the devil.

MR: What you say about sensation reminds me of Wordsworth's remarks in the preface to *Lyrical Ballads*. He said that the poet will bring sensation to the objects of science.

PR: Exactly, exactly. I think the masculine culture has differentiated its intellect so that it is without personal sensation and that enables it to do things on abstract grounds, things which are, to say the very least, counterproductive. Whether or not it's because they're a 'slave class,' or whether they are connected with their senses by the menstrual cycle, women may be more in the world than men are by culture. This is one of the things men learn by practising or reading poetry: to know what things are in the senses.

I have wondered about the reason why men drink. I think it's because they're creating sensation in their bodies. The alcohol stills thought and allows them to attend to sensation in the same manner as meditation will but also, of course, they're pissing, which is feeling the world pass through their bodies.

MR: But people say this is a very hedonistic time. Wouldn't that imply people would be very aware of sensations?

PR: The sensation function can be contaminated like any other and is likelier to because it's an inferior one. I suppose you mean that in this age people are very hedonistic because it's a consumer society. We may say that more people are drinking more wine, but is this good wine? Is it the wine of their country? Does it give the experience which good wine is said to do, the experience of the soil? To paraphrase Wallace Stevens: wine is the intelligence of the soil. These consumer goods are really reifications of abstract notions of what the consumer wants and what he will pay for. If one makes one's own goods, the sensation function is imbued. If one does weaving, cloth-making, this kind of thing, one's senses and one's skill are involved and one's symbolic imagination is involved as well, because the common objects become ritual objects. They become symbolic objects. One of the areas where this happens is in what is commonly called magical training, though I don't like the use of the word 'magic' very much because it suggests that the entire world is not magic and that there is a special corner of it which is. I don't believe that.

MR: That sets up another barrier.

PR: It sets up another barrier. Well, in training in magical lodges, what you have to do is to make your own magical tools. This is for people who have, as it were, lost their directions in the world and need to find symbols and bring them into the sensation function. Yeats did this. One of the greatest twentieth-century poets found his orientation by this means. You have to make your own magical tools. That is to say, these are objects which are present in both worlds, in the unconscious mind or the unknown world and the conscious world as well. Present to all four functions. And, indeed, the magical tools refer to the four functions, because there are four basic magical tools, for thought, feeling, sensation and intuition. You will have a knife, a wand, a cup and a plate, which correspond to these four functions. And you will, in fact, be manipulating in yourself, by ritual, these four functions with the things you have made.

Now this is the quality of life in a non-consumer society.

MR: Does this relate to your poem about TV in *The Apple-Broadcast* or *The Weddings at Nether Powers*? You distinguish between the TV image, which would relate to this consumer society, and the genuine image, which a person must find beneath his own skin. These are the images that 'cry out.'

PR: Yes. I think this is also in *The Facilitators,* a prose fiction in which I try to expound some of these ideas in a slightly cooler way. I mean, for me, poems are at the centre of things. The prose fiction is a little cooler than the poems.

MR: Do you therefore conceive of it as going to a different audience?

PR: Yes, I think I do, though exactly what audience prose fiction goes toward I don't know.

Let me see: prose fiction, dramatic work, psychological work. These will go progressively cooler from the centre. And the origin of all of these will be poems. You see, I make my prose fictions from my poems. I make my plays from my poems. And as I described with dreams, the psychological work is also connected with the poetic centre, but it is cooler. So of course, it would be a different audience in each case.

MR: Would you hope that someone reading your prose fiction might become interested in your poetry?

PR: Well, one would hope so, yes, but there are so many barriers in the literary world. A person who is writing novels is supposed to be a novelist, not supposed to be a poet or a dramatist. If a person is a dramatist, nobody will read his poems because they want his drama. But if he's a poet, they might just have to do with his drama, because there have been many poets who have also been dramatists. There are few novelists who have also been poets.

MR: Or psychologists.

PR: Or psychologists, yes. But this, I think, is more English than anything else. On the European continent and in America, I think, people are allowed to move freely among disciplines.

MR: To return for a moment to a previous topic, in *The Wise Wound,* you call the movie screen the mirror by which we look at the Gorgon's head, and then dismiss it, because it's 'pop' culture. Are you trying to release the energy that's available in such things?

PR: Yes. I think our culture breaks these things up. Take the example of horror films, again — magic horror films, not the sadomasochistic kind which are another kind of problem. In another time, the sensations that these give of exploration into mysterious places for fresh inspiration or for something surprising that you haven't thought of, which gives you a delicious titillation and makes your hair stand on end, is surely a description of the numinous. Normally, in another culture, you would go to a church for this, but this doesn't happen in church, or very rarely. I imagine because the images have become so involved with the state, or so Protestant that they become emptied of action entirely. Or one would become initiated into a mystery. There, of course, as part of the training, one will meet images related to those that one gets denatured on the horror screen. So it's really a fragmentation. But in it there are matters which are lost but essential and therefore mustn't be condescended to.

MR: This reminds me, too, of another genre that is often

relegated to 'pop' culture: science fiction, with its magical shifts of scale and time, strategies which you also use in your own work.

PR: This is traditional, too, isn't it, as in the notion of giants and dwarves in fairy-tales? People sometimes call my work surrealistic, which is very, very lazy. I think what the proper surrealists were doing was more distinctive to itself. I think this is a misunderstanding by a non-French people. I think nobody who has used a microscope would call my work surrealistic.

MR: There are these wonderful books that you read as a child that talk about these dimensional things. What tends to happen is that we're initiated into these mysteries and then we somehow bury and forget them.

PR: I wonder why this comes about. Do you think it is because it has some connection with the fact that our culture, generalizing, is the only one that has sexual latency? One wonders where the sexual latency comes from, the Freudian sexual latency, which I think is supposed to begin at five and go on until puberty when the sex comes through. It used to be thought that this was the universal condition of the human species, but I think anthropologists since Malinowski have known that there is not necessarily a latency period for other cultures, which are differently organized. Surely, this is schooling. I think children are taught to forget. I think they are taught in an extravert and intellectual fashion, and what is the commonest call of schoolmasters in this country, I remember, is: Don't daydream, Johnny! Well, of course, daydreaming is exactly what I have to teach my art students. I have to teach them yoga-nidra, which is daydreaming. To develop it into responsible fantasy.

There's this difficult passage in Coleridge about fancy and imagination. Now I think Coleridge is probably not being read right, or perhaps he was just making notes. What I think is the case is that what he called fancy is trivial and entirely contemporary. Fantasy is not that. Fantasy is spontaneous eruption from the unconscious mind. It can be entered consciously, or else can be unconscious, as in dreams. Fantasy is incipient imagination. Imagination is the responsible creative participation in fantasy, with moments of realization which I called a little while ago the fifth, the transcendent function, involving all four functions. In any art what happens is that thought, feeling, sensation and intuition are present at once. And that is the I Am that Coleridge talks about as being the utterance of imagination. I think the term that has been left out is "fantasy."

That is to say, by the use of fantasy, one arrives at the truth.

MR: Would 'pop' culture be a bridge between fantasy and fancy?

PR: Well, I think that people's fantasy is exploited and becomes fancy. The life goes out of it. Nevertheless, those commercial fancies are able to stimulate the fantasies of people who are growing up.

MR: When I was about five years old, going to the movies was like a religious experience.

PR: This is like a mystery religion. You go into an initiation chamber and you have an epiphany. Now if this is done unconsciously, it will still be done. I mean, the dreaming mind presents nightly to you images of your own integration and the things that you need to know. Nightly. Nightly, it presents a cinema show. Everything that humankind makes is a model of humankind. We don't do this in an interior fashion because we're an extravert culture. We do it in an exterior fashion in the cinema, so it is quite credible and proper, I think, to speak of the cinema in terms of religious experience.

MR: Fairy-tale and folk-tale, which we were relating to 'pop' culture, bring to mind the whole idea of enchantment. Do you feel that much contemporary poetry lacks enchantment?

PR: Well, I suppose it does, and if it does, I've become not interested in it (laughter). The trouble with the extravert culture, which is once again time-based and possibly this has something to do with the Christian notion of the Last judgment and time being unredeemable, is that we're hurrying to get things finished before the judgment comes, you see. To countervail this, the unconscious mind will tell one: well, everything is finished in every moment. Which is the meditative state.

MR: That reminds me very much of your poem 'The Apple-Broadcast' and also of the poem in the same book, 'Orchard with Wasps.' The poetry has a viscous quality.

PR: Yes?

MR: Very often, your poetry is grainy, like wood, but here it seems more viscous. Things flow over each other. The time sense is really altered through this technique. The moment is slowed and slowed.

PR: 'The Apple-Broadcast,' of course, begins with the strepitous, the sudden noise which becomes the seed of a returning meditation. I say it's 'A meditation experience at Boscastle.' It happened when I was meditating, this bird-cry suddenly set into resonance all these meanings and feelings. Of course, the matter of time stilling is another thing that happens in meditation. I can't remember whether it was on that occasion or another when I was suddenly — I suddenly opened my eyes and the birds were hanging still in the sky.

MR: You have an image somewhere of bird-cries hanging like lanterns in the woods.

PR: I think that came from this kind of experience.

MR: Philip Hobsbaum, in *Tradition and Experiment in English Poetry*, talks about poetry having lost a lot of ground, since the nineteenth century, to fiction. We've been talking about fairy-tale, fiction and I know that in a number of your poems, there is a strong narrative line. Are you conscious of reclaiming ground for poetry?

PR: I wouldn't claim — as I say, I'm not programmatic at all and this would be a very grand notion, and I'm not as grand as that. I'm just following what I need to do, really. I don't know how to answer your question. I think that fiction, prose fiction, uses very different muscles from poetry. I think in poetry what you have got is not only the subject matter but implicated also an account of the creative process. In prose fiction, the function of the narrator or storyteller as inductor or initiator is much more important. There is a greater sense of control and less of exploration. I mean, the narrator is expounding to you something that he purports to have seen, or at any rate, wants to direct your attention towards. And he is often the ironic master of the story. I think that poetry is, in the form that I favour, far more a matter of intercourse between the poem and the reader. It is an invocation. The poet is concerned with invoking certain energies in his reader. In prose fiction, you may have that purpose, basically, but that is not your craft. Your craft is to tell a story.

I think modern prose fiction has become contaminated also between . . . not contaminated. I think the uncertain distinctions between these forms have broken down anyway. And so, poets have been working in prose fiction, one thinks of Joyce and so on, and narrators have been working in poetry. I would much rather look at it in terms of the notion that I have already suggested. I find myself that poetry is the much warmer or hotter — is that a McLuhan thing? — medium. And there is more participation. As it gets cooler, the cooler and more removed faculties start to work, and the reader becomes manipulated. I don't think that the poet is trying to manipulate the reader. He's trying to share with the reader a discovery, and to stimulate in him parallel discoveries.

Then you get long narrative poems which are like novels. So these are prose fictions which use the methods of poetry. I think a distinction is very difficult to find. Then you get narratives like the Bible, which purport to be prose narratives but are, in fact, poetry. Or you get Russian novels which have the effect — in English translation anyway, I don't read Russian — of such clarity and scope that they go through to something else entirely, which is like a lyric feeling. When I read Tolstoy, there is so little effort in the scope he provides, one gets a lyrical feeling as though one has read not just a long book but a short poem about it as well.

It's a very strange feeling in the Russians.

MR: I'm sure you know that passage in *Anna Karenina* where — and this would relate to your Jabez poems — it's all from the point of view of the dog. It's the hunting episode, and the dog says: 'Here comes my terrible master!'

PR: (Laughter) Oh, I must look that up, I must look that up.
   I remember a story of Turgenev's where he's alone in the landscape, and his senses are expanded to the horizon and then somebody with a gun comes on, and his senses contract again. We use the word meditation as though it were something mysterious, but this is a direct thing. It's not a figure of speech. One's sensation seems expanded to the horizon, and something that happens over there seems to scratch the surface of it. Not by ESP or anything like that, but I mean, if one's meditating with one's eyes open, as one is when one is looking at anything with one's feeling as well, then a little movement over there would produce a gigantic tremor in his alert senses. One can cultivate this state, too.
   I think another thing that happened historically is that people are less accustomed to read aloud, aren't they? Both verse and prose. And so in private reading, I think different things happen. I'm not quite sure about that, because I don't know the extent to which verse was read aloud, say, in Victorian times, or in the time of the great English novel. I think these were read aloud, weren't they? I mean, Dickens used to be read aloud. He used to do his tours, and people used to read the serials.

MR: I remember reading in A.L. Rowse's *A Cornish Childhood* that certain members of his family read Dickens aloud to each other. It was a great tradition for them.

PR: Yes, that's right. The thing about verse is that it's easier to memorize than prose. Of course, as it is memorized it will be imbued with the speaker's nature, so it will be a cooperative venture, won't it? And the poet will be concerned with arousing a continuous, immediate interest. The prose fiction can move from climax to climax, so that the writer will not be concerned to make each line a certain event or a certain transaction. He can prepare with a great deal of diluter detail. This is, indeed, what one finds when one is using the different muscles in writing prose fiction from writing verse. Verse must justify its every word, but you can relax a little and furnish a room in prose fiction. In drama, it's a different problem. As Dryden pointed out, you must find the way of uttering sublime sentiment and also getting a servant to pull a bell (laughter).

MR: What about the prose poem? Doesn't it run counter to what you are saying, because you can't memorize it in the same way?

PR: I think a prose poem is a poem using a prose rhythm. And that's the only point of technique in prose that it uses.

MR: Let's take your own prose poem 'Really Gone.'

PR: Oh, that's a long time ago.

MR: It's like a little Borges story, or like what the Latin American novelists do, the self-destroying narrative, as in *One Hundred Years of Solitude*.

PR: It is a little short story, I think. But the modes meet, the modes meet.

MR: So I would disagree with you when you say it is just prose rhythms that are borrowed. I'd say it's a little bit closer to what's being done with prose now. Maybe not to the Victorians, but to the contemporary.

PR: Yes. You may be right. I hadn't thought about it like that.

MR: Sometimes your poems are like little short stories. Take the poem 'Born' from *Apple-Broadcast*. We were talking about the Russians. This has a very Russian flavour and reminds me of *The Death of Ivan Ilyich*. It works as a poem yet brings into poetry this feeling of fiction. Is there a sensation related to fictional technique?

PR: I think there is. I think that's very interesting. A book of prose fiction looks different, smells different, has a different visual quality, a different bulk to it. I think that reading a book is like devouring a book. It's like a loaf of bread, devoured slowly. I think this is present to the sensation function. Yes, I think it is. But I wouldn't want to dwell on that too much. I don't know, I don't know.

MR: Isn't rhythm quite important in 'Born'?

PR: Oh yes, yes indeed. Once again, present to the sensation function. Rhythm is present to the entire body, as both tactile and auditory. Rhythm is of vital importance, yes.

MR: In many of your poems, that one and 'Man of the Other Church' and especially 'Or Was That When I Was Grass,' rhythm is such a key. What role do you think it plays in 'Or Was That When I was Grass'?

PR: I'm trying to remember the poem.

MR: It's the one where you get a cut.

PR: Yes, that's right. I think it has to do with the quality of surprise. As I remember it, I wanted the movements of the line to be as surprised as the events that were described. The mimetic thing, yes. That's what I was trying for, but it is, of course, a kind of taste in the head which goes with the entire conception which one is trying to get down in the way the lines go, in the way the syntax goes. It's very difficult to separate one from the other, and very difficult to know when to, as it were, appeal to contrivance. That is why, I think, I take so long over poems, because I want to find out whether a contrivance diminishes the energy or enhances it. Whether non-contrivance diminishes or enhances the energy, whether non-contrivance becomes contrivance. All those things take time to decide, and of course meanwhile one becomes a different person.

It's rather like the dream experience. One may become very adept at this and a very meticulous dreamer indeed and be able to relive the dream. But one will not understand its significance to one's life at that time and one can approach it in various sorts of ways which the analyst will teach one. One may amplify it in the Jungian way. One may do active imagination on it, this sort of thing. But its complete significance will often elude one at the time. But then if one comes to it again after perhaps six months, one has grown towards the dream, with the dream's aid.

This is rather like when Robert Frost talks about poems in his introduction to Collected Poems. You throw down planks to travel into the future. So that after some months' time, one goes to the dream journal and can see what that means or how that operated or its significance in a portion of one's life which one neglected.

MR: Do you believe that, in analysis, the analyst should enable the analysand to do this for himself?

PR: That's right, that's right. I believe this is true.

MR: A Polish poet, Arthur Mydreziecki, has said that a key aspect of modern poetry — talking about rhythm again — is the fast breath. That the modern poem, from Rimbaud on, has a feeling of speed built into it.

I was rereading some of the Rimbaud prose poems in *Illuminations*, and they start with a dissonance and you're in the middle of something right away.

PR: Oh, I used to read Rimbaud endlessly, and he saved me from terrible things when I was starting out after Cambridge. I had to do these office jobs, you see, which were not right, they're not right for anybody. I used to complete my office work in the mornings, and I would spend a long time in the pub at lunchtime reading Rimbaud, and seeing the world like this. Which gave me strength to continue. I worked in an advertising agency and this kind of thing. Horrible.

MR: Was a poem like 'Lake Now-And-Again' influenced by Rimbaud?

**PR:** Undoubtedly. Yes, this is the drowned cathedral, this is the water that goes up and the cathedral that goes down. There's another very good book by Elizabeth Sewell, I wonder if you've come across it, called *The Structure of Poetry.* Best account of Rimbaud I've come across. You'd be fascinated with the charts of texture, suggestion and association which she produces, in showing his method of work, as she sees it. And this is a creative state on the part of the reader but, of course, contrived by Rimbaud himself.

**MR:** Among many contemporary poets, you perhaps use simile to the greatest degree. Take the beginning of the poem 'The Journey,' where you're in a railway carriage, which in itself is a compartmentalized separate thing. You look out a window and suddenly the similes start pouring. Do you think that simile, in your work, relates to an intention of shaking the ego?

**PR:** Oh yes, I think that's one way of putting it. I call this the correspondences. You see that things are real because they are part of a greater thing, that is to say, a bird is also part of the air and is shaped like the air; therefore, it's like living air currents, and immediately the similes begin. But also because in that particular poem, 'The Journey,' you have an oracular bird, a magpie, which for people is symbolic. It's a moonbird, a witchbird, that kind of thing. Seeing the bird is like taking an oracle, like taking a sortes from the Bible, from a living Bible.

The bird is connected with ancestral past and with one's natural energies, which seen subjectively are magical energies. And this is part of the reality of the bird to you, and part of your own reality, discovered by seeing likenesses, or correspondences, which resonate. Matters which resonate, one to the other. And, of course, the self, as seen by Jung, is a whole thing. I mean, it's everything. It is whole. Isn't it the Brahman? It's a traditional notion. Of course, one can't speak about it, it's ineffable. Poetry reaches toward it. The implicate order.

Of course, Jungian psychology says the centre should be in something which is continual, inexhaustible, instead of something which is exhaustible like the ego-complex. But, of course, in shifting the centre, the ego-complex is not dissolved entirely. It is simply that the ego reflects what goes on in the self. That is to say, the ego is like a child growing at the umbilical cord of its mother.

There's a very interesting distinction between Freudian and Jungian psychology in this way. Now the question often comes up in analytical circles: What is the end or finish of analysis? How do you know that an analysis is finished? Well, I've heard it said — I'm not sure of the source but I'm sure it's not in Freud, perhaps it's in an anecdote — the end or finish of Freudian analysis is when the counter-sexual impulse is entirely extinguished, in other words, when a man has no feminine elements and when a woman has no masculine elements. I think this is a calumny, whoever said it. However, in Jungian psychology, the end of analysis or the purpose of analysis is to live in a continual state of active imagination. In other words, to see the correspondences.

MR: Yes, that reminds me of a line in one of your wizard poems: 'I am startled by comparisons.' And being startled is being moved out of a narrower self.

PR: This is one's experience. I mean, I write — I think everybody does — out of episodes of closure. One is closed up in experiences of what is commonly called depression. Which I learned to regard as withheld knowledge. And the only way of getting out of, of transcending this depressed state in which every function is muted, everything is muted, is by seeing beyond the barriers which have somehow been created in oneself, or which one has created for oneself. It is in fact dissolving that ego, as you say.

People say that art should not be therapy. I think this is ridiculous. Of course art is therapy. Art develops the artist, and if it's good art, it develops the reader. It's ridiculous to suppose otherwise. I don't know how this could have got about. That's the origin of the misunderstanding of Jung's thing. He's saying that therapy is not art, you know, in order to train his doctors, so that they shouldn't start to think that they were artists, instead of healers.

In writing, and in developing the procedure that I have in dealing with my own psyche, I am in fact always trying to dissolve the barriers which seem to build up almost automatically and which are episodes of intense depression. It is my way of dealing — if I didn't have this way, I should probably suffer from this as an illness. I think an illness is nothing but this kind of thing. I think an artist is a man who is able to move around his psyche rather than get stuck in one portion of it.

MR: It strikes me as a kind of dance almost, and it's a teaching of the reader how to do this dance.

PR: Well, it should be, yes, if it works, and of course, this is what religion is also. Religion moves a person out of his small ego to an allegiance to something which is greater than his small ego. And to an increased likeness towards this greater thing, which is first encountered symbolically. And the techniques of religion, like the techniques of magic, are for doing this. For self-transcendence. Being merely in the ego is a depressive state.

MR: I find an interesting contrast between you and Ricoeur, in the sense that he seems concerned to predicate certain differences between poetry and religion as well as to bring them together. Do you think it's a better emphasis to talk about what they have in common?

PR: I think that the religious person will tend to cling to his images. The religious person is someone whose facilitating symbol — I think they call it now — or reconciling symbol has been found in a traditional form. Whereas the poet or the artist is somebody still in process. I think the artist will be as interested in the state of mind which creates poetry as in the images that are produced. More in the process, like Paul Valéry would say. But then a religious person would, if he's truly religious, be less interested in these icons than in his state of prayer or in his attitude toward these icons.

MR: Might some religious people even look at the process as dangerous, because it stirs up vital matters again?

PR: Yes, indeed.
   One of the things about Jung is that he does make obeisance

toward Christian doctrine, always. He says, what a great thing Christianity is and implies that Rome — which he could never visit, you know, he used to fall down at the travel agent's when he was trying to book it — is the heart of the universe.

I think this is another piece of camouflage because, for instance, whenever he talks about Christ, he seems to blame the Christians for making Christ so pure that he casts such a dark shadow, which is projected on the outside. I can't see what recommendations he has for that particular religion at all!

The redeemer in Jungian work seems to be not the Christian Christ but a guise in which he does appear in the Gnostics and in the alchemists, who were often of Gnostic persuasion. That is, the Mercurius, which is the infinitely creative variable stream of images or similes. This is one of the stages in the alchemist's work. You have the play of the universe in front of you and then you begin to make your choices. And, of course, he can mislead.

A church or a religion, by contrast, is a fixation. Not in the Freudian sense but a fixation of the feeling —

MR: That reminds me of your poem 'Song.' I love that verb 'chuck': I chucked my Bible into the fire. On the one hand, there's the Pentecostal and, on the other, the impulse to codify, just to use a shorthand. You seem to imply that you feel the pentecostal to a greater degree. Do you also perceive this desire to codify within yourself?

PR: Yes, because I'm writing it down, aren't I? You see, these are opposites, and the necessary things are in both terms of the opposites.

Now, the question is what of moral conduct in this situation? Scriptures will always contain guides to moral conduct, which usually set up classes of people and classes of abomination, don't they? The problem is well examined in Neumann's book, *Depth Psychology and a New Ethic*. The real thing here is the exercise of responsible imagination in moral conduct. Which is very difficult to describe in a short space, but I think you can follow what I mean from what I said about living in a state of continual active imagination or, if possible, the presence of all four functions. If you lack imagination and are moving entirely on an abstract, intellectual plane or you are projecting your shadow on a class of people, then, of course, it seems desirable, in the interests of purity, that this class should be expunged. And it will seem morally right to do so, because you're ridding the world of an evil. But if you regard these people's evil as at least in part a projection of yourself, you will be led towards self-examination before doing anything of the sort, and towards a state of imagination, which will see these other people as counterparts to yourself. That is to say, there is no state of feeling in these people which is not matched by a state of feeling in yourself. Therefore, how can you expunge them without expunging yourself, in an act of warfare or whatever?

MR: Would you say that poetry is more responsible than religion for the very reason that it is more provisional?

PR: I believe so. Yes, I believe so.

MR: You use many Christian symbols in your work. For instance, in 'The Weddings at Nether Powers' and in 'From an Ecclesiastical Furnishers' you use the image of a wasp stinging the crucifix. Do you use Christian symbols to deliberately violate them?

PR: Very interesting, this idea of blasphemy. They speak in the Bible, I think, of blaspheming the name of Jehovah. The true blasphemy — I think Robert Graves talks about this and Gerald Massey certainly does. Blasphemy is actually the revealing of an unorthodox truth, because the name of Jehovah is the name of a goddess.

MR: The earlier worship covered over by the later, as Graves asserts in *The White Goddess*.

PR: I was brought up in a sort of non-Christian Christianity. One was supposed to go to church as a duty. My parents were in themselves of a curious religion, which wasn't really religion. I mean, they went to the Christian church. My father was a Mason. My mother used to think one ought to go but didn't believe a word of it. In other words, nothing happened in church. I had religious older parents. I mean, my paternal grandmother was extremely religious, but nothing happened in church. I also went to a boarding school where one had to go to chapel twice a day, so one had the benefits of listening to the Bible read, which was very good. But there again, nothing happened.

I find there is something about the Bible which is wrong. I'm sorry about this, because I know many excellent Christians, but I can't be like Jung and perjure myself. There's something about the Bible which is wrong. I want to have a book that I can carry around and which makes sense to me, like a good book of poetry. But the Bible does not do this. There's something wrong in it.

MR: Is that why you are writing your books?

PR: Yes. I think so.

MR: I think Whitman felt the same way.

PR: Yes, he did.

MR: And Blake.

PR: Yes, 'I must create my own system or be enslaved by another man's.' That's Blake. There's something wrong about the Bible, which is being revealed now in this historical moment. Things are changing. Male things have become so differentiated that there is no life in them anymore. I cannot approach a Bible which has a male supremo as God or as a male saviour. It is not Jesus but his sister that I am interested in, and there is no such Bible. So, as you say, one has to write it oneself, as far as one can. Or prepare the groundwork, or at least do the work of self-reflection for this.

When I use a religious symbol, it has to be reversed into a feminine or physiological context in order for its better meaning to come through for me. We were speaking about the last chapter of *The Wise Wound* which deals with horror films. There is, in fact, another chapter which was left out of the original publication, because the publisher said it was too long, but it is going into the edition of the book coming out I hope with Spring Publications, the revised one. This deals with the problem: What lies beyond the explicit Christian meaning of the Christian symbols? And I find myself in my poetry being an inquisitor of these symbols, and seeing whether if they are, as it were, inverted, they yield up further life of meaning. But I don't do it in hatred. I do it in love.

MR: Perhaps we can tie this into a specific poem, like 'Reverend Uncle.' Was this really an uncle of yours, or is he a made-up character?

PR: It's a composite man. It's a composite of many teachers, I think, many people that I met. You see, I was always attracted emotionally towards the man who dedicated himself to religion, the clergyman.

MR: Wearing woman's dress?

PR: Well, they do, don't they, but in all cultures men do in order to be holy.
    I was always attracted to these men. I felt very friendly towards them because I thought it would be nice to meet adepts of this kind. But on my acquaintance with them, I found that they seemed to know very little about God. And so I was disappointed, but I still felt friendly to them. But I had to make up a series of clergymen who would act in ways which the clergymen I knew did not. In other words, these were proto students of the strange.
    There's one in a thing called 'The Sermon,' which is a prose poem, who is simply and blatantly making things up to entertain his congregation, because he wants them to be fascinated by *something,* in God's name, because that's all, well, he knows about God. Let them be fascinated and go on from there.

MR: He wants them to 'carry on'.

PR: He wants them to 'carry on', exactly. The character in 'Reverend Uncle,' of course, has gone a little further with this. He still practises the Christian religion because he still preaches in church and wears his dog collar . . .

MR: Which is the last image of the poem.

PR: Hanging like a crescent moon, on the hat-stand or whatever it is, yes. But he also does these other things and says, well the congregation would not be quite ready for this, the bishop wouldn't like it either, but there you are, boy (laughter). The boy sees the point. The boy is delighted, absolutely delighted.

MR: An uncle is an indulgent father. This is a very good father.

PR: He's a male — an uncle would be a maternal uncle, that is to say, the male counterpart of the mother, and he would have some masculine qualities which the mother doesn't exercise. An uncle as an initiator is very, very important in anthropology, of course.

MR: Isn't it typical for a humorous relationship to prevail?

PR: Certainly. This can become very cruel, because the boy who is being initiated will be teased by the uncles, or even be the subject of homosexual initiation. He will be treated as a clown and will be the butt of jokes, as in a hazing I think. But in this case, I think of this chap as one of the Victorian naturalists — amateur scientists who were so clever.

MR: He has an ozone machine.

PR: Yes, that's a machine for using negative ionization. In fact, this is one. The electrical weather in Cornwall can be so terrible that we have to do something about it.

MR: In this poem, you're able to tap into the category of eccentricity and play with it, so that it yields up its riches. One of the strengths of your work is that you are never over-solemn.

PR: Well, yes, I like jokes (laughter).

MR: Campbell said in Hero with a Thousand Faces that humour is an important aspect of the mythological but not of the theological.

PR: That is true. A priest in Campbell, of course, is somebody who does not participate. He knows what's good for other people. He does not participate, and he contrasts with the shaman, of course, who does participate, who does his dance. Who is a conjurer and a commercial fake, too, but tunes into these deeper things. You can see shamanism practised twice weekly in the Falmouth Spiritualist Church. It's a very interesting process, because what happens — you have the clairvoyant or medium who is on the platform, and he looks over the crowd until he sees a likely prospect. I don't know how he chooses them. Then he ventures some generalities, saying: I see a woman in white floating above you and I get the sensation of May blossom. They say: Oh yes, that's Auntie Sally. Who has either died or was ill or beginning to be ill at springtime when the May comes. So somebody agrees with this. But it's a generality and can be made up. The person is agreeing with the shaman's trick. He may or may not see through the trick, he may actually see this as an intuition, but he is agreeing to the shaman's trick.

So the shaman takes it up a little later: Ah yes, this lady is now beckoning, and in her hand she has a vase of roses. Ah yes, auntie was very fond of roses. As any elderly lady might be, as anybody might be. All right, so he's agreed to the shaman's trick, taken a little further. Then it may go a little further, a little further, with these generalizations. To the scientist investigating, this is an obvious phony, conjuring tricks, bewildering these poor people, leading them into something. Then the shaman or clairvoyant says something that he couldn't have known: Ah yes, auntie made that will before this one. Ah, that's a different category of thing.

I was there, and this happened to me. He speaks and you make a response, you see. And if you agree with it, you make a certain response. I think the response is: God bless you. This man was there on the platform. He was an elderly man of a feminine appearance, carrying a little dog, which was tucked in his coat, like a familiar. He said: you in the twill jacket — or whatever I was wearing — I see a dead person, a person not in the body attending you. I say: God bless you. That is my brother, you see. Everybody's got some dead, at my age. Yes, I see something about your brother. He was a happy young man. Well, he was sometimes, sometimes he was sad. God bless you. So I agreed to the shaman's trick.

He said: I see a notebook in your pocket. Now that was a little closer, because not everybody carries a notebook in his pocket. He was out-of-town, he didn't know me, and I'm a little more visible in Falmouth now because of various things that have happened, but then I wasn't. I said: God bless you. He says: I see you're a writer. Well, that's quite remarkable, but somebody could have told him, I suppose. He says: I see you wandering through the flowering meadows, in your hand a notebook and the dead are helping you, and they are like bees in all the flowers. I was writing at that time a book partly about spirits called *The Beekeepers*. That was remarkable. I agreed to the shaman's tricks, and he homed in on something which was exact and comforting and which he couldn't have known. My agreement helped him.

MR: Because you didn't reject —

PR: No I didn't. And this is how this kind of work is done. I wouldn't seek to provide an explanation. It is simply that these things happen.

MR: This reminds me of someone who seems the most anti-shamanistic of poets, Philip Larkin. He describes a situation like this in the faith-healer poem. Do you think it's too deftly ironic? There's something deep about it.

PR: There is.

MR: It's not dismissive.

PR: No. There's something about Larkin which I just don't understand. I think that Larkin as man and commentator is quite different from Larkin as poet. I mean, there is a dissociation there. I know this is the case with certain poets. Their poetry arrives and, for fear of disturbance, they don't want to know where it comes from, or anything about it. And they may become very good in this way, I don't know.

I had to make a decision about this. When I went for this work with John Layard, which was a unique opportunity because here was a famous Jungian man in Falmouth who was offering an analysis on condition that I would use his methods in teaching and other work. And I had to choose between two alternatives. It was similar, I knew, to the situation Rilke had faced. He was offered an analysis by Freud, and of course he decided not to have it, because he thought it might get rid of his demons, but his angels might fly away as well, you see.

MR: That becomes almost an emblematic refusal, given who Rilke has become.

PR: Of the artist, yes. But I had to think, well is my poetry, such as it is, is it going to disappear as a result of this investigation, this analysis, this opening up — if it happens — that I want? I had to decide, well if the Jungian analysis gets rid of my poetry, perhaps the poetry wasn't worth having. So I went into analysis. I think I learned some things. I think I learned that the creative process is not something special to the artist, but is a continuum with every person, and that it is a redeeming thing in every person. I think, as Blake put it, the saviour is the imagination. He talks about Jesus the imagination, Blake does. And I think he's right. And it is what is needed.

But I think there may be poets — excellent poets indeed — who do not want to make any such investigation and whose poetry is so autonomous and so certain to them and so clear to them that they will let it have its way. I think Larkin is one of these. Hughes makes investigations of this kind. Because of his treatment of shamanistic practices and his adoption of shamanistic emblems and apparent procedures in the poems, he seems to, yes, he does see himself as a practising shaman. That is to say, an artist who is not merely an artist but a healer, and certainly his poetry seems to tend this way for many people.

MR: I'm reminded of that story — I think I'm getting it right — where he was studying for an exam, fell asleep and when he woke, found that 'somebody' had written on his exam book: 'You're murdering us.' A voice from inside him.

PR: Yes, that's right. I think that sort of thing happened to him. I think he has examined it and connected it with his knowledge of anthropology and so on. So later he gives a consistent account in his poetry of the artist as shaman. I think with Larkin, it's direct. But Larkin doesn't wish to bother it, he doesn't want to tamper.

MR: Do you agree with Philip Hobsbaum's evaluation of *Crow*, which is that it's melodramatic, overblown?

PR: I admire its ingenuity. Hughes is certainly a marvellous poet. But I feel about *Crow* that it was a transition phase, and a nigredo in his alchemy. He has always talked about the alchemical process. He has always understood Jung quite directly, I believe.

I think his best work is the work which is of relaxed and masculine clarity.

MR: *Moortown?*

PR: Yes, though there is torment in that, isn't there?

MR: The line is a little more relaxed.

PR: Yes, it is. In the early Hughes, it's poems like 'Full Moon and Little Frieda' or 'Gnat-Psalm' or 'The Man Seeking Experience Enquires his Way of a Drop of Water,' which is relaxed at the end.

MR: That one reminds me very much of your work.

PR: Yeah, Hughes was always a poet that I admired very much and so was Plath because they seemed to be among the few poets around that knew how much there had to be in a poem to make that quantum jump from ordinary discourse.

MR: Do you think that *Crow* might have been in competition with her mythology in *Ariel*, an attempt to create a comparable mythology?

PR: I don't think so. I think Hughes has been engaged in an inner process of his own. I don't think he was in direct competition. Very difficult to say. I knew him quite well at one time.

MR: Did you know him at college?

PR: Oh yes. In fact, I'll tell you the story later, so far as I recall it . . . The crow is the shadow of the hawk, of course. I mean, the hawk is an emblem of the triumph of the masculine conscience, free of the earth, the mother earth. Which is 'The Hawk in the Rain' that was crushed into the earth, but later the birds detach themselves more. The crow is the necessary counterpart, the shadow that the hawk casts on the ground in front. So it was necessary to go through that beastly, self-destructive, self-mocking, god-mocking, everything-mocking book, which justified itself I think by the extreme brilliance of its images, the ingenuity of its improvisations. I think it is justified in these ways. I think Hughes is at his best a serene poet.

MR: There's this very beautiful poem, 'That Morning', at the end of the *New Selected Poems* about the bear coming down to the water to fish for the salmon. It's very Faulknerian, and it's serene, not tortured at all. His ultimate vision of a beautiful communion, of the danger in it.

PR: There's danger in it —

MR: But as in 'That Morning' —

PR: Energy is not lost. It is a negotiation.

MR: Energy is not lost, but absorbed in some greater harmony. That's a very beautiful poem.

PR: I think this is true. I think, too, that there is something very remarkable about his inner ear and about the way his poems proceed by steps or pulses.

MR: That corresponds with the way they look.

PR: Yes. And he talks like this, too, you see. Talks very much like this. I think many of us in college ... Now what happened, as far as I remember, was that we saw some of his work in typescript before he was well-known. We'd either recently left Cambridge or were in our last year in Cambridge. Hobsbaum was one and I was another. And we saw this work was excellent, and I for one tried to get it on the BBC, you see, but the BBC wouldn't have it. I even got a BBC producer in my house listening to the tapes, and they wouldn't have it.

I think in reading it we had the benefit of hearing Hughes's voice, because the voice and the verse were always very, very close. And, of course, he had ... he has a very powerful personality. And a very strong intellect. A most excellent man to know.

There was this competition, wasn't there, run by Faber, the prize for which was the publication of a book of verse. Now, I think Hughes, from what I remember, trying to get some of these poems noticed as several of us were doing at that time — this would be in the early 1950's — met with no success at all in England. I think I'm right in saying that he had to run a review himself called *The St. Botolph's Review* to get some of them published.

MR: He originated that himself?

PR: Yes. But when he entered the competition, he entered in America, with Marianne Moore judging. I think it was Marianne Moore who saw his quality.

MR: Hughes has always had a very favourable public in America. I just picked up that '59 *Paris Review* with the Eliot interview, and I noticed that 'Crow Hill' was printed there. America has always been congenial to Hughes. The 'pulses' are quite different from your work, aren't they? You have the flow, with twists and grainy, but not so much the jumps.

PR: Well, if you like, some of his is phallic and a lot of mine is urethral (laughter).

MR: Which would go along with a lot of the imagery, too.

PR: Of course it would, yes. I mean this is the feminine side. I am a much more feminine man than Hughes is, I think. There's an interesting remark by Jung about the distinction between the masculine and the feminine spirit. He says the masculine spirit strives after perfection but not completeness. The feminine spirit strives for completeness but not perfection. So this would go with my interest in breaking down categories and boundaries.

MR: And the insistence on the provisionality of the work as a whole and each individual poem — that they are not sacrosanct or meant to echo down the ages.

PR: Yes, and water relaxes and spunk spurts. Naturally, to me, the best of Hughes is relaxed.

MR: Water is your element.

PR: Water is my element, the feminine element. Yes, so I think it's urethral contrasted with phallic. I mean, if one wants to use these kind of terms, this is what springs to mind. I don't know what the Jungian one would be, but that's the Freudian one. But I'm not interested in Freudian work, really. I don't know what one would say in a Jungian way.

I think, you see, there is a sense in Hughes of the hero winning the dragon fight. This is the Jungian one. The hero winning the dragon fight, the triumphant reborn hawk Horus, the triumph of the reborn, the ever-coming sun.

Me, I am interested in the works of Leviathan. I don't fight the dragon.

MR: There's a poem of yours about a church-window with St. George —

PR: Fighting the dragon.

MR: But it ends not with the domination of St. George but with the wind again, like a snake, which reminds me of the poem 'Serpentine'.

PR: Yes, that's right. 'Serpentine', which is the dragon. And in the succession of cultures, it is said that they begin with the stellar time — stellar cultures — and go to lunar or feminine and then to solar or masculine. Whether this is true of cultures one doesn't know, it's much disputed, but it certainly is a series of layers in the development of the modern man. The modern man has to fight with the dragon, has to detach himself from the mother. His culture requires it.

But now feminine consciousness is becoming differentiated and aware of itself.

MR: Do you read Adrienne Rich?

PR: A little.

MR: What do you think of her work?

PR: Well, great tracts of it are magnificent, aren't they? I just quoted some in a review that I did of the new anthology of women's poetry called *Bread and Roses*. It asked the question: Why aren't there more great women poets? You see, this question is often posed by men! And I'm saying the anthology perhaps offers another answer, perhaps great women artists don't always seem to be so because the idea of great art is greatly misconceived. By definition, it is only something that specially inspired great people, usually men, can produce. Most poetry anthologies set up their contents as examples of excellence, to be admired at a distance.

Now listen to Diana Scott in her introduction: 'Inspiration may be an experience accessible to people in all walks of life. Some poetry may empower us to recreate the experience for ourselves. Inspiration is one of humankind's most ancient experiences. The process is one of mental transformation, and every poem of quality is, along with what it says it is about, the experience of what it was like for the author to create it. That experience is there for the reader to recreate and thus to share.' That's her introduction.

In other words, as I say in my review: 'The true purpose of art is to inspire others to their work, whether it is an artist, musician, doctor, writer or scientist. An anthology of poetry should tune its readers into their own sources of inspiration. This common and most valuable basic human experience, when, as Hopkins remarks, 'one's best ideas strike into the mind unasked,' or when in Mary Shelley's words, 'my imagination unbidden possessed and guided me, gifting the successive images that rose in my mind with a vividness far beyond the usual bounds of reveries'. . .

Now this is very interesting, you see, because this magic of inspiration, what I'm saying is a common human quality and the redeemer in Jungian terms, is what the women's movement is offering us in the poetry anthologies. Not poetry as an icon to be worshipped but to be participated in to rouse one's own poetry. What could be better?

I had to avoid the question of how good some of the poetry was that arose in that particular book out of the women's movement, in my terms. A little side-stepping it. But I think the faults, too, are very, very important, because they mar perfection. This is what the traditional solar hero hates about the dragon, or as Freud said to Jung, We must stop the tide, we must stop the tide. The tide of the what? The black tide of mud of the occult, by which he meant the mother. And as we try and point out in *The Wise Wound*, this would be partly the menstruating mother, when of course for many women everything collapses. I mean, a woman can make herself perfect like a man, but then crash, then comes the period. You see, one might not want to do it, not in masculine terms. The masculine wants perfection, avoids the completeness. The point of *The Wise Wound* was to show the neglected factor, the positive power in the period, as a component of inspiration in both sexes.

MR: Did you publish early Hughes while you were editor of *Delta*? Or was that not at the same time?

PR: No, Hughes hadn't turned up yet.

MR: Did you start *Delta*?

PR: I started *Delta*. It ran 25 years before it was merged with *Argo*. That's one of the longest running things. I can't claim any credit for that, it was just a succession of editors. But there was a need for a magazine of this kind. I think Philip Hobsbaum published some early Hughes when he succeeded me. I had done two issues. I certainly would have published Hughes if I had had the opportunity. But the typescripts didn't turn up till later on, if my recollection is correct.

Yes, that's right. I'm sure Philip published him. I think he published 'The Martyrdom of Bishop Farrar,' a couple of things that were in *Hawk in the Rain*. I think so.

MR: Is it correct to say that that the difference between The Group and The Movement, which came earlier, is that The Group had more of an allegiance to a method, with a fairly catholic taste, whereas The Movement had more of a content in that it was in reaction against more apocalyptic poetry?

PR: Yes. Well, The Group was a working association or, as they say nowadays, a workshop. The Movement was never anything of the kind. It was a journalistic fiction. Members of The Movement were hardly acquainted with each other. It was simply that it was discerned that people were reacting against apocalyptic verse, which they regarded as sloppy at the time, with a sort of Augustan or Drydenic procedure. What's the word I want? God! Certainly Augustan, this kind of conduct of verse. They wanted something which was less, as they thought, less subjective. Many members of The Movement thought this was a great simplification of what they were individually doing and said so. And there were powerful poets, of course, who were caught up in this. Was Thom Gunn supposed to be a member of The Movement?

MR: Yes.

PR: Yeah, when he was writing in his own way by himself at Cambridge, I met him there. He looked just the same then as he does now. Dressed the same. He went across to America and continued. I think he's written essays, hasn't he, on other members of The Movement? Then there was somebody like John Wain, who was in provincial universities. Quite a difference. I think it was all facilitated by journalism. We ourselves as The Group were individuals, I believe, but developing in the workshop. The workshop had no prospectus or manifesto or easily discerned common theme. When they wanted to discern a common theme, they picked out certain poems and said that we were rather domestic, the household. This is partly because we wanted concrete images and so we were looking around ourselves, at our bedsitters and flats, you see. We had no money; we were poor; we had to live in flats. But this wasn't how we wanted to proceed or what we thought of ourselves as doing. And it wasn't a method. Except of discussion.

MR: Talking about schools and movements, is this Martian School a journalistic fiction, or is there something really to it? What do you think of it?

PR: Oh, it's very difficult for me to say, because what I think is that Craig Raine is a poet, and I think his poetry was liberated by suddenly realizing that he didn't need all the intellectual apparatus that his education had given him and which his nature is expert at using. He's a very clever man. And I think he saw that the innocent eye and the — how shall I call the kind of simile or metaphor that he uses? — the immediate metaphor gave a great deal of pleasure to himself and to people reading him, some of whom thought of these poems in the same way as one thinks of riddles. The world appeared as a riddle of brightly coloured surfaces. I think he has such spirit in him that this sort of Lewis Carroll method touches quite deep springs sometimes. But the notion that the Martians are a particular school of poetry, is a journalistic one, and rather a peculiar idea. Because what else has poetry of any kind been doing but approaching things with an innocent eye and with the use of metaphor?

I mean, if one wants to be unkind about the Martians, one thinks of Lewis Carroll's poem about the mad gardener, isn't it? I thought I saw a — what is it, a postage stamp flying, you know the rhyme, and it was the middle of last week, it mustn't be out so late, because of the damp, and this kind of thing. There's a sort of lightness and recoil, but Craig Raine is a man of quality and ability and his work does get quite deep. I think if it had begun deep, it wouldn't have enjoyed the success that it has, because I think the English do not like to take their poetry too seriously. I mean, in certain ways, it borders on light verse. I think it's a diversion for so much of the English. They recoil from anything which touches them. Now, of course he's able to do it.

Now there are people associated with Craig Raine who, I think, entirely lack his qualities and who display a kind of meanness of spirit or a small compass of reference, which is entirely antipathetic, and I'd rather not discuss those people. Craig Raine himself I think is an original and developing poet of a good kind. But I do blame the commentators who find in his method anything different from very much poetry that has already appeared through the ages. I just can't understand why that they should think this was such a departure.

**MR:** Philip Hobsbaum attributes a great deal of influence to the publication here of Robert Lowell's *Life Studies,* in terms of moving poets toward the use of the dramatic monologue. Did you feel that influence personally? Do you agree?

**PR:** I think Robert Lowell has had a good deal of influence but not on me. I mean, like Hopkins, I say I admire and do otherwise. He's not what I'm looking for. It's a poetry of malaise, I think, and it asks you for the poet's biography, really. I want to know something about the reasons for his troubles, the reasons for his drinking. I mean, we've had these, this life of Berryman, haven't we, just recently, and we've had Eileen Simpson's memoir of Berryman and Lowell, and so on. It seems to me that they were terribly self-indulgent people, terribly self-indulgent. They'd go off for literary prizes, academic fame and distinction and still want to be poets. They wanted to have their cake and eat it, rather like Sylvia Plath's impulse to a career. Of course, this produced tremendous tensions in their married lives, and produced tremendous tensions in their personalities, which they tended to solve by drinking and so they gradually destroyed themselves. Because they did not make the conflicts natural to their situation accessible to their contemplation or repair. Nobody can tell the pressures on another person, but this is what I get from the poetry. It's a broken landscape fitfully illuminated with jagged bursts of lightning.

The Lowell I like best is in the *Imitations,* where in fact he got away from the confessional, and did excellent versions of Baudelaire. He has some beautiful Rilke, rather simplified Rilke but good, and things of this kind. I enjoy the things where Lowell is away from Lowell, rather.

So the answer is, no, not on me, but on my contemporaries.

MR: You have a whole series of dramatic monologue poems. We've talked about 'The Sermon,' and Jabez. Was there anything in particular that influenced you to use that form, what Hobsbaum calls the interrupted monologue?

PR: The interrupted monologue, yes. Well, I don't think it was directly influenced by anybody, though of course one finds correspondences in a lot of people. I mean, Browning is the obvious one, and I was reading a tremendous amount of Shakespeare around this time.

I think where it comes from is, once again, a religious idea — the idea that a person at the Day of judgment is suddenly given the ability to discuss himself without concealment and that on the Day of Judgment, the condemnation is done by oneself, or the approval is done by oneself, in the clarity of that day's dawning. I get this from watching Shakespeare, too. For me, the pleasure is not so much in the plot or the politics of the plays, as in the way these people are able to see the world and speak of it directly. There is no inhibition in the speech.

We grope for words when we're in our normal state of mind. We can't satisfy ourselves with what we say. This is why an interview is such a difficult form. But on the Day of Judgment, the person will be able to speak to his full bent. And that's what I think of as the attraction of the dramatic monologue. It's a moment of understanding which a person has about a particular time in his life, or at least he's capable of saying it, even though he might be deceiving himself.

I think a reasonable definition of tragedy in Shakespeare or anywhere else is when the people involved are not gifted with sufficient understanding to see their situation. I mean, this is the idea of the tragic flaw isn't it, that there is a lack of insight before action. But the most moving thing, the thing which purges us and troubles us in tragic drama is when, by a sudden gift, the scales are lifted from our protagonist's eyes and he sees what he has done and what he is.

MR: So it's that breakthrough feeling which comes with the poem.

PR: It's a breakthrough into another mode of consciousness. There is greater understanding than our ordinary waking consciousness permits us. And this, of course, is the tragedy of man, that he doesn't have this, and even worse, he often doesn't want it either.

MR: Here's a next-to-last question, which I think is related. You say in *The Wise Wound* that all of art deals with giving voice to the antagonist within.

PR: Did I say that? Did we say that?

MR: I think so.

PR: All right, that's part of the negotiating process, yes.

MR: In which ways does your poetry do that?

PR: I think the poetry of mine which I prefer is poetry in which the antagonist has been revealed as a counsellor. This is Jacob's posture, isn't it? That is to say, he wrestled with the angel and refused to let him go, until he'd blessed him.

Now this, in Jungian terms, is the fight with the shadow. The shadow is the antagonist, who contains all those parts or qualities of humanity that you yourself have rejected and despised and which nevertheless exist in you. And in Jungian work, when the shadow appears in dreams or in projections, the task is to face the shadow. The shadow keeps you to your work. If you run away from the shadow, you are running away from the work, because behind the shadow is the anima and behind the anima is the self.

It's where this antagonist is, as I say, revealed as somebody who has information.

MR: What about the poem 'Noise'? Where the speaker says, I am the printer's ink, everything is going to come to nothing. Isn't it a voice of entropy?

PR: Yes, it is, isn't it. And of course, 'The Idea of Entropy at Maenporth Beach' is later than that. The blackness here . . . this is one of the few poems I think that I have let come through, that worked to a certain extent, where one faces a nothingness anterior to the negotiation. Because, of course, one doesn't, until one dies, really face a nothingness, and even then perhaps not. That is an account of the kind of depression when a person cannot even read — I'm talking about 'Noise' — when a person cannot understand ordinary writing, ordinary words, which is a very terrible feeling when it happens. And of course, the poem is saying that perhaps this is, might be a good thing, no it's saying that if . . . you might as well prepare by not relying so much on books, for that kind of experience. So it's perhaps preparing for the sort of negotiation with the black tide of mud, as it were, which comes in 'The Idea of Entropy at Maenporth Beach.' Which if you remember, is an account of a woman in a white dress who deliberately baptizes herself in the mud.

MR: Marie Peel says that poem was not written in response to Wallace Stevens. I find that hard to believe.

PR: Did she say that it wasn't? Perhaps that's not the primary purpose but I did write it in response to Wallace Stevens. The reason was that I disagreed with Wallace Stevens' philosophy there, and I think that Wallace Stevens' own poem disagrees with his philosophy, because he makes the sea so alive and says that it's only the woman's song that counts. Well, it isn't, so I'm putting this singer into a position where she is counselled by that which is usually despised, which is the mud and earth.

MR: Why do you use the verb 'shrugged' in the last line: 'The shrugged-up riches of deep darkness sang.'

PR: Well, if you observe mud as in the tidal estuaries here, you'll see that as it turns, the banks are turned like shoulders turn and shrug. The mud shrugs up to the side of banks in rounded shoulders. So that's why I say 'the shrugged-up riches.' Or, if you have a channel of water and the water is above the detritus or mud, it is moving spirally all the time and the heavier substances sort of shrug up round the sides a bit in smooth banks.

MR: Is there the connotation of indifference to what we would call order?

PR: I think it's opulent indifference to its own richness. It is rich without knowing that it is rich. Or it is so rich, that it doesn't care if it's rich. I mean, you're only rich if you don't know how much money you've got.

MR: That's true. Filthy rich.

PR: Filthy rich. Exactly, exactly.

MR: Do you regard 'The Haunted Armchair' as a sort of polar opposite to that poem? I disagree with both D.M. Thomas and Marie Peel where they emphasize the verb 'grants': 'Everything grants me withering . . .' They take that as a positive term at the end. Whereas I read the poem as an opposite to 'The Idea of Entropy,' and I don't see why so much weight is put on the verb 'grants', to suddenly turn the whole thing round.

PR: I was surprised at that. What it means, it 'grants' him so that he doesn't have to worry about it anymore. The body is in fact wearing out and decaying, and will eventually go and leave him, without responsibility, as simply a ghost in an armchair. A dirty stain. He's nothing but a dirty stain now, so he doesn't have to try so hard. It's a very pessimistic poem, it's a very nasty ghost. Yes, I was surprised at them saying this.

MR: It didn't make sense to me.

PR: It didn't make sense to me either, but I respect the thought.

MR: One of the great things about that poem is that it reads like a little Beckett drama. I've never seen anyone reproduce that quality of voice in a poem as Beckett can do so well.

PR: 'Lesslessness.' That's the one where you have the same words over and over again but diminishing, diminishing. So it is like that, yes. But there were poems like that where there was no counselling from the antagonist. I think up to 'The Idea of Entropy at Maenporth Beach.' That poem was in fact a turning point. That's why it's dedicated to John Layard. Where this notion of baptism in the despised medium, which is of growth, which seems dark but is not dark to itself, in fact it's very rich, was accepted.

I believe it has a menstrual significance.

MR: Yes, you mention that in *The Wise Wound*. You say, a menstrual initiation. I applied it to the poem. In fact, *Wise Wound* really operates to elucidate many, many of your poems.

PR: It should, because it is all of a piece. I think *The Wise Wound* was part of the work which moves into the kind of poetry which is of negotiation with the nether powers. Instead of an explosive visitation from without, with menace but with no discernible significance but only cruelty, one sees one's own lost self, and negotiates.

MR: One of the successes of that poem I think is that entropy does not only work as a concept, but is embodied in every aspect of the poem. To me, the poem courts the ludicrous. It dares ludicrous images and succeeds. And that risk is part of the negotiation with the entropy.

PR: Yeah, that's very interesting, because it is a ludicrous action.

MR: But it's brought off as a ritual.

PR: But you see, this is the characteristic of important ritual actions, or what you might call the magical image. I mean, what could be more ludicrous than a church procession? Almost any religious rite is, from outside, ludicrous. From Frazer's point of view in *The Golden Bough*, almost everything that these benighted savages do is ludicrous. That's why it's such a wonderful book. It's full of entertainingly malicious anecdotes. I don't much care for the commentary, but his sense of the ludicrous sharpens his observation. I mean, he doesn't experience these things but he sees them in books, and it sharpens his cleverness.

But he keeps on saying how ludicrous these things are. How ridiculous, he implies, to think that by copulating in a ploughed field, one can make the wheat spring. What he is unable to see, I think, is that what is happening in these magical rites is that one is engaged in a symbolic participation with the universe around one.

Copulating in a ploughed field may or may not make the wheat more fertile, but it sure as hell is sexy! And therefore, it makes the human persons fertile, because they are part of that field and that growth. So he's got it arsy-versy.

A ludicrous action deliberately performed as, say, by a clown who is performing it not maybe in order to forestall an accident or as a result of an accident, but simply as a deliberate ritual, is going to surprise people more than make them laugh. I mean, it's going to have a very strange feeling. You might say that the Jewish custom of rending your garments in the case of a calamity or a death, or rubbing ashes onto your head, is a ridiculous thing to do. Well, of course it is. When people tear the seat of their trousers on a nail, what a comic event. But this is deliberately done. It breaks the normal pattern of things, so that there is a sense of wonder there, which is only partly slapstick. A strepitous.

MR: That seems to tie in many things we've talked about: the sense of the comic, the wondrous, the religious — all very close together.

PR: Yes, aren't they.

MR: Maybe that's a good place to . . .

PR: Maybe.

# 8. Lazarus and the Visionary Truth

## Interview with *Arrows* (Cliff Ashcroft)

**C.A.** Why did you start writing poetry, was there any experience that gave you a sense of poetic vocation?

**P.R.** Yes, there was, but it came comparatively late. I was always interested in words as a schoolchild, but I went on the science side. What happened was that I met a woman who was an Art Student at the time, a sculptor. Work with 'art' was an entirely new thing to me. I was about eighteen. It was her person that opened the doors to this. She was the first woman I made love to. After making love, a silence came into my head and into that silence came my first poem, complete. I was so surprised I nearly fell out of bed. I did get out of bed to write it down. I now realise that happening was a call to vocation; I realised that what was occurring was a coming together of bodily happenings and mental happenings in a way I had never known before. In the act of love with a woman, it was not ordinary time, it was somehow out of usual time. Time stilled in me and to what had happened made an answer or response which was rhythmical speech, made up of images, a poem. I was astonished, it was like a voice, I think it was probably another personality inside me, the real Peter.

**C.A.** This image of a coming together of bodily happenings and mental happenings is common in your poetry. Indeed you were at first trained as a scientist, then took up poetry, and later psychology. In the universities, schools and colleges, these areas are split up into departments; similarly there is this notion of the two cultures. In your own life, as well as in your work, would you say you view a world that is perhaps harmfully and dangerously fragmented?

**P.R.** Yes, certainly the modern mental world is fragmented. This is the way it defends itself against transformation into something better. The Jungian view is that human nature is four-fold, that we consist of and exercise four functions; intellect, sensation, feeling and intuition. A person is not complete unless he is operating on all these four cylinders. In our culture what we prize above all are the extravert qualities. In particular, we esteem extravert sensation and intellect. Our culture-hero is the scientist, who is one who observes the outer world, not the inner world, reasons about it and seeks to control it. One needs to balance this with finding what the world does to oneself, that is to say what moves in oneself, not just what one moves.

It is the will that is over-developed. I think what is being kept out is this complementary matter which is the passive qualities. I think the artist is a man who is trying to complement the overt culture, not lead it, but respond to it and find these things in his nature that society leaves out. Whereas the active, masculine will is rather like a tower, there is also in this landscape, but perhaps covered over, a well. So there is a will and a well. The artist needs the will to find out and do his work, but he also needs the well to look into the depths. That is why we call our new book 'Deepening'.

Putting it another way, you could say the best moments people have, are when sub-personalities trained by the culture come together in unity. There is the intellectual sub-personality of the clever schoolboy trained by school, there is the feeling sub-personality which is perhaps the mother's boy trained by the mother, the intuitive, ghostly, magical one, spontaneously arising, trained by nobody in this culture; and the sensual one, trained to inferior satisfactions by consumer society. But when all four meet and interact then the world, inner and outer is real, four-dimensional. These four-fold moments of reality are the moments that the artist is trying to get at and perpetuate. At the cross-over (one can see the 4 functions as a 4-armed cross) is another function, the function of imagination, which comprises all four, and is another term beyond, quintessential.

C.A.  As well as the scientist and the artist, you also use the notions of magician and hypnotist in your work. The areas of magic, the pagan and occult are exiled, non-legitimate regions in our culture. A Christian educated person, like myself, and most of this country, may come to your work with apprehension. In what way are you advocating these 'scary' areas? Do you think reference to occult practices can be of help to people like myself?

**P.R.**   Well, in the first place, the Christian religion has a lot to answer for in terms of people's anxiety. In the 'Wise Wound', we pointed out how much Christianity had satanised women, satanised the body and satanised sex. One of the most important mental experiences I had, as I said in the last question, my call to vocation, was a sexual experience. It was not a physical experience only, and was not a mental experience only. It was a third thing beyond any experience I had had before. Now if you have a Christian culture which has satanised these sexual experiences which are also spiritual experiences, you can see that for some people something very, very important has been left out, call it visionary sex. In Christianity, vision is mental and apparently non-sensual, it is meant to be spiritual but I found visionary experience in the body and still do. I find vision in the earthly world. I find vision in matter. I think matter and spirit are two sides of the one coin. I think they have been separated, as reflected in your example of university structure, because the intellect can act like bodiless pure spirit, it can separate itself as much as it likes, without connections. Now I would wish not to be presented as an occultist. Naturally, I have studied occult matters, but from the point of view of Jungian psychology. Both Jung and Freud secularised 'magical practices' which are actually practical psychology in the same way as any religion is practical psychology, the purpose of which should be making people real to themselves and each other. Christianity in its present form tries to do this by leaving things out. What is being kept out is this complementary thing, the so-called unconscious mind, which is intensely creative, and compensatory. So if you are terribly sweet and pure, leaving things out in your conscious mind, then there is going to be a terrible, dark, scary shadow in the unconscious. So for a person, or a culture, to conquer unreality, these sub-personalities have to be brought together. They must learn to converse with and tolerate each other and eventually merge.

Freud secularised the Jewish Cabala which happens also to be the basis of western occult practice. The basic notions of the ten emanations of God are used as a practical meditation in occult societies. That Freud secularised a good deal of this occult matter, I think is beyond dispute. I am thinking of David Bakan's book on Sigmund Freud and the Jewish Mystical Traditions. It is certainly beyond dispute, in that in a like manner Jung secularised Gnosticism. Gnosticism being the various ancient movements that arose either in opposition or complementarity to the main stream of Christianity that was the form that presided over our own culture. Alchemy was an 'occult' practice developed out of Gnosticism. Jung secularised this. In his analytic practice he found very, very strange and non-Christian images coming through in his Christian patients' dreams. Sometimes there were actively integrative images. Yet the patients concerned had no knowledge of occultism or alchemy. The 'occult' dreams were spontaneous dreams, and had to be followed up, with healing results. In explicating these images Jung was in effect bringing back into practical therapeutic psychology an occult practice.

I know of at least one magical society that was founded by a practising analytical psychologist who found that this was the best way for her clients to continue their studies. Why do we separate out things like this? What we call occultism is only somebody else's religion. You have to remember that old anthropological adage that the demons of the present religion are the gods of the former religion.

C.A.   In the novel *The Beekeepers* would you say you also concern yourself with the dangers possible in direct practice of the occult? For example the sexual antics at the institute.

P.R.   Yes, they did seem rather naughty didn't they? It was the gross passions of the doctor in charge. In *The Facilitators* the daughter of that doctor David has set up a healing institute which is even stranger than the one in *The Beekeepers*, but is more explicitly healing. The healing process is shown going on there, without disaster.

C.A.   In *The Martyr of the Hives*, similarly would you say the occult practices are 'perverted'?

P.R.   They are 'perverted' only where they are used for power. The art of opening is a dual art. When you come close to these compensatory energies you get them double. They can be used for healing or destruction. They can be used for power-plays for confining other people, or they can be used for liberation. This is a very good reason for being scared of the 'occult'. What is in the psyche is extraordinarily powerful. One must remember that occultism is only another name for somebody else's religion. If you go into Christianity it is dangerous. If you go into the wrong side of things, the wrong side of Jesus, then you are in trouble. If you go into Christianity and you happen to be a powerfully sexed person it is dangerous. You may, believe that repressing your sexuality will eventually sublimate it, so you have a beautiful spiritual life with that dark demonic sexual shadow that makes you afraid of anybody else's religion. Hence the most familiar of historical activities, religious warfare.

C.A. Yes, Krishnamurti relates a story where a holy man in order to suppress his sexuality in accordance with his religion, castrated himself. Of course the problem still remained.

P.R. Well I should think so because now he cannot express it. If you want to have sex outside marriage or if you want to masturbate or whatever, orthodox Jesus would not like it. However, Morton Smith believes that Jesus was a gifted hypnotist and masseur.

C.A. Masseur?

P.R. Yes, a healer. If you have ever been in the presence of a healer, there is this experience of coming into a powerfully charged atmosphere. Everyone has this experience in some form. In the presence of a close friend you often feel your body response to him or to her like currents going between you, or what seem to be currents. Healers know these currents. In a man who has trained himself or is gifted in this way, his presence is palpable. Morton Smith believes that Jesus was such a man, a gifted magician who was able to impart spiritual experience by touching. Now this is a practice of massage. Touching is coming back into some psychology. Reich for example was a physiotherapist, and this was part of his psychological work. You are trained in humanistic psychology, to have this intense awareness of touch. Such healing is certainly a reality. Many, myself included, have witnessed it directly. One has to remember that the Christian religion suits and interests a particular kind of person. To say that this religion is the ultimate metaphysical truth for all people, well that is a sin, an evil. There are different kinds of people, I am not a Christian, I do not therefore feel inferior nor do I feel superior.

As far as sexual experience is concerned we meet again with the crossing over into the other world. There are two worlds, there is as you might call it the executive world in which we handle our ordinary small affairs, and there is the other world we go into whenever we enlarge our consciousness and allow ourselves to relax, consider, fall in love, get drunk, watch a good film, read a marvellous poem, in other words we go beyond the ordinary boundaries of our personality, that is the other one. Now as we do his, we go into what it is fashionable to call an Altered State of Consciousness. It can be the light, hypnoidal, soothed state we get from television. It may be as common as this, or as a daydream in which you have to say 'hello', and then ask 'HELLO' and you have to shake them before they come out, which is cruel. Or it may go to mediumistic trance in which a person proceeds so far into their reverie that they appear to see their dead ones. Or into the mysterious areas of E.S.P. which our science will not examine properly. But all these altered states of consciousness are a kind of 'trance'. Now one of the strongest ways in which that altered state of consciousness is available to the ordinary human person, to everybody as part of their birthright, is by sexual intercourse. It is much more common to achieve an altered state consciousness by sexual intercourse than it is, say, by 'prayer' in a church. This was my fortune, to find myself in a poetic trance as a result of sexual intercourse. The first time I had sex, how should I be so lucky? I realise now that it was extremely good fortune.

C.A. Many of your images, poems and novels well as the psychological work, contain the presence of Goddesses, the notions of feminine energies, feminine aspects of nature. Could you explain what you mean when you say you wish release the feminine energies in men'?

P.R. Well, I think gender roles are culturally conditioned. There are two sexes, but there are two genders. The way a man who is sexed as a man behaves is somewhat pre-determined; his clothes, behaviour, his business, what he does in life and so on, are imposed by our gender role play. He or she may desire other things that are not set out in their course as a masculine person, or a feminine person. This is one of the ways in which the past manipulates the present, through our gender roles. A good deal of human nature is wasted through gender role-playing. A sensuous, intellectual, egoistic man will regard his compensatory functions of intuition and feeling as feminine and project them on his wife, who he may have married for this very purpose. He will keep the wife at home to do the intuitive bit and the feeling, and when he goes to work he will take his intellect and sensuality into combat. I say he should have all four active inside himself. If he is a scientist of the highest quality he will be intuitive as well. To do his science he needs his intellect and his sense to do his observation, he also needs intuition and feeling. It is very rare when you get those four together at all. The neglected functions are usually projected on other people, sometimes as demonic qualities. Women are satanised by projection.

C.A.  Yes, Bronowski relates a parallel incident in *The Ascent of Man*, a mathematical problem solved by an intuitive leap.

P. R.  Exactly, done in an 'altered state of consciousness'. The creative process is the same in the two cultures, the same in science and the same in art and the most famous illustration is Kekule, who saw the solution to the structure of benzene by watching pictures in the fire. It was one of the cornerstones of modern chemistry. Now you see it is the same in the two cultures. That is how Blake got his visions. You see pictures in the fire, you go into 'trance': Everybody does this, you know a coal fire, it is lovely, it soothes you, then you start to feel very relaxed then maybe you start to have dreams, start to see images and so on, it is very, very nice, and very important . There is also something about the physical atmosphere, it is not just visual, there is ionisation there, the electrical atmosphere changes, mind and body start to soothe and tell sooth in their relaxation.

If you record over the skin when you are in this sort of condition instead of a pattern of electrical activity running all over the place it comes over, as it soothes, as a pulse. Blake used to make love with his married partner, Catherine Sophia, and they would watch the fire afterwards and from there would come his engravings. In the *New Scientist* this week in a letter, they are asking for opinions on what the differences and the similarities between the two cultures. I am going to write to them and say, ask this question, is or is not the creative process the same? This would mean that the teaching in Art Schools could be relevant to the creativity of the scientist, and vice versa, science departments to creative artist.

C.A. At the Greenham Common protest mission, women would not allow men to join their protest as they believe masculine values were responsible for war and such destructive nuclear weaponry. Do you agree that there is this separation, that men are violent and women peaceful?

P. R. The separation is in fact the source of destruction. To identify gender roles with moral qualities is the source of the problem. Obviously, the women regard the quality of life of infinite importance. So any real human being does. But I do believe it is much easier for a man to become detached from the realities of his bodily existence, one of the reasons for this is that he does not have a menstrual cycle so men can forget the body. But a woman with a menstrual cycle is always reminded of the body, its real presence and its capabilities.

C.A. Does this detached masculinity therefore repress feminine experience?

P. R. Yes. A woman says 'I had a strange dream at my period', the man does not listen to the strange dream, he says 'Ah yes. I do not want strange dreams at all, this is detritus'. So next period instead of daring to say she has a strange dream, she says 'Oh I have got a headache' instead. He says 'is that your period? Oh I am sorry'. And so each month the headache gets worse. because she is not listened to. The dress is the royal road inward.

C.A. In *The Wise Wound*, you mention at one stage that women in particular, possess the possibility of creating 'mental children, seminal ideas and insights'. What are these? What are these prophecies and dreams that are useful to the community?

**P. R.**  I spoke of the altered states of consciousness obtainable during sexual intercourse. Now if you are in possession of a medium or craft of expression, artistic design or a method of science, these altered states of consciousness because they dissolve the fringes of your ordinary ego and are going to be your artistic and scientific vision. These altered states of consciousness are particularly available to the woman and the man during intercourse which is often of a more powerful kind during the menstrual or pre-menstrual time. The quality of sensuality in a woman seems often to be of a different kind at menstruation than it is at ovulation. The ovulation time is infolding, it tends to be more passive. It is holding the egg like a nest. At menstruation, at the opposite pole of the cycle, the woman partner is likely to be full of initiatory energies, she is more likely to initiate the situation. For example. she is more likely to wish the clitoris to be involved in intercourse, whereas the woman at ovulation is not necessarily going to put a great emphasis on the clitoris. These things change throughout the menstrual cycles and so sexual activity will be of a varying kind as will your changes of consciousness and therefore your work. This is an observation that we have discussed with many people, mostly creative people of various kinds. We also find it is true in the Tantric tradition when the woman's energies at menstruation are thought to communicate to the man and enlighten him. It also seems to be part of the occult tradition. It is called, vulgarly I suppose or popularly, sex magic. I will give you an example which we say is magic, but the whole world is magic. If you have a problem, late at night, you are working on it, what do you do? You sleep on it, wake-up in the morning and maybe see a way through. Similarly, if you have an artistic or scientific problem, some piece of work, you go to bed with your partner, you have sex and the problem may very well answer itself in your reverie, or afterglow or when you are engaged in the one-pointed meditation which is sexual activity with your partner. The analogy between what is called meditation and what is called sexual intercourse is exact.

**C.A.**  That is a very shamanic image you use.

**P.R.**  It is shamanism, of course it is shamanism, people talk nowadays I think, of shamanism as if it is a novelty. Shamanism is done each time we make love. You disappear and re-assemble.

C.A.   Yes. You make a similar analogy in the poem 'The Housekeeper', the new communion.

P.R.   That's right, the bed that must he eaten whilst it is fresh! This is shamanism, but once again our culture because it is a kind of Christian culture says 'none of that black magic!' It is not black magic, it is human magic and it is available to everybody, it is everybody's birthright. If you read the sex books a little about trance experience and altered states of consciousness is just beginning to arrive, in some of the new hooks.

An addendum to menstrual sex: If the menstrual time is so powerful, a 'magical' time or a creative time, this makes all the crueller the menstrual taboo such as the Biblical one, in Leviticus. In other words, the most powerfully creative time in the mental sense is forbidden by the official religion.

C.A.   A universal fear is the fear of death; do you think your poetry faces these fears, comes to terms with them? I am thinking particularly of your references to the Eleusinian mysteries and poems like 'Tapestry Moths' and 'Silence Fiction'.

P.R.   There was this initiation that went on in ancient Greece called the Eleusinian mysteries. It would appear that all the notable Greek people, all the powerful dramatists, poets, philosophers and scientists went through this initiation of the Eleusinian mysteries. In it they were taken through a series of actions and ordeals and at the end were shown something which removed the fear of death. Somehow they learnt rejoicing in the presence of death, that paradoxically death was not the total disaster it would appear. These mysteries were more or less closed down, they were certainly given bad 'press' in Christian times. One of the things in Freud is that the fear of death is a cause of neurosis: maybe he means the fear of change or transmutation. An important subject of my own poetry is transmutation or transformation through various barriers or thresholds from one state to another. These barriers or thresholds can be as simple in our daily lives as walking through a door into a strange room, or getting up, or getting out of the bath, or if one feels tired deciding one must go for a long walk, to change. There is a threshold or division to it and I think our lives are made up of various degrees of willingness and unwillingness to pass from one state of mind to another. What Blake calls the 'states': he says the states are eternal, man travels from one to the other. Death seems to me what Kingsley Amis calls 'God's best kept secret', all we can know of it, is that it is different from now. Now when we go to sleep we become unconscious except sometimes we dream, we extend our consciousness into sleeping perhaps. But we are all going to die, so we must prepare for it somehow. We must become reconciled to the possibility of extinction, but how do we become reconciled to the extinctions and enhancements we experience in our ordinary mental life? That is to say sometimes we have good ideas, sometimes we have no ideas at all, sometimes we are depressed, sometimes we exult. How do we reconcile these things? Well, we learn to change, we learn to become Protean. One of the differences between Freudian psychology and Jungian psychology, is that in Freudian psychology nobody can quite decide what the purpose or end is, when the analysis is finished! In Jungian psychology this is much clearer, it is when the person arrives at a state of continual 'active imagination', that is to say anything or everything in its changes become interesting. This is an ideal state, and very difficult to achieve, seldom achieved. Proteus changing and changing and changing but held on to until he answers your question.

C.A. Yes, that is similar to Hughes' poem from *Crow*, 'Truth Kills Everybody'.

P.R. Whether this has anything to do with actual death or not, who can say? Now in the occult tradition people talk to the dead. In the occult tradition some people gain their living power because they believe that there is something beyond death. It is quite common for people to believe in reincarnation and take their personal power from this. In terms of what is going to happen, I do not know what is going to happen next year or this afternoon, neither do you. What is going to happen when we die? We do not know but we have to live so we take our personal power from having access to as much of our own nature as possible. The death part must not be shut away. If you are a believing professed Christian you have no fear of death and you take your personal power from that. Occult power you might call it but it is the same thing in all religion. Poetry about this does not seem very common but it comes into my work.

C.A.  In poems like 'Silence Fiction', and 'Or was that when I was grass', you posit a me and I that survives intact throughout these transformations. Do you believe this to be literally true?

P.R.  Beliefs are not really a matter for this discussion, experiences are. One forms one's beliefs from experience but too often people who compare beliefs are not comparing experiences. At the present time I have no experience that would lead me to believe directly in reincarnation. I do write poetry which for me often predicts or refigures further experiences. Robert Frost says we write our poems because they are planks into the future, like bridges we run across into the future. This can be literally true; for example quite a lot of investigation for *The Wise Wound* had to do with poems which were working, as it were at the fringes of the mind and bringing matters such as the visionary power of menstrual blood into the light of consciousness, that which we did not know about before. So it is possible that these poems which speak to me about surviving death may prepare one for experiences which will then result in beliefs about surviving death. Poems are, after all, experiences at a very deep level. A powerful Taoist image is that a person forming their individuality is like water forming a vortex in a stream, which persists even though the water changes. A person who achieves individuality persists in the Tao. This is an image that I like. I had another aspect of call to vocation which was an experience I had when I was eighteen. I had a rather remarkable home life which I will not describe in detail and suffered as a result an adolescent depression — rather like the girl in *The Exorcist* as in interpreted in the last chapter of *The Wise Wound*. At that time there was conscription, so I had to go into the army for national service. I was in no condition to be in the army. This became apparent and so the army psychiatrist got hold of me and instead of adolescent depression I was told I had incipient schizophrenia and I was given insulin shock treatment. Now insulin shock treatment is a barbarous violence on the body. I suffered this violence because I was growing up and my experiences were non-conforming and poetic, so I underwent this violence. What happens in insulin shock treatment is that they pump insulin into you, which reduces the sugar in your blood, until you go into convulsions, and you then go into a coma. Then they watch you very carefully. When you are on the point of dying they pull you out by injecting sugar. They did this to me fifty times. During these practice 'deaths' (because they were very near death) I had a number of visions and the chief one was rather like the one at the end of *Ivan Ilyich*, Tolstoy's novel, in which one is conscious of the world, of one's self and one's body and then this is taken away, pieces are taken away like a stage-set being dismantled, and gradually this dismantling reaches the part of you that is aware of the dismantling and then that is dismantled and there is nothing. I remember my last thought before nothing was, where's my soul? The universe has gone, there is nothing. I do not know what I expected to see. Did I expect to see Charon with his punt ferrying me across the river? The thing that knew there was nothing was taken away. Then I came across Keats' letters in which he said the world is a vale of soul-making. And I realised that I did not then have any soul, in other words I had nothing that I could take with me into unconsciousness. (Incidentally I think these transformations you mentioned in the poetry are what are called by Keats 'negative capability'). Also, about the same time, I came across Jung's book *Modern Man in search of a Soul*, I was in search of a soul. I got my direction towards psychology because the psychologists who were in charge of my case were in error. I believed them but they were wrong. And so I began my investigations into some of the things that seemed wrong in psychology. One example was the menstrual book. There is nothing about menstruation in psychology, half the world has it, what is wrong with psychology? I had the good fortune to meet John Layard who gave me my apprenticeship in practical psychology.

So now I think I am a little more prepared for death than I was, but whether this means I will survive death, how can I tell? But I have got a little more possession of myself you see. This is the human condition: we have pieces of ourselves taken away by our mentors and our circumstances and we are trying to get them back. In all the thresholds of our lives we leave a little something behind us; at the birth-trauma, we leave a little something behind us, in the toilet-training we leave a little bit of ourselves snagged up. We leave something behind at adolescence and we go back and recover these selves and bring ourselves together, soul-making. And so I do my bit of this and writing poetry is part of soul-making. It is the recovery of repressed contents. I am able to pass some of my thresholds consciously, like the mud-dancer in *The Facilitators*. One day this may include my threshold of death. Maybe the death poems are training for this.

C.A.  Peter Porter regards that 'a fundamental part of your canon is the ritualisation of language as art which gives man a tool which could make him a god'. Do you think this to be so?

P.R.  I would agree with that except that 'god' is rather a strong word and 'ritual' means different things to different people. First of all I do not see poetry quite as a 'ritualisation' as the word is too abstract, the image I like to use, which may sound a little naive, is it is a magic mirror; language is a magic mirror. By exercising language, it would seem we see more of the other world which is the completion of this world. Whenever you go into meditation or an altered state of consciousness you are going into another kind of time, it is not a time which has sequence. This is why I want to comment a bit about this word 'ritual'. Whenever one thinks of ritual, one thinks of a sequence of actions: it is not quite like that. The time which is Chronos, is the time which has a beginning, a middle and an end and then possibly a day of judgement, great anxious examination. This other kind of time is where you go when you make love or when you get absorbed in a book. It is not a clock time at all, it is another time, that is the time of the other world. Jung and Freud called it the unconscious: it seems a little absurd to call it the unconscious, it is ourselves that are unconscious of it. In an altered state of consciousness the time changes.

Now ritual is an approach to this other time. This is what, for example, the Australian Aborigines call it, the other time when the world is made. Whenever they do a ritual which is a religious ritual to them, but we would call a magical ritual, they go into this other time. They are then in that time in which the world was made and is being made. And they re-make themselves by doing so. If we go into a Christian service we are going to the time of the Last Supper, which is present; if we make love we get to our ever present roots which daily executive time forgets, the time is changed. We go through a ritual, we use symbols which are objects that exist in both times at once. The symbol takes you through, that is the meaning of the cross, it is crossing over. I use Christian imagery because a lot of people are Christian. I can use pagan imagery if required (laughs). A 'sign' of course does not point beyond itself, but a symbol participates in the reality it points towards, it is part of that reality, and leads towards it. A poem is such a symbol. I call it existing in the two worlds , but by the other world, you do understand I do not mean some misty astral otherness, I mean this world enhanced, completed.

C.A.  A common image throughout your work is the mirror, the glass, the reflector, *The God of Glass,* what function does this strand of imagery fulfil in your work?

P. R.  Here is something about a possible masculine role because the masculine side has got to make some sort of amends, there has to be some change of attitude. Instead of the man being, as we say in *The Wise-Wound*, 'a proud and envious aggressor', he has got to become the student. I was thinking of what you could call a mirroring relationship which is the ideal relationship between analyst and client. The analyst watches for what he considers or finds to be deeper and more real elements and reflects them. A glass is a crossing. The same thing happens in education, if you get a good teacher he knows what you are really able to do and he reflects it to you, a mirroring relationship. There is a Tantric saying that man is the lens or burning glass which concentrates the multifarious energies of the woman. If the woman is by virtue of her sexuality a tremendous dynamo and the man in our culture has allowed himself to be disengaged from that kind of life because he does not have, shall I say, the weight of his body's fruit always bringing him below the electrical surface of life; yet still by the same token he could adapt himself to calmed mirroring as well as participation. This would give him a complementary relationship as a kind of sender back of knowledge. It is part of a gender role he needs to learn, which women have hitherto taken — reflecting the man. Good partners learn from each other in this way. But so far it has not been the norm. What you do with other people is show yourself and in doing so show them in yourself too. We have had enough of the Illuminated man. What about the Transparent man? I wanted Geoffrey Glass in *The God of Glass* to do this.

C.A.   Many of your novels and much of your poetry seem to me to contain an important humorous element. Would you say this is an underestimated yet essential part of your writing?

P.R.   Yes, they are supposed to be funny, it is the most important thing. When we love something we always see absurdity in it. Why do I so enjoy the dramatic work? Because actors can inescapably underline humour where readers may tend to miss it, especially if they do not expect humour in serious writing, including poetry. Now I do not know what sort of humour you would call it; *Florent and the Tuxedo Millions* won the Italia prize, a great surprise to me. It is funny. I meant it to be funny. I tried to write it funny and it is marvellous to find these people reading it and acting it as I intended, funnily. When people talk about my poetry, they tend to avoid the humour, they do not like poetry to be funny. Mind you it is gallows humour and it is sexual humour. Another thing people do not like is sexual poetry. My poetry as I said, this call to vocation is to the mentality of sexuality. I think unless people have parallel experiences in their own sexuality, they are going to find some of the nature of the experiences described or evoked in the poems incomprehensible. One has got to be a sexual person, I think, to really like my poetry. In this I think I am also closer to the woman, because as Christians know women are more sexual than men are or maybe that is a projection of a despised element by the men. Now one of the secondary sexual characteristics that is different between men and women is that a man's skin is less erotically sensitive than a woman's; the erotic sensitivity which a child has in its skin tends to dwindle in the male to specific erogenous zones. In many women, however, erotic sensitivity of the whole skin is very easily evoked. As a man gets very old this erotic sensitivity seems to come back to him. Some men (I think it is called haptic) tend to retain the skin as an organ of explicit knowledge, rather than as a boundary or an armour. This is why some of my books have the title 'skin', *Sons of my Skin, In the Country of the Skin*. I think this is maybe one way in which my poetry takes me closer to the woman. This can mean that the masculine asexual man who is into poetry, will not like my poetry, and the woman who is defending women's rights find this kind of poetry written by a man and says that it cannot be poetry, it is by a man. So I tend to fall between two stools, I become slightly unpopular with feminists and slightly unpopular with masculinists. I think I may write primarily for women of intelligence and sexuality, who know sexuality is funny as well as spiritual. This becomes more evident I think in the plays which are much simpler than poems, there are more people who can listen to plays than can read poems, the poems are more concentrated. In fact everything begins for me with poems, they are the hot centre then they cool slightly and become plays, for instance *Florent and the Tuxedo Millions* was made from the poem 'Florent' in *The Wedding at Nether Powers*. Maybe then they cool slightly more and become novels, then they cool slightly more and become psychological non-fiction work.

C.A.   Yes, *The Glass Cottage* is written in prose but it connects together like a giant string of poetic metaphor , a cooled poetry.

P.R.   Now *The Sleep of the Great Hypnotist* was an experiment in this sense, that I became interested in trying to find out whether what people call meditation was anything like what people call making love and whether this was anything like altered states of consciousness as described by psychologists, and whether this is anything like hypnotism. So I went into a serious study of hypnotism. I remember the way the poem 'Sleep of the Great Hypnotist' was written. I went to Colgate University to do a teaching job, I went there particularly because a famous hypnotist was there and foolishly I did not write to him before I went. I got this job and I expected to talk to him. One of the first things I saw was his tomb in the graveyard with this great surname on the side of it, and I was furious, I said the bugger's died (laughs) and I wanted to meet him and study with him. So I wrote this poem 'The Sleep of the Great Hypnotist' in a fit of pique; the man is in his last trance and he is not getting out of this one. I did some studying and later thought to myself, that was a bit unfair, as a kind of apology I would see whether I am any good at hypnosis; what I will do is that I will use the poem as a seed for the novel. I will write a novel about hypnosis by using self-hypnosis. So what I did was study auto-hypnosis which is basically the same as meditation, but it uses different techniques to reach the same thing. I went into my trance on an evening and I brought into my trance my poem 'Sleep of the Great Hypnotist' and I made this hypnotic suggestion that I should write a novel on this poem and that in the morning the first words of this novel would come to me, so I went to bed, woke up in the morning and the first words that came to me was the opening passage. That day the first five thousand words came. I put myself back into the trance in the evening and I looked at what I had written, which you can do in an hypnotic state, I did not read it, I saw it in scenes and I wished it to go on. The scenes moved on of themselves. In this way I wrote the book in ten days.

So I said to myself this technique works. Having performed this experiment, and eventually finishing the novel, I said only now will I teach this technique. Since that time I have been teaching this technique at the Art School with success (laughs). So what I do is to teach a simple relaxation technique which in most people if performed correctly, produces a kind of suspended, contemplative state into which they can bring artistic work, as a kind of living mirror or glass. If the painter has got an unfinished painting, he can put himself into his 'trance'; call it a trance in inverted commas, an altered state of consciousness, bring it into his 'envisaging place', watch it complete itself, bring himself out of the trance and go and complete the painting. Or a person who is studying their dreams, which as I say are a continuum with the waking imagination; if you want to develop your imagination, your dream-life must come into it. You find dreams difficult to recall perhaps, you bring yourself into this envisaging place and bring all you can remember of the dream and the memory completes itself. Or if a dream-symbol is particularly strong, teasing, and you want to know more, you can bring that symbol in and it will enact a new dream, a waking dream.

It is a device for waking dreams. So I have been teaching this, it is not hypnotism, it is something else, one does not call it hypnotism because of the stock response; it is a relaxation response, that if properly done can lead to enhanced creativity. But I would not teach that until I had done it myself

**C.A.** Have you subsequently written all your novels using that technique?

**P.R.** I do not use that technique quite as explicitly but I find from practice it's rather easier to reach that condition. Yes I do use it of course. I mean it is only just the same as if someone asks you a question, you pause for thought, you go into yourself don't you, or you may sleep on it, it is the same as that. Everybody does this whatever they call it. But I think practice improves.

**C.A.** Is this some of the material to be included in the non-fiction work 'Deepening'?

**P.R.** Yes, this is one of the things for the new hook. We did a lot of work, we studied and practised various forms of meditation, hypnosis and contemplative prayer. We listened to dozens of tapes of hypnosis, Alpha meditation, relaxation, nidra yoga, all sorts of things like this and we worked out this three-stage technique, which is very simple to put down in a book and it is quite simple to teach, it is better to teach it. That is going to be the basis for the book, and I use this in workshops.

**C.A.** What is your own view of your development? How do you regard your earlier poetry which in some cases seems to contrast to the themes of your later work?

**P.R.** Well, as far as I am concerned I am in the middle of the process! It is not easy to take a surview. I do look back from time to time and sometimes certain poems seem impossible and certain poems seem to be tolerable. But I would not particularly like to sort out which was which myself. As each book comes out it does seem to be slightly more complete, it does seem to be getting more to what I want to say. It is like the passage in 'The Beekeepers', if you remember, the golden sexual encounter in which he says in that moment he learnt more than if he had been at the university twenty years. It may seem cheek, but I think the encounter with the unconscious is as important as that. Everything that he does subsequently will be an attempt to recover what he saw in that moment, or other such moments. It is a familiar statement from the mystics. In the mystical experience there is a complete feeling, sensation, intuition and understanding of something deep. Now we all have such experiences somewhere. I mean so many people suddenly have extreme experiences which are very, very solid. It is like seeing that is also touching. Some people have to get it from drugs. Now from time to time I have this kind of experience naturally, what I am trying to do is to get it into my, poetry. My poetry comes from that as a response to that fusion with the world. I have it in sex; I had it in my childhood too, everybody has it in some form. My poetry is trying to embody this. If a person reads my poetry and is reminded of that experience which cannot be described in ordinary language but can be evoked or enacted in poetry, I would have done what I wanted to. In every real poem that I write I meet that quality of experience again. If the poem works it is still there when I look again. If it is still there when I look again in those past poems then I say, that's done what I wanted to. But in the poems that are nearest to me it seems to be there but then in some it fails, in some it maintains, so I am always working towards that and it is this fusion I believe of the four functions that I have been talking about. Poetry is one aspect of that union. I am not suggesting that I am in any way special because as I have been trying to say all the time, that this is common human birthright. Why I write poetry? It is because it is a technique for approaching that condition of union and maintaining it in ordinary life, if poetry is treated as it should be, as a mode of knowledge, for poet and reader both.

C.A.   Why do you write novels?

P.R.   The novels have come with one exception, out of teaching, they are also supposed to be funny, but also they are supposed to enact things that I have discovered teaching, they are supposed to be all about the validity and strangeness of imaginative processes. They are trying to set out a kind of code of conduct towards the imagination. That is what we are all trying to do. This is true of *Terrors of Dr Treviles*, less of *The Glass Cottage, The Sleep of the Great Hypnotist*, it is certainly true of *The God of Glass*, which was my accompaniment to my work on *The Wise Wound*. It is certainly true of *The Beekeepers* in which I talk of drunkenness being an avoidable substitute for symbolic experience, which is occult experience, and it is certainly true of *The Facilitators. In the Country of the Skin* is different, that is the record of the most extraordinary eight weeks that I experienced, when I was with Penelope Shuttle when we first started living together, which was a time of the most extraordinary sexual and visual experience, it is a very strange book. I could only write it in that way to maintain that quality which is what I wanted to set down. Now, in the radio play I got more of the story, but apart from these qualifications, the novels are so far all teaching tales.

C.A.  You are often mentioned in the same breath as Ted Hughes, do you think your work is similar to Hughes or any other poet?

P.R.  I would not say my work is similar to Ted Hughes', I think we are very different sorts of characters, we write in different ways from different masters. For instance, Hughes' great master is Yeats, mine, Eliot and Langland partly, in the early work, but I have others as well. It is a compliment to be linked with Hughes. He is a marvellous poet, Hughes is, but I think we are different kinds of poet. Poets of the present time that I respect a great deal, I do not know whether they would like me or not, I just do not know at all; there is a poet very unlike me and that is Penelope Shuttle. We write together so much, we exchange images, there is a sort of circulation of images between us, a circulation of all that we do. She is different from me so that my things look different with her, and vice versa, like stereoscopic vision, which has to be from slightly different angles to be solid. That is one of the reasons I believe in complementary male-female relationships.

# 9. The Science of the Subjective

## Interview with *Poetry Review* (Neil Roberts)

NR:   *Most modern theorists try to define poetic language by distinguishing it from scientific or referential language, and I imagine you'd want to refute that idea.*

PR:   Well, so many thoughts go through my head as you say this. I'm thinking what kind of scientific language are these theorists thinking of, or which particular instances? There'd be a difference in feeling tone of course to us now if we read Pasteur's documents or Faraday's documents. They would seem different to us from say Einstein's account of his own theories. The scientific prose which appears — which is supposed to be — objective has in fact got a very strong feeling tone in it rather like a poem has, in its own way. This suggests of course that scientific prose is not simply as referential as it makes out to be. It contains personality and it contains history and as the paradigms change so the kind of attention we pay to a piece of scientific prose changes. Similarly with poems.

NR:   *Would you say then that all language is on a continuum, is of essentially the same kind, and there is no distinguishing feature of poetic language?*

PR:   This is my experience in reading. If one reads Darwin or if one reads Harvey on the circulation of the blood, these expositions are like different kinds of poems. The Harvey is like a meditation on wonderful internal hydraulics; the Darwin is a man alert in his world. I think a continuum is a very good way of expressing it.

NR:   *Do you think that there are any distinguishing characteristics of the kind of language that adequately acknowledges the inner or subjective reality?*

PR:   Poetic language in this way uses the same devices that dream language does — condensation, symbolism, displacement, these kind of characteristics of dreams. I certainly wouldn't be the first to point out the likeness of poetry to dreams. As people still debate whether dreams are useful in any sense at all so people tend to debate whether poetry is any use at all. I take the position that Trilling does . . . I recently came across this . . . Trilling quotes Charles Lamb. He says the poet dreams, being awake. That is to say, a dream does possess you. In the kind of waking dream we call poetry you have, as he says, dominion. You have the kind of control that a navigator has, the yachtsman has over his yacht. He is obedient to the natural currents and winds and to the construction of his vessel but he has, within limits, a certain will. This is one of the differences between dream and poetry. Of course you have lucid dreams too, and you have automatic writing in poetry. It depends on what comes out, and what degree of attention anybody is paying at the particular time that we're talking about. Contemporary poetry has a very strange fate in England I think as compared to America and possibly on the European continent. We seem to be party-going poets. Contemporary English poetry is very show-off really — it dresses itself up. The kind of inward absorption that you get with a magnificent poet like St John Perse, really wrapped up in his subject, is a great rarity in English poetry at all I think, since the Great Victorians or since Wordsworth perhaps; I think the egotistical sublime has gone out of poetry.

NR: *You'd take it as far back as that would you? You don't think even Eliot has the quality you're talking about?*

PR: Eliot is always present isn't he? He's always a critical presence in his own verse, he very seldom lets go in the interests of discovery. Even the momentary visions are ritualistic. He very seldom allows himself to be blown off course towards the Unexpected Isles. But I think Wordsworth deliberately seeks to learn from these spots of time, where he loses himself. That amazing passage, isn't it in Book VI of the *Prelude,* where he loses himself in the Alps, and as he comes to, he remembers that he's seen something wonderfuul, something of the invisible world, which was too much for his ordinary senses, which are nevertheless enlarged by it. Now we don't get many poets losing themselves in the psyche or in nature at the present time, do we?

**NR:** *No. Do you think this is a cultural loss of nerve relating to what I said at the beginning, that poetry tends to be defined as non-referential, as pseudo-statement, as fictional, and so the poet becomes too self-conscious to be able to do that sort of thing?*

**PR:** I think so, yes. The reaction the poet has come to expect is 'Very amusing, but completely subjective, of course'. 'Subjective' is one of those elastic words. It has come to mean not only 'the only truth we can know', but, as a corollary of despair to this, 'untrue' as well. The point of the poem is the process that you go through as you read it and what it does to you. So it's not only what the poem is talking about, but what it's doing to you and enabling you to see, and this is both objective and subjective at once. I think one of the reasons for the loss of nerve at the present time is that the scientists have given us a picture of nature which is competitive, alien, empty, mechanical, and a universe in which we are complete strangers, and in which — talking about continuums — there is no continuum between ourselves and nature. This is the great romantic quest, that a continuum between nature and mankind should be proved . . . Science still proceeds on behaviouristic principles. Scientists, for instance, have to be very careful in testing drugs, or in doing any psychological experiment, not to allow suggestion to enter into it, no suggestion of the result, no placebo effect must be allowed in. But the placebo effect is a very wonderful thing indeed. It means you can take a sugar pill believing it will do you good and it will do you good. This is worth looking into I would have thought, but it's the very thing that science keeps out: the power here — the Romantic idea — of the mind over the body, that the material world is responsive to the energies of the mind, or to immaterial energies. We live in a situation where these things are systematically undervalued. The Enlightenment was concerned to display everything visibly, with every factor controlled — and this is when the idea of the scientific controlled experiment came in. The Romantics were in contradiction to this. They wanted to know what was invisible. They protested against 'the tyranny of the eye'. There is so much in Romantic poetry about weather for instance. Weather influences us profoundly. It is an invisible and visible series of changes which alter our moods and alter our access to ourselves. We are inspired or depressed by the weather. It is both objective and subjective in its effects. Thirty per cent of the population are intensely weather-sensitive. There is a kind of feeling-knowledge of the world which arises from meteorological changes. There is a response, an invisible response which is not accounted for in medical science. The facts are that very many diseases, very many sicknesses and illnesses, are intensified by the processes of storm. Heart palpitations sometimes synchronize with radio static from storms. You can watch, on a computer, the meteorological pattern say over the city of New York, and superimpose the deaths from heart attacks, and you can see that these two patterns follow each other, and there is a causal connection which appears to be electrical. We know that many people suffer from weather-sensitivity to a psychiatric extent — you get this very much in Cornwall, which has a great deal of weather as they say. But what happens? How are these people treated? Well, of course, the tranquillizer and antidepressant. There is no study of medical climatology, there is no school of it in this country as far as I know. There is no school of bio-meteorology. This romantic thing, the weather, this daily demonstration of our response to the whole situation of the earth and the atmosphere, the temperature of it, the humidity of it and the electricity of it — we can't deny this any more — is just ignored, because of course, to adjust this, to treat weather-sickness — well, there are certainly herbal and homeopathic remedies for it, and another solution is to move, which may not be viable economically. What is viable economically and which props up our system is to prescribe another of these invented drugs, at great cost. The alternative is to seek union with the invisible but actual world, as the Romantics did.

NR:     *You were talking about the effects that poetry has, and I imagine that that is a physiological effect in your view?*

PR:     Yes. I.A. Richards didn't go far enough in this. If you record blood pressure, skin resistance, pulse rate and this kind of thing, when people are listening to poetry, if you can persuade them to do it — it's a bit difficult — you find that there are profound changes. You can do it on the E.E.G., that's the electro-encephalogram, the brain-waves, this is sometimes done, but it's much better to do it on the skin, which is covered all the time by a kind of rainbow of electrical patterns, which run over the skin and seem to bypass what we call our conscious minds. If a person is reading poetry or having poetry read to them, or indeed any complicated or emotive utterance, the results of this — they may be paying very little attention or they may give very little account of this in their conscious minds, but the body becomes alive with, if you like, the colour of the poem. It's a very extraordinary and beautiful thing, that. I think we are very used to repressing this kind of event. If we relax of course we can feel into our skins and our emotions much more deeply, and poetry is providing an induction into this deeper life, without a doubt. It is — whatever else it might be doing — connecting us with our physiology, with areas of our physiology which we are inclined not to use in daily life, and which we of course are encouraged not to use by the paradigms of what I must call commonplace science . . . As I said, poetry is both subjective and objective at once. Goethe said that the human senses were the greatest and most accurate physical apparatus there can be; and it was the greatest misfortune of modern physics that it recognized nature only as it was manifested through artificial instruments. Science is getting it both ways now by using incredibly sensitive biochemical processes in its most delicate chemical instruments.

If you look at a picture of the earth's magnetic field, generated by the bow-shock of its motion in the sun's field, it resembles nothing so much as a great winged figure, folded in robes, it's an angel shape. This is very, very Romantic, but this is the kind of imagery scientists who are closer to naturalists, I think — though of course it has its defence budget aspect, studying geo-magnetism — are coming up with. They're coming up with a confirmation of the Romantic experience of a continuum between mankind and nature. That geomagnetic field reaches right into the protoplasm.

NR: *Would you say that all poetry, regardless of how the poet himself might define it, is essentially Romantic?*

PR: It's doing a Romantic thing. It's taking you into a world which is enhanced. Even the most Augustan of poetry, which is concerned with, as you might say, social adjustments or the adjustments of one person to another, of one man to another if you like, one man of sense speaking to another man of sense, gives, by its articulation, a sense of body, of speech. When we are speaking we are altering the feelings in our body through circulation and respiration; we are taking thought of our speech, we are engaging in a kind of inner dialogue with our physical capacities. Poetry has to be spoken, is spoken; even when you appear to be reading it silently there is a voice going on. I'm thinking of the heroic couplet - the Augustan heroic couplet is a most bracing measure, one feels braced by it as by a walk in a stiff breeze. It's physiological. As we read, as we do anything, but especially as we are closely engaged in something, so the atmosphere changes round us. Others know this. So we give off these strange substances which are called pheromones, these scents, these olfactory hormones. I like to think of a poetry reading . . . you try and watch this, if you don't smoke, and you can smell, you can actually smell an audience paying attention; this stimulates the reader, so there is feedback, and in a good reading or performance, the creation of a total atmosphere.

NR: *When you look back at your earliest poetry, how much of the real thing do you find in it; is it something that you feel it took a long time for you to develop, or was it there from the start?*

PR: It is always a terrible struggle to get the poem, to find again in the poem the experience that had made one need to write the poem. I'm not at present content with anything that I've written either in prose or poetry, because what anybody's prose or poetry is reaching for is far too terrific to be grasped in the terms of our present culture. It's as though I've always felt this — we need another culture. We're working in the wrong culture for poetry. This led to my work in womanism, I'm sure of that, because one of the missing things is the place of women's influence in our culture. The things that women can give on the personal level by their companionship, their motherhood, and their sexuality are so close to the things that I want to say in poetry. All of my poetry in that sense is love poetry. I'm looking for the missing half, if you like, of the Platonic body, trying to find this in my poetry. In the same sense as the world talks to me, so does my poetry talk to me, and I try to understand its language, as in a dialogue with a Sphinx. But I will not respond with the Oedipal answer that destroys her. I try to shape it so that the two, the inner thing and the outer thing, touch as they speak. This is the love-experiment I'm doing. My poetry is one continuous aspiration towards this. The early poetry has a — it's not a violence, it's an ardency of perception and surprise, which of course is one of the things that one may sacrifice as one goes on to reflect increasingly on the work. But the later poetry, I think, knows more of what it's necessary to put in a poem so that it can be accepted as a kind of discourse which leads the reader gently into other states of mind than the one-dimensional non-sacred personality that we develop to deal with the world.

NR:    *There's a great deal of fear of death in the early poetry, isn't there?*

PR:    It is natural to fear death. We must accommodate the fact that we are all going to die. I'm sure that the little deaths that we experience in sleep, in the transformations that occur in sex, the transformations that occur each night as we go to sleep, in our dreams, are ways of approaching the big transformation that nobody knows about, the best-kept secret, as it were, of death; so that it is right to rehearse the imagery of death, that the more imagery of death there is in the poetry the more the poet, and hopefully his reader, is prepared for the kind of transformations that occur in his life. One of the things that exercise me greatly in writing poetry is a very common experience that everybody has, and that is the contrast there is between our best states of mind and our depressed states of mind. There is such a vertigo between the state of inspiration, or the state of joy, the state of alertness and responsiveness to the world, such as one experiences for instance waking up on a good morning or after making love in an exceptionally beautiful and satisfying way, or after having a wonderful dream, or when a poem is coming out — there is such a contrast between that kind of experience and the experience of dumbness, dullness, stupidity, frustration, and the narrowing of the chinks of one's cavern, until everything that one values or believes in is gone. This experience of depression and recovery from depression is very common to our age . . . The subject of my poetry is like that of George Herbert's poem 'The Flower', in which he says how his life sinks down to the roots, just as it does with a flower, but then there can be a change, a sudden change in the psyche, so that 'I once more smell the dew and rain,/And relish versing'. Now, he says *smell* the dew and rain'. His *animal* senses have become alive again. It's not just a visual thing. There's been a change in the weather, his own weather, or the outside weather. If you look at Coleridge's Dejection Ode, you see that it's almost the weather speaking those thoughts, it's the weather which solves the problem of his depression. There is a change of weather. Perhaps human beings are the intelligence of their air and of their ground.

NR: *In comparing poetry to dream are you implying that in some sense the poem is already there? That the drafting of the poem is a process of recovery as much as a process of production?*

PR: Yes, I think so. I think that every person has a central poem. I don't know what else to call it. The word poem is better nowadays than using the word spirit or soul. I think it's easy to understand the statement that every person has a central poem. I think — this has a Wallace Stevens ring to it, so I may be quoting him — I think the poems that we retrieve are fragments of this central poem. I always think of those lovely Victorian pictures of various poets marching into the Day of Judgement or going to the Hall of the Muses after they're dead with their books, or their souls, tucked underneath their arms. I think that we are trying to re-compose that original poem, and I think what this in part consists of is a very deep and compendious image or experience of the real universe, in a state which is superior to the nature of the conditioned waking personality that we develop. The poem is a discovery, the personality is a construct. It is what we call our conscious minds which are the constructs. The poem comes from the interface between conscious and unconscious, and there is far more to that than the conscious mind is used to, as in Wordsworth's 'visitings/Of awful promise' when in the

Alps the light of his ordinary senses went out, and his greatness switched on, as he tells us. It's true that as one goes on in poetry there is sometimes a sense of recovering something which one already knows — maybe a central poem. I myself believe that the foundations of this central poem were laid in the womb, during the process of our making, from molecule to organism to person: the whole natural continuum. Every live person, to be alive at all, is formed by the co-operation and harmony of a milliard influences, inner and outer, current and past. I argue in my *The Black Goddess and the Sixth Sense* that the knowledge of this is retrievable, that it is poetry, that it is the model or Tao of our proper relations with the universe, and that it is *synaesthetic* — but more of that later.

NR:   *And yet the poem is different for everybody?*

PR:   As everybody's face is different, yes. The poem is different for everybody but it's related in everybody. As the skeleton or the birth-process is, if you like. It's true, and I think everybody's work is finding that central poem and declaring it. We've become very metaphysical there. I'm thinking of Traherne's *The Praeparative* at the moment, in which he talks about this womb-experience . . . I don't think he's usually understood in this manner, but it's here, in the *Centuries of Meditation,* in these words. He says . . . he's talking about illuminated experience . . . He says, 'Those pure and virgin apprehensions I had from the womb, and that divine light wherewith I was born are the best unto this day, wherein I can see the Universe. By the Gift of God they attended me into the world, and by His special favour I remember them till now. Verily they seem the greatest gifts His wisdom could bestow, for without them all other gifts had been dead and vain. They are unattainable by books, and therefore I will teach them by experience'. 'Those pure and virgin apprehensions I had from the womb . . .' And that's my belief.

NR:   *I'd be interested to know what you have to say about the Jungian idea that the unconscious is feminine in both men and women.*

PR:   Are you sure that's a Jungian idea?

NR: *Well, it's in Neumann.*

PR: Neumann says that the unconscious is feminine in both men and women?

NR: *Yes.*

PR: Yes, I see. He says that the ground of being is feminine. Yes. Yes, I seem to have said that just now (laughs). The ground of being is feminine. This is echoing T.F. Powys, isn't it? He said the ground is goddess. But I also think that the ground changes. The unconscious is compensatory. If the conscious mind is masculine the unconscious mind will be feminine. Culturally our conscious minds are masculine, with a masculinist society. This means the ground, now, is feminine.

NR: *So this is a culturally determined thing, it's not a fact of nature that the unconscious is feminine?*

PR: You're asking me now to define the place of the male principle in the modern psyche, and I can only do this by allegory, as Graves did. I can only say that the masculine principle has taken the throne and has not known what to do with its power, and has to be ousted. We just don't know what's there now. We don't know what the ground is now, really. It is not matriarchal. We've passed from matriarchy to patriarchy. Now there is something else coming, and who can say what it is? I certainly can't, but it's in the ground. And the ground of it I myself call feminine, yes. I call it black and I call it a goddess. That is to say, it seems to me that the important things that are growing from the pysche are feminine and are invisible. We were talking about the magnetosphere . . . there's an image for you, the magnetosphere, the diagram of it being like a robed and winged figure, as it were clutching the earth to its heart. The magnetosphere is shaped around us, in space you understand. And that might be an image for the Black Goddess. It's clearly a feminine figure. It is a spirit of the earth which is seen in another way as magnetism. And it's also black, because it's not visible. But it also reaches into the protoplasm of each and every living thing that there is. We as organisms have a magnetic field which interacts with the earth's magnetic field. It is once again the continuum. There is not just *one* Romantic continuum; there are several of them. There's what I call the pheromone maser which is the equivalent to the classical magical aura, which is a free-floating cloud of organic molecules which surrounds the body, which is produced by the metabolism of the body, which is then irradiated by the infra-red of the body, so that you get a sub-visible fluorescence. It detects and decodes kinds of electromagnetic radiation beyond the visible; was first described in moths by pest-control scientists.

NR:   *Like most contemporary poets, you don't write metrical poetry. Do you think it's a loss that you can't, or that somehow it doesn't work for you?*

PR:   I think that people nowadays don't sing or chant very much, that we're trying to write a sort of poetry that comes from explanation, or the voice of one person speaking to another as a companion. We don't ordinarily sing to each other. Domestic music doesn't happen very much. The things that happen to us which are deepest to us are those things which are said in daily life and which suddenly become illuminating, or which . . . even lovers don't often sing to each other nowadays at all, but they will speak, and they will speak with a particular searching or expository rhythm, which can't be accommodated very easily in most exactly regular forms of metric. I think that another purpose of prosody is to emphasize the shape in sound and therefore stimulate a sense less-used than that of the eye, which is what we use day by day most of all. It as it were caresses the ear like a touch. It alters time. In the poetry that is being written now I think what we're trying to do is a further thing, which is not only to arouse the non-visual senses, but to weave them together with sight. George Whalley says that this 'synaesthesia' is almost a definition of poetry. In an age with no shared faith, poets must demonstrate from experience. I think we're trying to get a synaesthesia by persuasion and demonstration, so we will use persuasive rhythms. Now what happens in what is commonly called hypnotism, which I prefer to call (with pun intended) 'trance-formation' is that you work out, with your client's co-operation, what is their . . . or you can tell of course, what is their most-used sense. And you ask them to pay attention to this, perhaps by means of guided imagery, you set a scene, and this will usually be a visual scene. So you'll set this visual scene, you'll speak to them about this visual scene, and then you will introduce into this quite deliberately what is their less-used sense. It may be the sense of touch, it may be the sense of hearing. You will introduce the sounds of the waves, you'll give a metaphor for this. You will let the sand under their feet have a particular touch. And as you do this so you can see the process of inner attention deepening. And that is the process of hypnotism or the formation of trance. Now this is exactly the way in which poetry operates, I think. Charles Hartman says, 'A poem is an act of attention', and that its prosody is the poet's method of controlling the reader's attention. A poem may be persuading into trance by prosodic but not necessarily metrical skills and at the same time subverting ordinary consciousness by bringing another sense in or an illustration from another sense. One will look at a stone, one will describe its shape, and then one will suddenly introduce a notion of its taste. What does that stone taste like? And immediately it's a different stone. And immediately the poetic process begins to operate. When Rimbaud said that what we must have to become seers is a reasoned disorder of the senses, he was not talking so much about an upset or an explosion as a synaesthesia: the joining together of all the senses and their mutual illumination thereby. I think you could argue that synaesthesia was the central characteristic of poetry . . . The Vedas say that there is only one sense, and that the special senses that we use in the world are diminished versions, shielded versions of that one sense we knew as spirits, or in the womb. Blake says that all the senses are cursed except the sense of touch, through which a man may pass out to infinity any time he pleases, and I take his meaning to be that all the senses are basically a touch (of air, of volatile and dissolved substances) and that the experience of infinity is tactile and synaesthetic. It's a characteristic of mystical experience. It's a characteristic of poetic experience, of experience of the hypnotic trance, of waking dreams. The characteristic of the central poem must be that it has a unity. In mysticism, in Middle English mysticism, there is a great deal talked about the non-visible or synaesthetic presence of God. Christ appears simultaneously as a beautiful smell and a wonderful touch; or as melodious food. This happens too in Hindu yoga, where the spiritual experience is often described in terms of simultaneous touch, warmth, odour, rather than visually, which is what we usually seem to think our religious experience ought to be. It's a very intricate sensuous process, as poetry is. And this is why I consider the poetic experience and the religious experience to be in essence the same thing.

## 10. Rimbaud My Virgil

I.

Rimbaud escorted me many times through Hell and back again, something he was not able to do for himself in the end. My first Season in Hell was without his company, and emphasized the need for such a guide. During National Service an anxiety condition was mistaken for incipient schizophrenia and I was incarcerated in a mental hospital where I was tortured into convulsions and coma by insulin shock treatment. The idea was to inject enough insulin to draw all the sugar out of your blood until you were nearly dead, then bring you back with another injection. I had many visions and other experiences in the insulin coma, but I had no scheme or net to catch them in, or mentor who knew the way, so for a long time I lost the quality and significance of these journeys. I learned however that there was another world, which was this one deepened on the way to death, and that it was possible to pass through its jaws, and return.

A second season came when I had drunk sufficient bad alcohol to produce at the last a reasonable likeness of the insulin coma. Again I saw many visions, but now there was a difference. I dreamed intact the entire text of the Norman Cameron 'Saison en Enfer' with Keith Vaughan's amazing illustrations, in multimedia and synesthetic form. I woke screaming, but grateful because I had travelled this region 'holding on to my eyes' with the help of the imagery of somebody who had been there before. I would rather have had many more such nightmares than run the gamut of the office jobs that followed University, but I had been (on the one view) far too disturbed, or (on another view) too far into visionary experience, to profit from the formal university instruction, and I left without a degree, which meant that I had to take many ad hoc jobs rather than stay in the academy where I now believe I could have worked profitably — it is after all a kind of asylum.

I had been a compliant child, not as precocious as Rimbaud, but near it, and my desire to please everybody had created that sort of false personality which easily entered the consumerist fantasy by acquiring wife, home and children, responsibilities I was entirely unsuited for. I read now 'Les Poètes de Sept Ans' and wished I had growled much harder, and rebelled earlier, as Rimbaud did. Yet because of my nightmare I knew him to be somebody who spoke the truth: I knew that what, otherwise instructed, would have seemed to me perverse impulses were reality-communions when I travelled through Nature 'heureux comme avec une femme' and had my first sexual experiences this way. I learned something too under his instruction of the 'Comédie de la soif':-

'Chansonnier, ta filleule
C'est ma soif si folle,
Hydre intime sans gueules
Qui mine et desole.
J'aime autant, mieux, même,
Pourrir dans l'étang,
Sous l'affreuse crème,
Près des bois flottants'

(Singer, your god-child is my mad thirst, mouthless bosom-hydra who mops and mows and ravages . . . I had as soon lie dumb and festering in the pond among the driftwood and beneath the horrible scum . . .)

In fact the furrows of my husbandly mask were the protective whelks and ridges of a high-pressure chrysalis cooking. I found that during any office day I could deregulate my senses by taking a mere half-pint of beer twice or thrice and improvising my own versions of *Les Illuminations*; later on I preferred to do the whole thing on an empty stomach and take speed prescribed by an over-friendly doctor, finish my advertising copy by lunchtime, and spend the rest of the day brooding over the Rimbaudian look of the world the drugs and drink offered to me. I feared it was an artificial paradise, yet with careful and rational regulation in the spirit of Rimbaud it did give me things I could use; later on I found it was not merely artificial, since I was able to achieve it by natural means, mainly sex-magical, towards a daily sacramental vision. This is what I believe Rimbaud was working towards, and he must be counted as one of the exemplary masters and martyrs. He had not the benefit of his own guidance as I did (this does not make me Dante) and he could not visit himself like a time-traveller. He was probably unable to lift himself out of his last 'Saison en Enfer,' and the depression probably lasted the rest of his life. We mourn and salute him. I will say later how I believe he could have found a companionship Verlaine could not offer.

My first marriage broke up, largely, I believe, because I was unable to compromise about my visionary life; (I acknowledge that women may not need to break through with such vehemence and violence, as the menstrual cycle can take them through all human modes, from visionary to domestic-sacramental and back again). The break-up was accelerated by meeting an ancient Rimbaud with white hair, a dream visionary and a rebel who was at the same time a world-class anthropologist and analyst, John Layard; who restored my job-eroded visionary faith and with his dictum 'Depression is withheld knowledge' showed me again that the doors of Hell were revolving doors, and that the secret was to go the right way round, just as in the Northern hemisphere you must fly round a hurricane to the right. Dream analysis with Layard led directly to my book with Penelope Shuttle (The Wise Wound) on the menstrual cycle, the taboo on which is arguably the way the masculine non-menstruating spirit prevents women from achieving their own visionary riches by shutting them into a hell of disinformation and stealing the one half of their sexuality — the tabooed menstrual half. Seen in this light, Rimbaud's remarks in the 'Lettre du Voyant' are not condescending: 'This language will be of the soul, for the soul, and will include everything: perfumes, sounds, colours, thought grappling with thought. The poet would make precise the quality of the unknown arising in his time in the universal soul . . . When the eternal slavery of Women is destroyed, when she lives for herself and through herself, when man — up till now abominable — will have allowed her her freedom, she will be a poet as well. Woman will discover the unknown! Will her world of ideas differ from ours? She will discover strange things, unfathomable, repulsive, delightful: we will accept and understand them.' I had the paramount good fortune to live and work with a woman who had undergone this mighty process of female liberation and who was a poet from the time she was a woman aged 14, and who wrote strange and vital novels which were a feminine replay of 'Saison' and 'Les Illuminations.' And how like the 'hysterization of the skin' of the French feminists, the exterior cunt of outer contact seen potentially as deep intimate and sensuous as the womb experiences of love, masturbation, menstruation, birth, is Rimbaud's programme, though he may have underestimated the extent the women could be teachers, after the exile of the feminine during 2000 years of Christianity. Read Hélène Cixous' 'The Laugh of the Medusa' — would our Rimbaud not have written this had he been she? Such are the habitations for our visions. I wish Rimbaud had met the grandmother of one of them. She would have companioned him out of Hell. Here is a cento from these Rimbaudian feminists:

'A world of searching, the elaboration of a knowledge, on the basis of a systematic experimentation with the bodily functions, a passionate and precise interrogation of her erotogeneity. This practice, extraordinarily rich and inventive, in particular as concerns masturbation, is prolonged or accompanied by a production of forms, a veritable aesthetic activity, each stage of rapture inscribing a resonant vision, a composition, something beautiful. Beauty will no longer be forbidden.' Cixous. This is sheer Rimbaud sex-magic, called *jouissance*.

'But *woman has sex organs just about everywhere*. She experiences pleasure almost everywhere. Even without speaking of the hysterization of her entire body, one can say that the geography of her pleasure is much more diversified, more multiple in its differences, more complex, more subtle, than is imagined . . .' (Irigaray).

'Women's *jouissance* carries with it the notion of fluidity, diffusion, duration. It is a kind of potlatch in the world of orgasms, a giving, expending, dispensing of pleasure without concern about ends or closure.' Marks and de Courtivron.

II.

What Rimbaud was up against of course still remains. Alvarez called it 'the gentility principle'; Freud had a formula for it: if you want to rid yourself of an uncomfortable reality, first sublimate or idealize it, then repress it; and the actors hold the mirror up to human nature by saying 'No sex please, we're British.' The plain fact is that the sacramental is erotic, true magic is a turn-on, and by magic we should mean 'unwounded perception' — 'If the doors of perception were cleansed everything would appear . . . as it is, infinite.' Rimbaud having opened himself by 'deschooling the senses' was perhaps choked by the pollutions of patriarchy. Many have been so afflicted, and fallen. Sylvia Plath, who by the measure of her creative energy suffered abominably from the repression we call PMS, could find no woman-information or solidarity in the 1960s academic and literary atmosphere of Freud, Graves and the rest, and ended up 'believing nothing' just at the threshold of the feminist revolution. Nevertheless she hysterized the skin so that her inner and outer were one, and wrote poems of protest and rebellion which puzzle male commentators with their vehemence of feminine energies frustrated of their meaning. For me, she inspired because she was one of the few poets writing in England in the sixties who knew how much has to go into a poem before it was a poem. She makes the quantum-jump through that revolving door into the palaces of hell the fires of which Blake said were 'the enjoyments of genius,' as Rimbaud does in *Les Illuminations*. You will have noticed that I have subtly deregulated the word 'dérèglement' in Rimbaud's dictum because it has been misused by people who are not serious about the 'Alchémie du Verbe' and are anxious for poets to dissipate their gifts merely, so that the editions can be closed early and become more manageable to the scholar.

'Dérèglement' does *not* mean dissipation. Anyway, it is 'raisonné dérèglement.' Rimbaud always designed that the poems he wrote would induct his readers into the same world from which the poems came. George Whalley says that Rimbaud's statement is the essence of poetic; '. . . metaphor disorients the individual senses so that they excite and fertilize each other . . . In this way Poetic establishes a novel interpretation of thought and feeling . . . In Poetic, sight can be converted into sound and texture and even scent; single words can assume physical shape, contour, fibre; groups of words may take on meanings not implied by their grammatical relations; savor, aroma, cachet may be conveyed in texture and rhythm.' This is *jouissance*, which 'carries with it the notion of fluidity, diffusion, duration . . .' Such writing not only comes from actual experiences of jouissance but creates them also, after de-schooling. Rimbaud would have liked the way Virginia Woolf's Orlando fell in love: 'These details were obscured by the extraordinary seductiveness which issued from the whole person. Images, metaphors of the most extreme and extravagant twined and twisted in his mind. He called her a melon, a pineapple, an olive tree, an emerald, and a fox in the snow in the space of three seconds; he did not know whether he had heard her, tasted her, seen her, or all three together.' As Whalley also says: '. . . the appeal is not to any one sense but to an interinanimation of all the senses combined into a tactual impression of great power — a condition that psychologists call synesthesia. This may very well be a prime characteristic of all poetic perception, of the poetic sense of language, and perhaps of all our refined and developed sensory experience.' The tantric version of this is that the senses may appear to be five (or seven or seventy-seven) when they perceive outwardly, but inwardly they are the one, all-embracing sense, which is mind as well . . . So instead of saying 'the point is to arrive at the unknown by the disordering of all the senses' let us cease to distort the message and say 'The point is to arrive at the unknown by the rational de-schooling of the senses.' It is in school that we are first systematically taught gentility. It is not so much that we must 'make strange' as to be prepared to find life as strange as it is, and it is a function of gentility to conceal strangeness.

Which is to say that society needs its poets — people who know something other than the genteel so strongly that they are able to re-arouse even in the genteel the true self, which is never genteel. Gentility is a convenient way of behaving in ritual forms for superficial and necessary purposes. If there is only gentility it is as stifling as England is today. We need something else, clearly. And that can be the poetry of really-knowing what is beyond gentility.

This the poet must be a specialist in; if he does it by dissipation then he may expect his useful life to be shortened; alcoholism and writing are nearly synonymous, it seems, in America. But Auden said we must be fit, in case the Muse requires us to climb mountains. If we call ourselves Muse-poets we should know that this means express knowledge of the death and resurrection each month of the personality in tune with the moon, amplified in every household by the menstrual cycle of the woman; and if we are the woman. . .then we must have enough knowledge and companionship to avoid the fate of Sylvia Plath. If we open ourselves by yoga or meditation and/or sexual practices to what is in here and out there, then we must expect experiences of comparable intensity — say of the fruition, death and rebirth of the year (as of the month) still felt in country districts, but a rhythm overpowered by the cities, as all these ancient but actual rhythms are. We should become technicians of the sacred and study not the abstract ramifications of physics, but the actuality of psychological and biological sciences, remembering of course that any psychology which neglects the inner experience of the woman — and they all do this — is suspect and almost derelict unless we can give our own personal and poetic testimony from actual experience; as Freud said 'if you want to learn the truth about women, go to the poets' which may not have meant to him women poets, but it must always do so now. We must look for what is neglected in genteel life, for it is the stone that the builders rejected that became the cornerstone of the building. This means sex, and the metaphysics of sex; nor am I here counselling promiscuity, which is the stock genteel mistranslation, as in this alchemy one can only progress through long practical study with one's Soror or Frater Alchymica. We must study our dreams; the visions of the night that show us so directly that 'I is someone else' are neglected too so must be studied. Sex, a language adequate to express its intensity with its camaraderie an erotic vision of the world — this is the vocation Rimbaud calls us to; we can share his adventure and take it further than he did. The world has moved forward enough for the urgency of the 'Lettre du Voyant' to become directly intelligible even environmental — I paraphrase — 'The first study for a poet is self-knowledge complete . . . I say that one must be a seer, make oneself a seer . . . by a long, prodigious, and rational de-schooling of all the senses . . . to search oneself and consume all the poisons in oneself.. . faith and superhuman strength is needed . . . for the poet arrives at the unknown . . . is responsible for humanity, even for the animals;

must see to it that poetic inventions can be smelt, felt, heard . . . A language has to be found . . . the time of the universal language will come . . . of the soul, for the soul, containing everything, smells, sounds, colors . . . The poet would discover and name the amount of the unknown awakening in the collective unconscious at any time so that it need not catch the world unawares . . .' For poet' read 'everyperson' or 'Pilgrim' for there is nobody who is exempt from this Work.

### References

The quotations from Cixous, Irigaray, Marks and de Courtivron come from *New French Feminisms: An Anthology,* edited by Elaine Marks and Isabelle de Courtivron (Harrister 1981).

## 11. Mapping the Great Mind

### Review of *The Mystery Religion of W.B. Yeats* by Graham Hough

I have overheard scholars quarrelling about the nature of Yeats's magical grade or degree in the Golden Dawn. 'Adeptus Exemptus, indeed! exempt from what troubles of ordinary mortals?' Auden couldn't stand the magic either, and expostulated 'How on earth, we wonder, could a man of Yeats's gifts take such nonsense seriously . . . so essentially lower middle-class . . . Mediums, spells, the Mysterious Orient — how embarrassing.' It was in this same year (1948) that Graham Hough himself wrote on this subject that 'the beliefs underlying any great poetry must represent a permanent or recurrently important phase of the human spirit, and cannot be merely individual or fashionable fantasy'. Nevertheless Auden's has remained a widely held attitude.

*The Mystery Religion of W. B. Yeats* derives in part from lectures in which Professor Hough set himself the task of presenting Yeats's occult philosophy to a general literary audience. It does not, as the publisher's blurb claims, give an 'extensive history of the occult tradition'. Graham Hough makes it clear that he is aware of the radical simplification he is engaged upon. Its contribution is that the turning to and fro of its reasonable scepticism, always deferential to the poetry itself, will assist the kind of reader for whom the magic stands in the way of the poetry.

Fortunately, this type of readership is less influential than it used to be, as it is beginning to be understood that the modes of consciousness from which a good poem arises, and the changes of consciousness that it gives rise to in the reader, are not so different in kind from those types of experience that we call 'magical' or 'religious'. It is also widely understood that when we speak of 'magic' we may signify contemplative magic, which is the art of causing changes in consciousness by the exercise of will. Thus the discipline of the poet, the Jesuit exercises of St Ignatius, the combinatory play and thought-experiments of an Einstein, the active imagination of the analytical psychologist, and the pathworking of the occultist on the Cabbalistic Tree of Life are not different in kind, but are all attempts to enlarge the range of the conscious mind by techniques of willing, and thus to come into relationship with the powers that move us. As George Mills Harper puts it in *Yeats's Golden Dawn,* 'By means of magic, as Yeats conceived it, man can understand, not control nature. Once he understands nature as a sentient unity, a Great Mind or Memory, he may discover the secrets of the universe, of the past as well as the present, of the invisible as well as the visible.'

Thus also does Yeats's magic stand squarely in the Romantic tradition of the 'runic script' of nature or *Chiffernschrift*, that 'marvellous secret writing you find everywhere' of Novalis, of Blake, and Boehme in *De Signature Rerum*, right back to Plotinus and Plato and maybe beyond.

Hough spends some time establishing the reality of this rival to what has seemed to many the only possible tradition worthy of the name, the Eliotic one of the Catholic Christian theological orthodoxy. He finds plausible that the former emanates from the Greco-Roman world of late antiquity, and recurs in our own age because of similar social and political conditions. I think this is a simplification, as is his insistence that this occult tradition is life-denying and world-escaping.

Hough is on firmer ground in discussing the rewards he feels Yeats gained by occult study. This poet is no Faustus torn to pieces by demons, but an affirmer, whose whole occult myth was 'an indefinite extension of the phenomenal world, as though it were that which Yeats wishes to make eternal' and who would arrive at the gates of paradise, with all his sensual baggage intact 'to be received and legitimated within the holy city'.

We see these rewards, according to Hough, both in the poetry and in the person, in the life as well as the art, which Yeats himself doubted was possible. It is in the poetry because that is informed by the occult idea of correspondences 'as above, so below', so it rests squarely in 'the idea of a vast design, so intricate that all experience could find its place within it, and yet be part of the same pattern'. The Christian myth, with its various territorial exclusions, did not have the same claims. Yeats was able 'to situate friends, enemies and indifferent contemporaries in their due position on the Tree of Life so that they became inhabitants of something more fundamental than an erotic or heroic legend'. Hough can find no analogue to this power nearer than Dante, and it came from occult study (as indeed William Anderson's *Dante the Maker* suggests was true of the older poet too).

As to the personal reward, Hough recalls Virginia Woolf's meeting with Yeats in 1930 (the poet then being sixty-five). He notes that her diary entry was an act of homage and respect 'not very common in the annals of Bloomsbury'. Yeats talks about dreams and states of the soul, about modern poetry and its deficiencies at the end of its era, about another system of thought that was due to arrive. Virginia Woolf, not accustomed to being over-impressed by distinguished men, calls him 'vital, supple, high charged and altogether seasoned and generous', felt her own ignorance in comparison to his 'complete psychology', spoke of the intricacy of his art, 'also of its meanings, its seriousness, its importance, which wholly engrosses this large active minded immensely vitalised man'. The actual diary entry (November 8) is a little more ironic than Hough's account suggests: 'he seemed to live in the centre of an immensely intricate briar bush; from which he could issue at any moment; & then withdraw again. And every twig was real to him.'

The suggestion is that other people could see the magic that Yeats knew introspectively as in 'Vacillation': 'While on the shop and street I gazed / My body of a sudden blazed; / And twenty minutes more or less / It seemed, so great my happiness, / That I was blessèd and could bless.' In the prose version of this poem he says: 'It seems as if the vehicle had become pure and far extended and so luminous that the images from Anima Mundi embodied there . . . would burn up time . . .' 'Vehicle' in this context I understand to mean the semi-electrical aura that is reputed to surround all human beings, and which the magical exercises are said to render conscious and sensitive.

Where I differ from Hough is in his insistence that the occult tradition he sketches for us was in its essence life-denying, so that Yeats can be seen as a particular exception. Indeed, Yeats was a particularly gifted and able practitioner, but the practices of training in the Golden Dawn were intended to bring about such results as these. There were, for example, rites of assumption and transformation which were intended to bring about a state of expanded perception such as an incarnate god might enjoy: 'It seemed, so great my happiness, That I was blessèd and could bless'. Arriving at the gates of the heavenly city with 'all one's sensual baggage intact' would be part of an occult assumption called 'The Bride's Reception'. The influence of Gerald Massey's (1828-1907) earthy anthropological and philological works about the Egyptian mysteries was strong, and Massey maintained that the mysteries were constituted in order to protect the marvels of the commonplace from the abstractors who would devalue them.

Then again, three most important aspects of the occult tradition are sidestepped in Hough's account. One is that it is not vicarious, that is, it is not a congeries of metaphysical statements conveyed by a priesthood, but a series of initiations into an immediate experience. So the tradition is more truly a series of techniques than what we ordinarily understand by 'tradition'. Hough does apply the distinction between *pistis*, faith, and *gnosis*, knowledge; but not I think with sufficient emphasis between priesthood and shamanism. What we are talking about here is a tradition of techniques of European shamanism.

The other two aspects derive from this. One is that there are female shamans as well as male ones, and very likely the former have the greater natural ability. Thus women have always been important in the occult tradition, as in the Romantic. Hough mentions Madame Blavatsky with sympathy though with some over-stressing of her conjuring-tricks (which were often the prelude to any shamanism) and that Mrs George Yeats was initiated into an offshoot of the Golden Dawn, but he fails to remark that Yeats's order right from the beginning had an important and distinguished female membership; in 1896 almost half the members of Yeats's temple were women, eighty-four of 189, according to Professor Harper. The other aspect is that it has always been believed in the occult tradition as elsewhere that important changes of consciousness take place if you can achieve relaxation, the deeper the better, and that one of the deepest and clearest ways to magical visualization was the sexual trance.

There is evidence that there was an undercurrent of Tantric teaching in Yeats's order, and indeed it is difficult to imagine the highly sensuous rituals being concluded without some sexual feeling. It is possible that the religious teachings of Thomas Lake Harris began to influence some members of the Order at the same time as Yeats's refusal to initiate Aleister Crowley into the Second Order started the contentions which eventually broke up the Golden Dawn, to Yeats's great distress. The evidence is that Yeats staunchly defended the chastity of magic within the Golden Dawn, but that the female and sexual side of it became increasingly important to him. In a very early essay he spoke of finding 'divine love in sexual passion' and there appears to have been a mystical or visionary marriage with Maud Gonne, if not in the carnal sense then in the dream or astral one: 'we melted into one another till we formed only *one being, a being greater than ourselves*, who felt all and knew all with double intensity', according to Maud Gonne.

What is certainly true is that *A Vision*, the culmination of Yeats's occult practices, came through the mediumship of his wife, by a sort of conjuring-trick arising from boredom on their honeymoon. George Yeats began by pretending automatic writing, but the gates once open, it took hold so hard that it quite overrode Yeats's previous magic training over more than thirty years. As he says 'my initiation into the "Hermetic Students" had filled my head with Cabbalistic Imagery, but there was nothing in Blake, Swedenborg, Boehme or the Cabbala to help me now'.

The result was what Hough describes as the 'literary kind' of an apocalypse, 'forbidding and bizarre', nevertheless 'stylistic arrangements of experience' (Yeats's words) in which its chief instrument — The Great Wheel of the Lunar Cycle — 'with its twenty-eight phases represents twenty-eight incarnations which fulfil the whole possible range of human experience; and this pattern is so fundamental that it appears, on a larger or smaller scale, in every aspect of human life. Man passes through the same phases in a single incarnation, in a single judgement or act of thought. . .' Nevertheless Hough finds the Great Wheel quirky, idiosyncratic and full of puzzles, and it is here that his apologetics show the strain.

Again, I believe that this Great Wheel, though it is certainly a departure from the Cabbalistic Tree of Life in which Yeats trained, is much more in the occult tradition than Hough will acknowledge. The communications occurred with the companionship of a woman, and in a sexual ambience. The Tree of Life is sometimes described as 'The Anatomy of the Body of

God'. This was Yeats's early study. Now, as it were almost as a defiant extension of the magical work of the man he hated and despised, Aleister Crowley, described as an 'unspeakable mad person', a true Anti-Self, with sexual workings and his Scarlet Women and Goddess 15 (which would correspond to Yeats's dark moon and full moon), Yeats now sought to make as plain as he could his complete Vision of the Anatomy of the Body of Goddess.

The puzzles in A Vision concerning this wheel become much clearer as one sees the movements of the interpenetrating faculties Will, Mask, Creative Mind and Body of Fate are, like the ancient pattern of the woman's fertility compared to that of the Moon as Goddess, movements towards and away from physical incarnation. This is an immensely ancient and traditional magical idea, with the full moon representing ovulation and the dark moon menstruation. In Richard Ellmann's words, 'At phase 15 the urge to incarnate is strongest, and at phase 1 the impulse to mate is most powerful.'

Recent anthropological work by Chris Knight ('Lévi-Strauss and the Dragon', Man, March 1983) suggests that these two culminations of the moon imaging forth human fertility stand behind much, and possibly all, tribal legend and folklore. The interplay of full moon, ovulation, incarnation, husband, offspring, subjective (supplied with ample social symbolism) human speech, antithetical, with dark moon, menstruation, male sibling, magic children, transfiguration, prophetic speech and shamanism, primary and secret, might be said to fulfil in 'stylistic arrangements' 'the whole possible range of human experience'.

As I've pointed out before, and John Montague in a recent Guardian review (June 14, 1984) of the new edition of the Poems reminded us again, Yeats gave the game away In 'The Gift Of Haroun Al-Rashid': 'All, all those gyres and cubes and midnight things / Are but a new expression of her body . . . Awnd now my utmost mystery is out.' Perhaps the tantalising frustrations and fragmentation just as a voice was about 'to explain a new branch of the philosophy' that Yeats experienced during the communication of A Vision, were because it was a precursor of the feminist philosophy now beginning to return out of the occult regions where it had been exiled so long.

## 12. The Moods of God

## An Introduction to the Stories of T.F. Powys

### I.

I first encountered T.F. Powys' work in *The Evening Standard Book of Strange Stories* (my copy is undated, but it must have been in the 1940's). At that time, not long after the war, 'Strange Stories' merely meant tales with that pang of the unconventional that can range from the odd to the horrific. Powys' *The Two Horns* is not one of his best, though it is still a troubling little tale about an old village Doctor worried that a precious white stuffed sparrow might be stolen. On his honeymoon he buys a couple of immense Swiss horns like blunderbusses which he takes back to use as burglar-alarms. He is disturbed at night by what might be burglary, but it is his wife trying feebly to be unfaithful, whom he trumpets back home for ever with his ferocious horns.

My point is that it is perfectly in order to approach Powys' tales as Strange Stories, or as Horror Stories if you like, or Tales of Terror, or Mystery Stories. Why I am sure of this will emerge shortly. They are also Tales of Romantic Love, of Overbearing Malice, Pastoral Beauty, and of perhaps the greatest Horror Tale in the World, the Jesus-Murder and the Treachery of God,

I would not like them approached as Religious Tales, unless one were absolutely positive that by religious one could also mean Pagan. Thus, to begin at the end, Brocard Sewell reports that 'When Theodore Powys was dying a friend read to him from the *Revelations of Divine Love* by Julian of Norwich, and this drew from him one of his most Theodore-like remarks: "I like her. I like that thing she said, 'God is GROUND.'"... He had taken it to mean that God was actual ground — EARTH.'[1]

### II.

As well as approaching Powys through paradox, by saying, for example that his stories are both holy and wicked, malicious and forgiving, lecherous but not prurient, that they concern happiness and horror simultaneously, I think one can give the flavour of the tales by telling stories about Powys himself, for he lived as he wrote. Many of the terrors of personality which he found in his characters, he found in himself, and much of the paradox too. Part of his writer's working-day was his walks, during which he ruminated creatively. Sylvia Townsend Warner remembered him 'coming back from one such walk, but sooner than usual, and looking troubled. "I heard a noise in the hedge. I said to myself, It's only a rat. But then I thought, Who made that rat?"'[2]

In Powys, nothing is so small as to be trivial. Small is beautiful too, and nearly all his tales take place in small villages, in the heart of rustic countryside. F.R. Leavis showed critical acumen in commending Powys: 'It does not seem likely that it will ever again be possible for a distinguished mind to be formed, as Mr. Powys has been, on the rhythm, sanctioned by nature and time, of rural culture,'[3] but, as so often in Leavis, one wonders where his sense of humour had gone. For small is Moral, as Leavis wants, but it is also holy and horrifying and very, very funny.

The story is told that there was a certain troublesome and loquacious Mrs. Ashburnham, who had rented the rectory in East Chaldon, where Powys lived. She loved to waylay him on his working-walks, for conversational purposes. On one occasion Powys saw her approaching, and hid from her in a field of stubble, lying face-downwards, close to the ground, not very well-concealed. Mrs. Ashburnham's dogs discovered him easily: 'He remained motionless as the Scotties scampered up and sniffed at him, then he heard a footstep, then silence. At last Mrs. Ashburnham asked brightly: "Communing with nature, Mr. Powys?" She had been standing beside him for a full minute.'[4] The Scotties later appeared as the ghostly hounds of death in one of the novels, *Mark Only*. One wonders how long the communion would have extended if she had not spoken.

This tale fits, but only by paradox, with the dignified figure described by David Garnett: 'A grey-haired, elderly, heavily-built man, with a big head and powerful rugged features. His very sharp eyes under bushy eyebrows summed one up; he was a moralist and a shrewd critic of men. The grey eyes were those of a relentless and severe judge. But . . . he was exaggeratedly polite and spoke with an excessive humility and gentleness, as though he were an unarmed man addressing gunmen ready to shoot on sight .'⁵ In this vignette Powys is seen as both monumental and sensitive, as the earth is, and as his narrative style is. Again, Elizabeth Munz tells us that when she started sculpting a portrait head of him out of Purbeck Stone he remarked 'Cut out of one of the far hills that I look at when I walk on the cliffs . . . To be carved out of the heart of one of those noble, ancient hills, older than time itself, *that is a great honour.*'⁶ Compare this to the reply he made, a year or so before he died, to the question as to whether there was any way men could transcend the positive evil they had been born with. He said 'Oh yes, there is. There is Eternity, and God knows what that is more than I do. To the Elements we go, and there is no kind of evil in them. We pass to the Elements, and then we pass further. To that which was and is and is to come. All is redeemed then, all is salvation. Yes, there is only one way, and that way is the same for all creatures.'⁷ Powys, in this dignified statement, lacks all stiffness or human pride. Just so, in his tales humanity is no arbiter, but more seriously lost and puzzled than the creation which surrounds mankind. In *John Pardy and the Waves*, for example, the sea speaks to his terribly damaged hero 'Our great joy comes when we break, yours when you are born, for you have not yet reached that sublime relationship with God which gives the greatest happiness to destruction.' In *The Dog and the Lantern* Powys tells of the sheepdog who thinks that God is the flame of his master's lantern, and because he has a strong enough faith, this becomes the truth: 'The Saviour of the World,' says the truly humble Christ in this story 'can be everything. Little Betty may find a lucky stone by the seaside — that stone am I. Dig down into the clay where poor Tom, the madman, lies buried. His coffin-boards are rotted, his flesh is clay — I am he. The sexton stole the church oil — I was that too — and sold it to the shepherd, who filled me with it.' Creation is a continuum, not a privileged arrangement on behalf of humanity. All are pilgrims. It is not surprising that Bunyan was among Powys' favourite reading.

There is every kind of serious sin depicted in Powys, with a kind of saintly glee. God's irresponsible error in creating man imperfect, and his appalling repentance now it is too late (as in *The Only Penitent*) is a sin like any other, maybe greater than any other. Perhaps this accounts for the thunderstruck innocence of Powys' clergyman. It is as though the Christian pastoral of Langland's *Piers Plowman* were revised by the Seven Deadly Sins, or *Pilgrim's Progress* by the citizens of the City of Destruction. There is one exception; I can recall no cowards in Powys. The good people suffer with fortitude; the bad people are only as wicked as plants in nature that compete for sunlight by strangling each other. Compared to Powys' rustics, Shakespeare's are bumpkins; in Powys they are alight with malice. He seems to say, how can a person live the good life without the joys of innocence or the satisfaction of malice? There is the occasional saint also, like Charlotte Bennet a magical good fairy type of character (like Hester Dominy in the novella of that name) to be distinguished from a 'goodness' which is only fortitude. The innocent and thunderstruck religious I mentioned above who so frequently appear, innocent and helpless, like Mr. Summerbee in the masterpiece *The Left Leg* or the possessed mystic James Gillet in the same story, are set against the monumental activist greed of Farmer Mew which is both a sin and a natural force.

There is also the slyness of the greed of the sexton in *Archdeacon Truggin*; many of the stories, as by paradox again, operate slyly: a wicked kind of story that delights in sliding sideways like a spider, with a glimpse of some unexpected wickedness — or blessing. Powys' brother, John Cowper, once remarked that Theodore couldn't help being like that, for he was the one who always stood in the shadow. Yet this Vision of a Field Full of Folk takes place in a landscape which is also involved in the drama of redemption or whatever is the alternative, where the bones above ground converse underground, and which is as full and round and gorgeous as a Stanley Spencer canvas or a Samuel Palmer, for at times 'all the village spoke of plenty, peace and quiet labour.' (*The Left Leg*)

That village is Madder. Or God's Madder. The pun is intentional, and is an important clue to Powys. It is not quite that God is insane, any more than the Jehovah in the Book of Job is insane. C.G. Jung implies in his 'Answer to Job' (1952) that God is curing himself of a kind of psychosis by conversing with his creation (just as God comes to confess to the clergyman in *The Only Penitent* (1931) which antedates Jung's radical work by 20 years). It is that God's moods are dangerous. Powys himself, as before, gives important testimony here in his first commercially published book *The Soliloquy of a Hermit*: 'I know how men move under the shadow of the moods of God, and I know how I move. Some try to hide in the Garden, and some try to hide in the beast's belly. I have tried to hide amongst grassy hills; but the moods of God have hunted me out . . . As I could not hide from God, I tried to hide from myself, and watch the moods as they passed by . . . To believe in God and not to believe in yourself is the first duty of a priest . . . All human laws are made to trap and snare God's movements; men are always trying to get at ease with themselves and away from his terrible ways . . . I see the awful Majesty of the Creator come into our own Grange mead, and lie down amid a joyous crowd of buttercups and red clover.'

### III

Theodore Francis Powys was born into a truly extraordinary family. He was the third child of the Revd. Charles Powys and Mary Cowper Johnson, and his eldest brother was John Cowper Powys, the great novelist. A younger brother to Theodore was Llewellyn Powys, who became a famous essayist and controversialist, and in the family of eleven children, three of the sisters of note, Gertrude Powys, the painter, Marian, who became a world authority on lace, and Katie, who was a poet and novelist.

The pressures on the family were not economic, especially as Charles Powys inherited a fortune when Theodore would have been four. The controlling forces in the family seem to have been the clash between the opposing personalities of the clergyman father and the powerful natural paganism of John Cowper, who confessed that all his life he wanted to be a magician. With this ambition he spun towering and toppling fantasies he created for his brothers and sisters, a powerful swords-and-sorcery world of strange games and fantasies generated in direct opposition to the paternal beliefs.

According to their biographer, Richard Perceval Graves, John misused the power he had over Theodore, finding 'in his imagination a quick response to some of my most devilish games and some of my most scandalous experiments.'[8] However, the Revd. Charles thought it his duty to form and shape his children. He took them on immensely long walks, and John remembers 'little Theodore, white in the face and with great forlorn eyes like an over-driven animal, as he was dragged along some dusty road where the very flies joined forces to persecute them!'[9] One must suppose that the father expounded his religion on these walks, as in all other departments of his life, and Theodore must have been wrestling with the paradoxes that became the heart of his work later, just as walks on which he saw more than a mere rat in a rat, were always part of that work. He probably developed as a protective gambit, the beginnings of that irony which is one way of approaching ultimates without losing heart. One could also call the tales of his maturity 'devilish games.'

He found a private sanctum under the shrubberies of Rothesay House, their home, which he called 'Bushes Home', another protective device which was probably later continued in his lifelong need for country solitude; and while the other brothers became collectors, as was expected of them, for their father collected things — John collected birds' eggs, Littleton fossils and butterflies — Theodore, in his elder brother's words, 'always so terrifyingly original, did actually collect nothing.' Graves says that Theodore at eight and a half attracted bullying in the family because he was so unlike everybody else;[10] and later on John claims that he was the most original of them all. He was certainly the first of the brothers to make a substantial literary reputation. But 'original' also means 'concerned with origins', and in the family tumult Theodore kept a profoundly considering balance between the rival claims of upper middle class Christian Anglicanism and the contrary power of John Cowper Powys' pagan imagination. Thus Theodore glimpsed issues that were to preoccupy him the rest of his life. Had he not been a writer, and spun his extraordinary vision of human life which is simultaneously good and evil, his frequent attacks of depression would have been likely to lead to permanent illness. A great psychologist of recent times, John Layard, made his watchword in therapy the saying that 'Depression is withheld knowledge.' Theodore Powys' watchword for these his Tales of the Ultimate is '. . . once in the darkness one learns to love what is profound, lasting and sublime. "Let your light shine" should rather be "Let your darkness deepen"' (*Darkness and Nathaniel*). In that deepening darkness of depression extraordinary illumination shines. In his conflict he sought the ground, to have his feet on it, for that is an ultimate too.

The only way out then for Theodore, was to get down, as low as he could, as in his encounter with Mrs Ashburnham. He saw clearly the worst in human nature without losing his love of people and life, and this is an extraordinary achievement. Because it is so original, of the origins or ultimates, it generates paradoxes. These are not gothic stories. It is not as if *Pilgrim's Progress* had been re-written by E.A. Poe. Powys is an earthier writer by far, of his ground. The nearer comparison is with Hawthorne's great allegorical power. But Hawthorne is short on humour, as Theodore Powys is not. What is behind our cruder contemporary tales of horror or terror is a fear of the opposing contradictions inherent in reality. Theodore Powys saw them steadily, and so in him even the horror has a glow of holiness. In solitude, Love wrestles with its intolerable opponent, Death.

That solitude is a kind of fortitude. In *Soliloquies of a Hermit* he said 'Only the same kind of day must come in order that I may be able to remember the past, and I must have that same kind of feeling that I had on that same day; the same old crippled man must hobble past; the same wind must howl in the chimney; the same white cow must chew the cud at my gate; and then I remember. And often it is something ugly that brings me to this happiness.' What if man is 'a collection of atoms, through which pass the moods of God — a terrible clay picture, tragic, frail, drunken, but always with claws holding on to his life while the moods pass over him and change his face and his life every moment. The people of the earth are clay pieces that the moods of God kindle into life . . . Then the change comes. The first change — the forerunner of Death — is Love. When the sun of Love rises and a man walks in its glory, he may be sure that a shadow approaches him — Death. Love creates and separates; Death destroys and heals,' (*Unclay*) and 'I want to cultivate the kind of mind that can turn stones into bread, a dull hour into a heavenly glory, and a dull life into the life of a king. For what we call dullness is really the best soil we can dig in, because the gold it yields is very precious and lasting.' In my opinion this refusal to skate on the surface of what is now fashionable pessimism and anomia makes Harold Pinter look like an amateur of life and Samuel Beckett a trifler with the feelings of honest people.

To any outward view, Theodore Powys led a most uneventful life. He became apprenticed to a farmer in his twenties, and went on to run his own farm at Sweffling in Suffolk, which was not too successful. He then moved to Dorset, married, and published privately his first book, in a limited edition, *An Interpretation of Genesis*. He was rejected for military service in 1916. By 1922 he was a well-established author, though he hardly stirred out of Dorset, but was exceedingly productive; in 1927 he published the novel by which he is at present best known, *Mr. Weston's Good Wine*. He continued publishing many books, though increasing illness slowed him down; he died at Mappowder, Dorset in November 1953. The present book now reprinted, *God's Eyes A-Twinkle*, was the last he published, in 1947.

Sylvia Townsend Warner, his great friend, gives this picture of Theodore Powys at work: his 'Books grew like stalactites and stalagmites. He deposited them, secretly and methodically — a process taking place in a cave. After breakfasting, rather late, and leisurely, he went off to the parlour, sat down before a large solid table, read for half an hour (usually the Bible) and then set to work. He wrote uninterruptedly for three hours or so, put his work back in the table drawer, and began again where he left off, on the following morning . . . When I happened to pass the window, I saw the same grave, dispassionate countenance, pen moving over the paper, dipping at regular intervals into the inkpot.'"

IV.

Readers new to Powys might feel that they could do with a short guide to these luminous parables, which are also a psychological minefield. I had thought of giving short vignettes of each story, so the reader could begin by picking the sin that interested him most, and go on from there. In the great novels

*Unclay* and *Mr. Weston's Good Wine* one has ample space to grasp Powys' tone and intention; the stories on the other hand tend to sidle up and bite, and no condensation or précis would do justice to the immediacy of the mingled pain and pleasure of that bite in the best stories.

In my opinion, the book in this arrangement becomes increasingly Theodore Powys as it goes on, with a kind of peak at *The Left Leg* which is a comic masterpiece which no-one else could have written. I believe that in absorbing the stories, one has to be firmly prepared for opposites to clash together with the production of completely unfamiliar feelings, for just as the terrible Deadly Sins are not proof against Powys' irony and sweetness, so not even God is sinless. In this sense, the book is seamless, for the vision is entire, and it can be read from beginning to end as it were a novel. If one prefers to approach with a fondness for the Strange Story, one might read first *Christ in the Cupboard* and then *The Gong, John Pardy and the Waves, Darkness and Nathaniel* and *My Money*. If one is more interested in the kind of paradox that punches a hole through the appearance of things into non-ordinary reality, one might sample *The Only Penitent, Bottle's Path, Jesus Walk, Charlotte Bennett, The White Paternoster, Mr. Pim and the Holy Crumb* and especially *The Dog and the Lantern*. If one prefers black comedy, one can start with *The Left Leg* and proceed with *Archdeacon Truggin, When Thou Wast Naked, The Candle and the Glowworm, The Golden Gates*. But I think that whichever way one begins, one will end up with the whole, because behind all these different categories is the one thing without a name, which Powys called the Moods of God, which he wrestles with on behalf of us all. Only in awareness of this existential contest with reality and its occasional truces are we likely to come to maturity as individuals or a species, for, creation has hardly begun, and, to use religious terminology, God is still moulding humanity out of the clay, 'The people of the earth are clay pieces that the moods of God kindle into life' still. To know this as Theodore Powys knew it is to have one's feet firmly supported by the Ground.

# References

1. *Theodore: Essays on T.F. Powys*. Edited with a Foreword by Brocard Sewell. Saint Albert's Press 1964. p. ix.
2. *The Brothers Powys*. Richard Perceval Graves. Routledge & Kegan Paul, 1983, p.172.
3. *New Bearings in English Poetry*. F.R. Leavis, Chatto and Windus, 1959, p. 92.
4. *The Brothers Powys*. p. 172.
5. Ibid. p. 158
6. *Sewell*: op.cit. pp. 19-20.
7. *Sewell*: op.cit. p. 13.
8. *Graves*: op.cit. p. 11.
9. *Graves*: op.cit. p. 11.
10. *Graves*: op.cit. pp. 11, 14.
11. *Graves*: op.cit. pp. 171-2.

# 13. Windings and Conchings

Review of *River* by Ted Hughes and *The Achievement of Ted Hughes*, ed. Keith Sagar

Water is one of those substances that seem to take care of us, to guarantee human significance in the physical world. It appears to have both mental and physical properties, like numbers or breath. Evolution would not have been possible without water, with its high latent heat guaranteeing against lethal extremes of temperature, and its curious and unique property of becoming lighter when it is cold (otherwise the seas would freeze solid). Its windings and conchings reproduce the organic forms out of which the mineral, plant and animal worlds are constructed; it is the working-fluid of the sun-earth heat-engine; and it is a kind of liquid crystal whose properties alter with the approach of gravitational fields such as the Moon's. One can see its function teleologically, as if transmitting cosmic influences to the living world. Writing about water must be, then, one of the great reconciling meditations.

In reading Ted Hughes's *River* I was reminded of all this, and of a story by, I think, Richard Brautigan, about a scrap-metal yard with a stream of special water running through it, the property of which was to reflect images of all the events and places it had passed through. I was reminded also of Henri Michaux, in *Au Pays de la Magie* (1941), and his magical Water-Shepherds, and of Ruskin's Eden-streams in *Praeterita*. There is a kind of magic that comes with the contemplation of water which is also a science, since water and its creatures are so undoubtedly *there*.

Hughes in the farming poems in *Moortown* was able to reconcile his sharp observation of the external world with his mythical and philosophical strain, though on the whole it was an uneasy book, interested in pain, troubled because it dealt in part with the death of Hughes's admired partner and father-in-law — Jack Orchard (the 'good shepherd' of an excellent essay on *Moortown* by Craig Robinson in *The Achievement of Ted Hughes*). *River*, however, moves towards something I have been anticipating and hoping for since *Crow* went hunting Hare, and lost the magical battle ('Crow Goes Hunting'). As John Layard has shown in *The Lady of the Hare*, this animal, in contradistinction to the fighting, fumbling Crow, all over the world stands for the relenting and feminine aspects of nature, the willing sacrifice, the creature that never closes its eyes, and whose reputation as a witch animal and for uncleanness comes from its identification, like water and blood, with the Moon. Crow thought Hare the greater power, and 'gazed after the bounding hare / Speechless with admiration.'

In *River* the method of exploration is important, It is a tentative, vulnerable feeling-out, like waking up out of sleep. In 'October Dawn' in Hughes's first book, ice 'got its spearhead into place' in a half-glass of wine: 'First a skin, delicately here / Restraining a ripple from the air; / Soon plate and rivet on pond and brook'; in *River* it is like the reverse transformation. 'The Morning Before Christmas' begins with frozen 'Buds fur-gloved with frost' a 'standstill' and a 'stillness' in a 'blue haze'. Then at mid-morning the sun pushes dark spokes across the fields, the water wakes and the river steams, showing its colour 'flint-olive'. Now there are close-ups of dead salmon: 'lolling lilies of fungus . . . Nothing / So raggy dead offal as a dead / Salmon in its wedding finery'. But quickly there is a hen fish 'lurching alive', and the sun 'embellishes her beauty / Her red-black love-paints, her helpless noble mask', the mask of sacrifice. Men appear, the 'solemn' regulators of nature, and squeeze the eggs out of the hen fish and the milt out of a surviving cock salmon, 'precarious obstetrics', and the fish go free. Nature would not be so abundant without the men's careful husbandry, and as a consequence of this act the world is now 'Wrought in wet, heavy gold. Treasure-solid.' Cell-shocked: 'That morning / Dazzle-stamped every cell in my body'. A thought-fox muse presides: 'A flood pond, inch-iced, held the moment of a fox / In touch-melted and refrozen dot-prints.' Something spoilt and frozen is redeemed by the magic of animal husbandry, which is also a kind of science.

The pattern repeats as we read through the book: a waking, and some act of perception which transforms. In 'Japanese River Tales' snow in the night hurries like a bride to her river-groom, who 'rejoices all morning / In his juicy bride': unfortunately this is daytime magic, her destroying talons are 'lengthened by moonlight . . . And the river / Is a gutter of death'. Or, as in 'Flesh of Light', one may start with an abstract proposition, the sun being the generator of radiation which makes the atoms dance on earth, and proceed to waking instances of the muzzles of the cattle drinking and dripping that same radiant light of which both their bodies and the shining 'mercury creature' of the river are made. This comparison of the river to mercury recurs, as though the shining water were at the same time the alchemical Mercurius, the living imagination.

In 'Whiteness' the waking is disorderly and restless, until the sun establishes itself; in 'Four March Watercolours' the river, at first much occupied with 'twistings and self-wrestlings', progressively organizes itself into 'river-epic'. If the hills remain 'locked in snow', like dry dugs refusing their springs, the eye nevertheless wakes to 'lit queenliness . . . / The high, frozen bosom, wears this river / Like a particularly fine jewel' ('Dee').

In some expositions, it is as though the skin of water separated the narrator from participation in the thriving depths, and once penetrated, all is changed. 'The Merry Mink' stops being a magical star and romps and topples into the river like a goblin. Then a celebratory religious element enters: 'the river is in a resurrection fever' in 'Under the Hill of the Centurions', the cock-minnows 'abandon contemplation and prayer in the pool's crypt' and do their work, which is also a 'Stag-party': 'In the clatter of the light loom of water / All singing and / Toiling together / Wreathing their metals' and their work-song is imagined. We 'Join water, wade in underbeing' in 'Go Fishing' and in 'Milesian Encounter on the Sligachan' there is the spontaneous shock of falling into the 'sheer cavern of current piling silence . . . Such a brilliant cut-glass interior' through the raddled surface of a bog. Some mythic parables supervene, of 'Ophelia' and 'Creation of Fishes' (the Moon's children, saved from the parching sun, by a sleight) and in 'West Dart' the sudden eruption of torrents without preliminary warning breaks what has hitherto been the pattern of most of the poems.

Now the fish watch the poet through their skins, and the whole river whispers 'We've got him' ('After Moonless Midnight'). Just about half-way through the book, in 'That Morning', in a country where there are bears 'Two gold bears came down and swam like men . . . And dived like children./ And stood in deep water as on a throne / Eating pierced salmon off their talons . . .' It is as if the poet is declaring after his explorations that the seeing eye, like the Hare's, is now open for always, for after that point the poems enact and record confident vision, freely entered: 'So we stood, alive in the river of light / Among the creatures of light, creatures of light.'

There is more religious imagery, in the title poem explicitly, of the willing sacrifice, the softness of the water of the Tao, which, yielding to everything, conquers everything: 'So the river is a god / Knee-deep among reeds, watching men. / Or hung by the heels down the door of a dam', like the Hanged Man in the Tarot, and one notices the word-play on 'dam'. But the river can also have the softness of an idle woman who stretches and 'an ecstasy tightens / Over her skin, and deep in her gold body / Thrills spasm and dissolve', for this 'Low Water' is also a 'love-potion' across which Hare eyes Crow 'steadily from the beginning of the world.'

There is a lot more to say about the poems, but not now. To my eye, the photographs are not of the same interest, and present an embalmed or chocolate-box appearance: they are not awake.

*The Achievement of Ted Hughes* is also distracting in a not-dissimilar manner. People who prefer to read a poet because he is marked down as 'great', rather than because they find him good, will receive an excellent massage here, as most of the essays seem to take the standpoint that Hughes can do no wrong, a declaration contradicted by the long section of uncollected poems, which are naturally uneven in quality. The editor, Keith Sagar, says right at the beginning that Hughes's is 'the most penetrating, authentic and all-embracing poetic vision of out time'. I have considerable sympathy with his enthusiasm, but I wonder whether he really means what he says. What is the span of 'our time'? Does he mean, in any language? Should we confine 'poetic vision' to literature, and if so, why?

But enthusiasm about Hughes is justified. He has helped bring back into English studies in this country a sense of poetry 'not as a vague ornament of life but as one of the great living disciplines of the mind, friendly to all other disciplines, and offering them and accepting from them new sources of power'. These words are Elizabeth Sewell's, from *The Orphic Voice*, a book not cited here, but which would be of considerable interest to the contributors if they don't already know it. Indeed, it is one of this book's shortcomings that in speaking of shamanism and other religious matters, Hughes is not placed in his full European context, So to place him would be very interesting, for he is obviously not the first poet 'of our time' to quarrel with the Christian Church, or to suffer from a Crow-like conflict between spleen and ideal, horror and ecstasy, supernaturalism and irony. Besides Baudelaire, one immediately thinks of Rimbaud.

The poetic descent into the 'underworld' as part of a search for 'accommodation' in the world, is not new and exclusive to Hughes, as the majority of these essays suggest it is. Comparison with a line of poets that included, say Novalis, Nerval, Mallarmé, Rilke, Valéry, Yeats (Hughes's strongest early influence), Trakl, Eluard, Supervielle and Perse (I recalled the last's great 'Pluies: Neiges' and 'Amers' in reading the smaller *River*) would be fascinating indeed, and would do better service than the essays here which make of Hughes an isolate, and rather bookish figure struggling against patriarchy, the Movement and the sins of the rational intellect. Exceptions to this are good essays by Craig Robinson, Graham Bradshaw, Terry Gifford, Neil Roberts and Seamus Heaney, and an interesting one by Ekbert Faas.

Yet, as Dr Sagar says, 'poetry is religious or it is nothing. Its claim to be taken seriously . . . is its ability to keep open and operative the connections between the depths of the human psyche and the hidden sources of everything in the non-human world' though that 'non-human' will be the question for Christian and other religious, including Blakean ones. It has taken a poet of Hughes's energy and commitment working as he may have been out of an individual distress prompted by collective causes, to allow such an important declaration to be made, friendly to other disciplines. But so anxious are many of the contributors not to lose this treasure of feeling that they often become tiresomely sycophantic.

With regard to those 'other disciplines' it is good for example that the world-wide phenomenon of shamanism is seen as a type of pattern of the healing creative process in romantic poetry; though this thought will not be unfamiliar to those who read Nora Chadwick in the 1940s. It is good also that parallels are drawn between the patterns of poetry and Jungian psychology as a practical healing method; though one is sorry that in the animadversions against the rational intellect the true Jungian position is not seen, which is a balance between four functions, including intellect. The anguished negotiations are between three of these functions and the 'inferior' or undifferentiated or deep function which I believe to be 'sensation', diabolized in our culture, the life in the physical world of the fully sensuous body. As Wallace Stevens says 'The greatest poverty is not to live / In a physical world . . . / The adventurer / In humanity has not conceived of a race / Completely physical in a physical world.'

I take *River* to be an adventure into or working model of such negotiations, the thinking, feeling and intuiting by things, which leads, when successful, to the fifth function, which is the 'treasure-solid' imagination. But is *River* 'good' — 'good' as Blake, as Shakespeare (for these comparisons are implied in Sagar's book)'? Is *River* 'worthy' of the most 'all embracing poetic vision of our time'? Dr Sagar's editorial policy will want it to be and thus confuses the issue. *River* will take nearly all of its readers much further into imagining with the four-fold taste of quality, and into making it their own, 'dazzle-stamped', than they could go unassisted, and this is perhaps one of the principal 'great' things we should ask of any poet of our time.

# 14. Healing, Creativity and the Black Goddess

## The 1984 J.R.R. Tolkien Lecture,
## The Lincoln Clinic and Institute for Psychotherapy

### I.

Anybody who has performed conjuring tricks for an audience, or led hypnotism or meditation groups, knows that an altered state of consciousness in the audience is announced by a quite palpable change of atmosphere. The leader or performer usually notices this before his audience does, and it is his business to feed it back to them. That is why they came. This has also been known to happen during the course of a lecture.

At the very least there is a tingle in the skin which means you've got them (and they've got you) an impression maybe of an elastic fragrance that has begun to fill out and define the contours of the room, and perhaps an enhancement of light and colour so that what you're doing and the people you're doing it with become vivid and everything seems larger and the show, whatever kind it is, begins to go right.

I remember watching a performance of the play *Sleuth*. There is a point, you may remember, when the phoney Inspector discovers blood on the stairs where there cannot be any blood; we the audience know this. But when he said 'Blood, Sir' and the other actor replied 'Blood', I felt the whole audience opening to the stage, like the petals of a one immense flower.

Or on another occasion, at the Cornish Miracle Plays at Pirran Round, Jesus had escaped from his tomb and the centurion sent his soldiers to look for the escaped criminal. 'Cor Lucius,' said one of them, 'you're in a right mess. You've lost Jesus. Where is this Jesus?' Then the Roman soldier turned to the audience and shouted cut, 'Have you seen this Jesus?' From all and between all the spectators sitting in their tiers in this Ancient Round Theatre there was the escape of breath on a one high extended note like the sound of a harp-string snapping, then echoing, in a one uncalculated act of unity and wonder.

The orthodox scientist scoffs at the importance of such 'feelings', but everybody knows they exist, and, if they are wise, uses them. I want to suggest this evening, among other matters, why and how such 'feelings' are to be trusted, and treated at least provisionally as perceptions of actuality, equivalent and maybe superior to the conventionally-acknowledged senses. In fact, when we fall in love, make friends, influence people, give Tarot readings, feel compassion, do magic, make prophesies and even converse with the gods, we may be exercising a sensory capability that has been concealed by the paradigms of science and by a misunderstanding of religious experience. 'Intuition', fantasy, subliminal perceptions, 'feelings', 'vibes', dream-life, psychic and healing powers, are perhaps a continuum, different in quality but not in kind, the use of which is a kind of prophecy of what could come about when humankind has put off its intellectual arrogance, condescends to learn from nature, and develops its 'unconscious senses'. What has a writer to do with this? Freud has a concept particularly interesting to writers as I think it describes the way most of us use words. This is the 'watching agency' which develops in the infant between primary narcissism, self-absorption, and the Oedipus Complex, of which more later. The Watching Agency is the conscience. Its operation is concerned with the emergence of speech and the use of language, and its products include the ego-ideal, speculative systems, memory, the sense of time, dreams, and self-regard.

Why this idea becomes interesting to a writer is that he seems to preserve consciousness of this stage. Not only is his conscience the words he uses, but language in his watching agency also.

It is a very simple notion. The writer watches what is happening by means of his craft of language. E.M. Forster remarked of the writer's speculative gift, 'How do I know what I think until I see what I say?' Language itself for the writer has become the watching agency. It is as if a writer's language is a magic mirror, in which a person may teach himself things he did not consciously know. As Robert Graves put it, language is like the shield which Perseus polished up so brightly that he could see the Gorgon in it without being turned to stone.

For the writer, and for the reader too, language is capable of describing both objective and subjective events; it unites the inner and outer worlds, particularly in poetry. Speech, and therefore language, is made of breath, which testifies to the basic and ineluctable link between conscious and unconscious: one may breathe consciously, or let the breath come and go on its own.

But if the watching agency gives rise to dreaming and introspection in parallel with the development of speech, what can one learn of the outer world by introspection? That is the enigma. For if one learns only about oneself, then that could easily be a meaningless self-indulgence in 'feeling'. Yet that itself is an assumption; there is surely an a priori case for regarding each person as a part of the universe; thus we should learn as much or more about the universe by going deep within ourselves by introspective techniques as we can by travelling the outside world. But there is a persistent idea that the universe and ourselves are not a continuum; we are 'ghosts in the machine'. There is the assumption. And that subjectivity is purely personal, and full of merely individual information, feelings, fantasies, symbolic enactments. I'll try to suggest that 'feelings' are neither meaningless nor self-indulgent.

Introspection. It's a dangerous business, this opening up of the gates of the inner world. Being on this podium, I must give my own example.

A book that terrified me from my teens was Robert Graves' *The White Goddess*. It seemed to be saying that the universe was controlled by a female principle that was capricious and exacting, and whose purpose was to bring night to the mind of the poet in order, if he was very lucky indeed, that he might be reborn to a better light. As I wanted to be a poet, and I knew, as most of us do, the difference between the joy of our best moments and the hell of our worst, I made a superstitious allegiance to this powerful figure, and did my best to do nothing to offend Her. It was much as Dylan Thomas in the preface to his *Collected Poems* remarked that 'I read somewhere of a shepherd who, when asked why he made, from within fairy rings, ritual observance to the moon to protect his flocks, replied 'I'd be a damn fool if I didn't'.'

The story is told of the publisher who refused to accept Graves's book being found hanging in his garden on an alder tree, dressed in bra and panties. T.S. Eliot who accepted and eventually published the book, on the other hand was shortly afterwards awarded the Nobel Prize.

I was terrified and in awe of the mere appearance of the volume, as a devout Christian might take especial note and care of his bible, but this bible was bound in a frightening blue-green or glaucous colour, like the blue-green of jade or that of a mouldy corpse; one of the sacred colours indeed, one of the Goddess colours. Under *The White Goddess'* auspices I made my strict respect towards women. I married, and tried to settle to my writing. I had children as much because it would please the Goddess as out of my own passion. I got various unsuitable jobs in order to support my dependants, and my marriage began to shake to pieces.

Why, when I had been at such pains to be good, and White, did another matter keep on coming through in that cellar of my mind where my magic mirror was kept? I would sit down at my desk, and open the cellar door, so to speak, and descend into myself, and compose this mirror of language, settle it, to see what I might see (how did I know what I knew until I saw what I said?) Why then did this mirror show blackness, accompanied by strange and powerful feelings? What was this apparition:

A boggy wood as full of springs as trees.
Slowly she slipped into the muck.
It was a white dress she said and that was not right.
Leathery polished mud, that stank as it split.
It is a smooth white body, she said, and that is not right,
Not quite right; I'll have a smoother,
Slicker body, and my golden hair
Will sprinkle rich goodness everywhere.
So slowly she backed into the mud.

What was this illegitimate, and black goddess, who, after her mud-baptism comes up:

Dressed like a mound of lickerish earth,
Swiftly ascending in a streaming pat
That grows tall, smooths brimming hips and steps out
On flowing pillars, darkly draped.
And then the blackness breaks open with blue eyes
Of this black Venus rising helmeted in night
Who as she glides grins brilliantly, and drops
Swatches superb as molasses on her path.

Who is that negress running on the beach . . .
She laughs aloud and bares her teeth again and cries:
Now that I am all black, and running in my richness
And knowing it a little, I have learnt
It is quite wrong to be all white always . . .

(And the apparition or vision ended . . .)

Ah, watch, she runs into the sea. She walks
In streaky white on dazzling sands that stretch
Like the whole world's pursy mud quite purged.
The black rooks coo like doves, new suns beam
From every droplet of the shattering waves,
From every crystal of the shattered rock.
Drenched in the mud pure white rejoiced,
From this collision were new colours born,
And in their slithering passage to the sea
The shrugged-up richness of deep darkness sang.

A way of putting this appearance of a kind of black door
opening to a new light of many colours, that might appeal to
a Jungian, is this. My conscious devotion to a great archetype
or basic symbol, the White Goddess, had constellated in my
unconscious her compensatory opposite, the Black Goddess, and
the two met in one, and created a rainbow, the 'cauda pavonis'.

But it is all very well having these visions, which, as I am a
writer, came to me through the incantation of my verse rather
than by direct seizure; one cannot live in *that* world; the poem in
a way brought the vision into *this*; but now (in Jungian terms) we
must do the work of amplification, and find some meaning that is
practically active and useful in this mysterious blackness, or deep
and dazzling darkness, that had come to my poem; and not pure
either, but with a sexual squidginess that was totally unexpected;
a measure of its inner energy.

The problem is that nobody seems to know much about a
Black Goddess. Graves tells us about a White Goddess, whose
correspondence is with the waxing and waning brightness of
the Moon; could the Black Goddess have something to do with
the darkness of the Moon? Our official Christianity seemed to

be much in the same state; it knew bright and virtuous demi-goddesses, like the Virgin Mary, and Mary Magdalen after her conversion from whore to saint, the one who must not touch Jesus, but was the first to see him after the resurrection; and there were rumours of secret blackness in the Black Virgins kept in the crypts of many European churches and cathedrals; especially in Poland (and the present Pope [John Paul II] appears to have a special devotion to the Black Virgin). Close to hand, in the bible itself, there is that poem of Tantric vividness, the Song of Solomon, called the Song of Songs, where the Shulamite says of herself 'I am black yet comely'. I have since found two essays by the distinguished analytical psychologist Ean Begg that explore these areas, and another by the Italian Jungian M.T. Colonna.

I must then unpack this archetype, for myself, for the archetype is both intensely personal and also universal, by exploring its possible analogues and associations as far as I can through the worlds of science, psychology, literature and art. And here I will try by indirections to find directions out, and will change direction a little, temporarily.


II.

Ever since the beginning of the Christian era, human kind has laboured under an all-pervasive misapprehension. This fallacy is so deep that we have no direct words for it and have to use images. It can be stated thus: only the light is good, what is in the dark is bad.

'And God said, let there be light!' And out of the black chaos the world emerged. All the devils were left behind in the darkness. In most European languages, 'see' and 'understand' are synonymous words. To see is to understand. This illustrates how important to us sight is, and how the information we gain from the world is mostly in terms of sight. When there is no light, most people feel uncomfortably disorientated and suffer 'sensory deprivation', as in the psychologists' 'black room', and begin to see strange imagery and hallucinations by 'inner light' in true darkness, as though there were more in darkness than science admits, as though darkness were always dreaming, despite science. Perhaps it is time for darkness to wake.

Now I want to introduce an idea which may at first seem rather at variance with psychoanalysis. We have the notion of the unconscious mind as a kind of repository of all the things that have happened to us which we have in various ways endeavoured to forget. In forgetting, we lose natural energies and conscious energies, and diminish ourselves. We become a little more unconscious, a little more dead. We may transform or sublimate what we wish to forget into art, religion and noble idealism, the flowers of civilisation which are rooted in the black earth of animal feelings, which we deny we have. In this unconscious mind, time stands still, and the nursery is contemporaneous with the marriage bed.

The discovery and exploration of the unconscious mind is one of the greatest means we have at our disposal for our evolution as a species. But are we not, in using that word 'mind', leaving out all but a quarter of our being? A Jungian would think so: mind is only one of the four functions: the others are feeling, intuition and sensation. There is a fifth, the transcendent function, the imagination. Perhaps it is best to say 'unconscious psyche', and this begins to imply a part of our being which is active and living, rather than a repository of repressed matter. I want to take this a little further, then, and consider a newish idea. Rather than dwell on the unconscious mind, let's consider the unconscious senses. As Freud pointed out, in becoming human, we lost a lot of what it takes to be an animal. Freud was there referring to the sense of smell, use of which had become so much diminished by our rising from our four-legged state to our two-legged one. But it is not only in the sense of smell that animals excel.

Animals receive extraordinary quantities of information not only through their ears and noses, which are many times more acute than our own, but through magnetic and electrical senses also. Let me say that these are the 'dark senses', since they do not use visible light, upon which we so depend as human beings.

To take odour first, the German sheep-dog's sense of smell is about 1m times greater than our own, measured on the olfactometer. An expert in perfumes must be able to distinguish about thirty thousand nuances of scent. A dog, however, would find an individual smell in every being of this world. He will be able to distinguish his master's scent on a door-knob that has been handled by a hundred people who have passed through it subsequently. There is an anatomical element, in that the olfactory area, lying deep in the human nose takes up a mere five square centimetres, on average; whereas the German sheep-dog's measures about 150 square centimetres. However, the human sense of smell and discrimination is very much greater than is usually supposed, and can be increased by yoga-breathing and other exercises. Some people have this olfactory area naturally much enhanced or enlarged, and its sensitivity is also greatly increased in so called hysterical conditions, and in the hypnotic trance. In normal life, experiments have shown that a mother can distinguish by smell the tee-shirts of her children among many others after several washes.

It is a common experience particularly in the interview or analytical situation to experience a range of strong emotions during a discussion, and it is often possible to locate these in the sense of smell. The intuitive detective will smell out the criminal: Inspector Hound. I know an analyst who declares he can smell the thoughts and emotions of his client, of certain clients, and can almost read their minds by this means.

Harry Weiner in the 1960's published an impressive series of papers in the New York State Journal of Medicine in which he advanced a theory of schizophrenia. It has often been maintained that the over-sensitive individual picks up many cues from the people around him, body-language and so forth, that contradict overt verbal statements, and that this split in meaning on the part of the parents or others, between the latent and the manifest meaning of a statement, 'Stay out as long as you like Johnnie' 'But make sure you're back no later than half-past nine' leads to the double-bind conflict, and in certain people, to illness. Weiner maintains with an impressive array of evidence that this process is brought about principally by the agency of pheromones, which are highly-active hormonal substances given off by all living things, including human beings, that carry very fine degrees of discrimination and information with them. Edward Wilson, of 'Sociobiology' fame, said that they are the chief means of communication in most, possibly all, animals.

If a parent acts kind and smells cross, that is a double-bind; and the pheromones as well produce strong physiological reactions of emotion and 'feelings'. A person likely to become schizophrenic according to Weiner, is one who reacts consciously to these smells, which may have the seeming property of a radiation; and the one who also produces such pheromones in response to his conscious thought.

This means that the people around him, including his therapists, react more strongly towards him and more anomalously than with people whose pheromones do not abruptly alter, but who smell more 'tribal'. This gives rise to the 'schizophrenic aura', a strange feeling on the part of the doctor that is sometimes used to diagnose the condition. It leads too to the frightening situation, often reported when the patient seems to read the doctor's thoughts (instead of vice-versa!); this being done by pheromonal sensitivity. Eventually the victim of this gift goes into withdrawal, for the reason that the experience of life to him, and the accepted consensus of what reality is, are too much at variance; the rift between what people say is happening, and what he feels or perceives, is too great. It is possible that psychotropic drugs used in the treatment of schizophrenia work by cancelling or diminishing this primitive and apparently socially inappropriate sense of smell; a dark animal sense indeed.

Then there is another dark sense, the sense of hearing. Once again, the extraordinary sensitivity of domestic animals is well known, and that of animals in the wild. The spectrum of hearing in animals extends far beyond the human 16 to 20,000 cycles a second. Most fish, as you'd expect in the slow-moving medium of water, respond only to low-frequency vibrations, and to them human speech is like an ultrasonic twitter. On a summer night the air would be an intolerable din with the sounds of nightmoths and bats, were we ourselves normally able to hear ultrasonics. The ordinary brown bat's cry goes up to 50,000 cycles a second, which makes it able to echolocate the tiny particles of flies, mosquitoes and moths on which it lives. These insects, in their turn, by using the vibrations of their wings, send out jamming echoes which cause the bat to miss its mouthful.

Birds also can detect low frequency sounds inaudible to us by using sense organs on their legs; and the altered behaviour of many animals before an earthquake — the Chinese in particular have attempted earthquake prediction by studying the behaviour of animals — may partly be due to their sensitivity to the very low-frequency grinding sounds of the geological strata in slow movement, which also produces environmental electrical changes.

But is the human limit to the hearing-sense so set? We know how the spectrum changes with age, so that older people hear a different sound picture from younger ones. A blind person, perforce, must make use of the dark senses, and her self-training may very well uncover capabilities which look positively magical to the sighted. Certainly low-frequency echo-location comes into this. A blind person may stand still in a room and get a sense of its size and shape by means of the echoes of his heartbeat. In the sound ambience, the background-noise which is always going on, (for the air never ceases to be in motion), every object and movement casts its sound-shadow; and blind people learn to read the echo-shadow of houses, trees and may even recognise people this way before they speak or before they touch them.

A clairvoyant also in a trance-state may pick up sub-vocalisations in his clients, and converse, as it were, on the subliminal level with these. The above mentioned analyst who responded to smell-talk from his patients also says that he can sometimes detect sub-vocalisations and respond to them; most practitioners would maintain that sometimes they speak and listen into two voices at once, to latent and manifest spoken meaning at the same time, to explicit and implicit, to conscious and unconscious; and indeed this may be the basis of any deep relationship between people, that we communicate almost magically on many levels.

It has also been shown that human beings respond to weather in a manner which suggests it is the sound of the wind, the frequency of the stratospheric jet-vibration, which is responsible for certain types of illness; and it is also thought that some kinds of seasonal sickness in seaside towns is due to the subsonics produced by storms far out at sea, a kind of landlubber's sea-sickness, partly conveyed through reflection downwards from cloud-masses.

There is the sense of touch too, but I think we have not time to go into every aspect. Again, this is a dark sense: just as for a dog 'smell' and 'understand' might be synonymous, and for a barn-owl, 'hear' would be equivalent to 'know', so a fish would comprehend its world by 'smell' and 'touch' — indeed with its sensoria of the skin a fish would as it were touch the whole river in which it lived, as I like to think the stump of the severed head of Orpheus felt the river as his whole new body as he floated upon its ripples and currents, singing.

Then there are the electro-magnetic senses, which have long been well demonstrated in animals, and are now known to operate in humans. What we call visible light is of course electromagnetic, but it represents only a tiny sliver of the whole electro-magnetic spectrum. The eye is as it were cramped between lavender and violet, between the colour of veins and of arteries, while the electromagnetic spectrum itself ranges from the very long low-frequency waves that emanate from outer space — there is one sort, the Schumann waves, the distance between whose wave-crests is greater than the diameter of the earth; right down to the incredibly tiny and fast gamma rays; and indeed right down to the ultimate particles which are the basis of matter, which are also electromagnetic wave-forms.

Just as cats use smell to mark out territories, and birds use song, so do the electric discharges of the elephant-fish mark out its territory underwater. Tuna orient to direct-currents, and trout arrange themselves in obedience to magnetic fields, which also affect their fertility. The *Gymnarchus*, one of these electric fish, sends out a continuous 3-10 volt pulsed current, 300 a second, and this produces a spherical field of force round the animal which is like a sensitive radar globe. The feats of homing pigeons are well known, and it has been shown that the pigeon navigates substantially by responding to the geomagnetic field of the earth, and its recognisable anomalies. The clap of the pigeon's wings as it ascends produces a kind of radar-blare around it from the electrical effect — piezo-electricity — of the compression of the keratin in its wings — which serves to orient it within this field. Evidence of the electrical senses of animals shows their occurrence to be the rule rather than the exception.

But it has been the scientific orthodoxy that the only electromagnetism that human beings could respond to was visible light and radiant heat and (if it is electro-magnetical) gravity. It is clear that this is not so. Robin Baker at Manchester, studied the homing sense of his students in a series of excellent experiments in which he sent them carefully blindfolded out in buses, and required them to point the direction home. The women were substantially better than the men at exercising this dark sense, this black magic. Baker wondered whether it was geomagnetic, so fitted a proportion of his subjects with helmets on which were soldered bar-magnets. Indeed, these magnets apparently temporarily destroyed the homing-sense, and disoriented the subjects.

Now we may see perhaps where this is leading. What is our sense of home? What is our sense of a good place? We *feel* that it is good. But how much of that feeling is perception, in the dark senses; for instance, in the magnetic sense. How do we express such inchoate feelings? By symbols. By symbolization we indicate that this mountain is the breast of our mother-goddess, who will shelter and nurture us, for her magnetism feels right, and we can find our way home to her even in the dark.

I know several dowsers, and have been taught dowsing myself; this is probably also an electromagnetic response to the static field produced by water flowing. Thus I know my mother hill by my dark senses also as a place which will, like my own mother's breast, provide me with water, and with water, fertile soil.

There is also no doubt whatsoever that people respond to the electrostatic charge of the air, its ionisation. Negative ionisation is beneficent, certain rocks and waterfalls will produce it; thus my mother-mountain gives me the energy of life, she gives me a zing in the wind that breathes from her; and the desert beyond, whose hot sands strip off the electrons from the nitrogen atoms of the air and produce a terrible positively-ionised sirocco; why, that place is full of demons.

That is the transpersonal mother of my environment, but my personal mother too, why she smells good, and she feels right, and she has the right electromagnetism! It turns out to be true that every human being is surrounded by an aura, as in the old tales; the subtle body, the etheric body. The head, the brain; the heart; the womb; are places of immense electrical activity; and the skin itself is made of what is called an electret substance; that is one like a magnet, only electrical charges stand in it, and move around in it, altering with posture and blood-supply. The skin forms a dialectric waveguide, in the electronic parlance, and the beating heart an oscillating circuit, with the blood and the bones; an adjustable circuit that can be tuned by emotion and feeling, by blood and glandular supply, by posture and gesture. The skin and the lungs emit an immense population of physiologically active and sub-odorous molecules, part of whose activity is supplied by electric charge or radiation, as in the device we call a maser or laser. Thus, surrounding the body is a complex chemical cloud, upon which pour microwaves or black body radiation from the pulsing heart, and the cloud pulses with sub-visible fluorescences, which can by some people, under certain conditions, be seen. The clinician Kilner could diagnose by aura, and invented special goggles to help others not so gifted to use this ability. This subvisible cloud of glory is, in scientific terms, an amplifying pheromone maser which receives EM radiation also from the outside world, and responds to it, wobbling, as it were, in the environmental field, like rainbow raisins in a vibrantly coloured jelly.

No wonder — you may have seen a Channel 4 programme on this subject recently — that people have begun to wonder exactly what effect all the microwave and other radiation unleashed into the atmosphere by domestic and defence radio has on the human being. No effect while it was thought we were shielded from all EM except visible light, heat and possibly gravity; but now it is understood the living body is an ineffably sensitive electrochemical radio-receiver and transmitter, microwave pollution gives grave cause for concern.

Once one looks for these effects they are there. Bones are healed by magnetism and pulsed electric fields; lung cancer cured by tiny battery implant; suicides increase where the high-tension wires run; unearthly glows of gamma-rays seen in the vicinity of nuclear reactors; a sinister hint of electro-magnetic microwave warfare, with the Americans and the Russians beaming at each other immense quantities of energy by means of semi-secret microwave transmitters in both hemispheres; frequencies which are supposed to have deleterious mental effects. Now the classic radiation fantasies of schizophrenics are beginning to look sane. In case this is beginning to sound too mad, let me summarise the electric effects operating now, on you, in this room, that have been demonstrated to have physiological and therefore potentially conscious effects, and are a part of the tone or background to everybody's thoughts and fantasies, and, potentially, also, capable of entering conscious knowledge.

Under the heading of 'electric stimulation' we have first the atmospheric fields, which include aero-ionic currents, which affect your sense of touch, respiration and blood-pressure, and which vary with cosmic radiation, soil radioactivity, fluctuations in the potential gradient of the air and the earth; with humidity, temperature, atmospheric pressure and the presence of metal conductors.

Then there is the plain potential gradient of your own height, about 200v between head and feet; this changes according to how well or badly you're earthed, with the ions, with the tone of your nerves, with the feedback between yourself and ionic currents, with the topography of houses and trees, with the weather; clear, air, fog, rain, impending rain, thunderstorm, snowfall; with the daily, yearly and sun-spot pulses, with earth currents.

Then there are the geophysical fields, and these include the influence of the conductivity of the soil, which has an effect on the rate at which your electricity leaks, which in turn has a feedback effect between you and the environment, and is changed by rock composition, water content, porosity and permeability of what's under you, and the soil structure. Also the travelling earth-currents, with which you interact, change with local geology, the presence of conductors, faults, folds, subterranean caves, ore bodies, stratification, ground water level, distribution and shape of standing and running water, with the magnetic field and the atmospheric field, the presence of rails, pipes, power circuits, foundations of houses and their shapes, etc.

Remember, these are all things that act measurably on us, and therefore of which we are potentially conscious.

We also have our own electric field, its polarity between head and feet, left and right sides, its daily fluctuations, altered if you approach a conductor, with your own nervous tone, dust potentials, and all the effects already mentioned. Your field interacts with that of everybody else in the room and with the environment around you above your heads and below your feet. Your skin potentials, a part of this field, include diffusion potentials, membrane potentials, injury potentials, compression potentials, these are direct current; your pulsing, or alternating currents include your heart, diaphragm and brain-electricity, the skin nerve-endings and your muscular movement. Your skin resistance fluctuates with posture, temperature, humidity, your sweat, daily rhythm and yearly, with drugs and emotion; there are effects from capacitance changes in the body, photo-chemical and photo-dynamic effects, the menstrual cycle, and the presence of animals and plants and fellow humans, besides interaction with everything already mentioned.

Then we proceed to magnetic stimulation, which affects everything, including the dimensions of the body (magneto-striction), the fluid crystals of the cell's protoplasm, ionic movements within it, elotrolysis, oxidation and nerve induction currents, and with what kind of magnetic field it is, which varies with locale, and changes hourly, with the sun and the moon, to say nothing of magnetic storms. There is also induced magnetism in conductors, rocks, lava flows; a kind of echo effect.

There is simply not time to go further with this, or the EM, acoustic and pheromone effects — the great webwork in which we live of unconscious senses.

Readers of C.S. Lewis's *Out of the Silent Planet* may remember the moment when the kidnapped philologist Ransom leaves earth's atmosphere and is surprised to find that the darkness of outer space is not dark as science teaches at all, but full of vibrant and tingling radiations that are to him health itself. This is also the Medieval image of outer space, and in his non-fiction work *The Discarded Image* Lewis also speaks of a walk by starlight, and how the medieval man would imagine the heavens, He says: 'Darkness, our own darkness, draws the veil and we catch a glimpse of the high pomps within; the vast, lighted concavity filled with music and life' for the space of night is not empty but alive with beings and influences that are all-pervading, and we live within sound of the Music of the Spheres. Before moving on, let me compare this with a picture afforded by more recent contemporary science, of something of the appearance of the real world once the accustomed limits of our senses are transcended; a picture of what is really there, the environment in which we truly live.

'If I could wave a magic wand before you and give you the power to perceive all the invisible sights and inaudible sounds around you at this moment, what would you see and what would you hear? Shall we try to query. Close your eyes for an instant. I wave the wand. Now look around you. The room is ablaze with dazzling light. The chairs, the tables, the floor, the ceiling, shades of red, yellow, green and blue such as you have never in your life seen before. Your clothes are on fire with a million microscopic rainbow flames. Your nose, your cheeks, your hands are shining ruby, emerald and sapphire. You open your mouth and a shaft of amethyst light beams out before you. The air itself sparkles as if millions of miniature meteors are darting all around you, as if a cluster of sky rockets had just exploded. This is the realm of the unseen and the unheard that shines and pulsates around you and within you unperceived during every moment of your life. But though invisible and inaudible, it is just as real as everything that you actually see and hear and feel. It is the domain in which scientists are beginning to discover more and more of the secrets of life and of the universe.'

Of course everybody realises that in this passage, for the purpose of metaphor, (a word which means 'change-bearing' or 'bringing across',) these radiances and resonances have been transposed into the octaves of visible light, in much the same way as Liszt would transpose the multiplex orchestrations of a Beethoven symphony into music for the piano.

What, however, would one experience in the presence of such an opening? Well, everybody knows, in their own way. As Blake says, 'if the doors of perception were cleans'd, then everything would appear as it is, infinite.' It is certain that such experiences, since they engage the whole person, every fibre of their being, carry not merely reference with them, as in the ordinary world, but deep meaning too. One might have the vision of a rainbow light, but it would be that kind of rainbow which has traditionally seemed to the religious the automatic reaction of space to the appearance of Deity.

One might experience in the presence of an event that so filled the accustomed senses and therefore the mind, an episode of black depression, as the accustomed operation of those usual senses became, as the mystics say in their exercises 'ligatured'. As a great analyst, John Layard, used to say, 'Depression is withheld knowledge.' It might then be that that depression was a resistance to a state of entranced understanding, for we know that in what is crudely called hypnotism, a way into trance-formation is to establish which of the five is the most usually-used sense, (most often sight in this culture) and to supplement it with imaginative evocations of a less-used sense, smell or touch, maybe by means of hypnotic passes.

Then the experience grows and extends into a synaesthesia, in which the barriers between the senses are down, the dark senses join with the visual and 'when the bells begin/Song colours, colour sings', the fog 'tastes a misty shade of purple' one hears 'the white voice/of the water in love.'

Now your theorist will say that synaesthesia is a literary device used by certain poets; it is not; it is the way the info comes in. It is like the person who has been released from his chains in Plato's cave, where he with his fellows around him has always watched shadows, with his back to the light; now he runs out into the true light and is dazzled; and when he returns his companions, who have all the time been watching shadows thrown on the cave back-wall, cannot understand his stories of how 'the morning light comes creaking down again' and that above is 'Azure: blue sound/of the inexplicable/horizon'. If we cannot cope with what is out there, or if we have not somehow seen it ourselves, then we will diagnose a psychosis, and more firmly bind and double-bind our companion to his bench, his head facing the one way. The Vedas speak of the One Sense, which is divided and diminished in the physical man; it is possible that synaesthesia is the natural mode of pre-birth perception. After all in adult sex, the touch of the lover can be both light and perfume; and the hypnotic trance, with its moulding reflex, has been shown to be an analogue of womb-life.

It is in this sense that imagination is reality; we encounter a sensation, a mystical experience, a sexual orgasm spread out of the bedroom into our lives, which we may call 'being in love', or any deep sensation which has dark as well as light about it, and in order to preserve this experience, and to make a way back to re-experiencing it, we make an analogue with our imagination, or an analogue is made in us. This analogue is a touchstone or magic object that carries with it that experience, it is an aide memoire, it is an obsession, a fetish, a poem, a religion, a symbol, a doorway to a further reality, a dream that can be worked with, it is the praxis to the vision, the knowledge that there is more to the world than the agreed reality principle affords.

Thus it must be obvious that the blackness of the Goddess is just such a symbol, a 'deep but dazzling darkness' 'noire et pourtant lumineuse' black and shining with it, black but comely, 'Thy plants are an orchard of pomegranates, with pleasant fruits; camphire, with spikenard, spikenard and saffron; calamus and cinnamon, with all trees of frankincense; myrrh and aloes, with all the chief spices: a fountain of gardens, a well of living waters' as the Song of Songs has it; just snuff up those pheromones.


III.

Why then is this Goddess black? Let us say again because she is the symbol of all the things we could know in the blackness beyond visible sight. Because she represents all the forces that surround us which are not perceived in the eyes, but which extend from the visible spectrum into unexplored modes of being. Because she is the Goddess of the vision of the night, the dream, and all those things we see by inner light when our eyes are closed. Because she is the Goddess of Second Sight, and of First Sight too, the touch in the womb, and the lover's light of touch in bed. She is the Goddess of intimacy, of being 'in touch'. And perhaps because she lives in the blackness which men have created by their blindness she is therefore sometimes represented as blind, the Goddess of Justice, the blind Sheckinah weeping for the exiled people, Jung's blind animal figure, Salome.

And what other symbol would there be in such an almost purely-visual culture as our own as the symbol of the rich darkness? and in a patriarchal culture of the female mediator, anima and anima mundi, the welcomer to neglected riches, the initiator? The legends say that Adam's wife, before Eve was created, was Black Lilith, and that she coupled with Adam to produce dreams and imaginations, and that the offspring of these were all the legions of demons. But where do these demons come from? We know Freud's opinion on this in 'A Neurosis of Demoniacal Possession': 'One thing, however, is certain: gods can turn into evil spirits when new gods supplant them . . . It requires no great analytic insight to divine that God and the Devil were originally one and the same, a single figure which was later split into two bearing opposed characteristics'. Our Goddess has also been thus divided into Good White and Demonic Black.

Indeed does our almost solely visual culture recall the Thebes of cerebral and sighted King Oedipus, the king living in unconscious sin with his mother Jocasta, while the city and Kingdom decays around them full of plagues, threats, anxiety, peril and strange portents.

Could it be that Oedipus' sin was knowing carnally the one woman only, the woman who bore him physically, and whom he could *see*? Before his sin could be eased, it was necessary for him to put out those misleading eyes ('I stumbled when I saw') and to descend into the kindly darkness of earth at Colonus. It was as though he would not know his second mother. He had to know the invisible, the Supernal Mother. He had to know the second mother. And this would not be the Eve to his Adam, the mother of visible children; but the black mother Lilith, mother of invisible children, children of the spirit, of spiritual imagination.

Let me put this into an anthropological context. The anthropologist Chris Knight has been showing in published work that behind possibly all tribal legend and folklore in Europe, Australia, America and Asia there lies a common duality. There are two pulses in culture, which relate to the woman, as the source of that without which there cannot be any culture at all, human beings. He contends, as Penelope Shuttle and myself do in *The Wise Wound*, that the fertility cycle of the woman, and consequently the whole series of deep psychological experiences which are normally unconscious without knowledge of that cycle, has two culminations of a differing and opposing kind.

One is ovulation, when the creation of physical children is an option; and the other is menstruation, when the woman is full of strange energies and depths and is very frequently treated as an ill person or a tabooed witch, as our book shows.

The taboos on menstruation are very complex and strong. It is said that denying this experience its validity is one of the chief ways in which women are manipulated by the patriarchal non-menstruating culture; and the strength of the taboos on considering menstruation a positive resource is encapsulated in George Devereux's aphorism on this subject in a famous paper on the Mohave Indians 'You don't bother to tie up a harmless puppy with steel cables'.

Chris Knight shows that ovulation, traditionally associated with the full moon in its bright whiteness, is associated with family behaviour, physical children, offspring, their upbringing in the culture, with union with an exogamic husband, with public tribal rites; while the menstruation is associated with vision, shamanism, imagination, prophetic speech, association with fellow-women; the male partner is the brother, and there is endogamic, intra-family behaviour and rites, and a return to the mother's hearth. A frequent symbol of this return is the entering of a paradise inhabited by oracular serpents, or being swallowed by a great Rainbow serpent who takes all the menstruating women up to heaven.

To give just one great example of this pattern appearing in sophisticated European culture, there is the poet Yeats' *A Vision* partly originating in automatic writing by his wife on their honeymoon, and the system of thought or 'stylistic arrangement of experience' which led to his late, great poetry . Its chief symbol is the Great Wheel of the Moon's Quarters, which represents movements towards and away from physical incarnation.

Let me recapitulate: the interplay of full moon as emblem of ovulation, incarnation, husband, social symbolism, public and human speech, secondary process; crosses in interplay with dark moon, menstruation, male sibling, magic children, transfiguration, prophetic speech, shamanism, primary and secret process. This might be said to fulfil in a 'stylistic arrangement' 'the whole possible range of human experience'. Yeats himself said of his magic 'All, all those gyres and cubes and midnight things/Are but a new expression of her body . . . / And now my utmost mystery is out' ('The Gift of Harun al-Rashid').

IV

Shall we find another name for this Goddess? Black is usually associated with death, not life. Freud in *Civilisation and*

225

*its Discontents* remarked, 'Men have brought their powers of subduing the forces of nature to such a pitch that by using them they could now very easily exterminate one another to the last man . . . And now it may be expected that the other of the two "heavenly forces", eternal Eros, will put forth his strength so as to maintain himself alongside of his equally immortal adversary which is Thanatos, Death.'

Freud however was not noted as a feminist; his primary forces were male; for feminism, he implied, for the mysteries of women, we must go to the poets. Preferably the women poets, but I have to quote here Robert Graves, who after all knew the black Goddess, and said of her in a late essay that she was merely a whisper among the fortunate so far, but that she 'promised a new age, and a new pacific bond between men and women'. This is Eros.

And by a paradox, it will be seen that the White Goddess, presiding over the population of our over-populated world, with the many material problems that will and do entail, the goddess of physical fertility, because she is the only aspect of the Goddess that the patriarchal culture will allow, that is, women as human breeding-stock, not as equal partners; has evolved to become the goddess of rampant materialism and territorialism, and therefore of war, and thus the representative of Thanatos. In a sense this was always so, for as soon as we are born we begin to die; and who has not been made to feel older as their children grow. The White Goddess then is involved with secular time. And the black Goddess of invisible love, of the dark senses, the senses of the night, the lovers' senses, returns as our mysterious partner, eternal Eros, eternal because timeless, of the timeless interior world.

The Freudians here will have noticed that I am counselling desublimation. Up to that point, I have been in fair Freudian accord. As David Bakan points out, Freud was in agreement with the Cabbalah, which hints 'at least symbolically, at the psychoanalytic notion that the depths of sexual satisfaction are in having intercourse with the Mother. The sex act in the *Zohar* is symbolic of the relationship to the supernal Mother', the Goddess. I have also quoted Freud on the splitting of the God-Image into acceptable and unacceptable, Good-Evil.

I would now continue to distinguish the two images by suggestion that the way to the White Goddess is by genital cathexis, the man's way, investment of sexual energy in the phallus, conscious senses, striving, sublimation, ideals, territory and state religion. It is the province of the genital orgasm at ovulation, that is most likely to lead to the conception of physical children. Thus the taboo on menstruation in most world-religions.

The way to the Black Goddess on the other hand is by genital de-cathexis the total or skin orgasm in the man, which is more a spreading, a seeping, a merging than an ejaculation, by desublimation the development of the dark, nightsensitive senses, by an interest not in abstract ideas but in concrete particulars, by simply being there. I speak of the man's approach to the otherness of feminine nature; in the woman this is surely an approach to her own core-nature, by re-instating its completeness, and sexually would be differentiated in the different quality of orgasmic experience at ovulation or at menstruation.

How then shall we desublimate the visual-genital cathexis, glaring eye and rampant phallus, and develop our unconscious senses and enjoy a new being; our animal senses, while still remaining human? This was the reason the ancient Egyptians worshipped their theriomorphs, their gods with the heads of ibis and dog. Paracelsus remarked, and I call his healing blend of magic and rational medicine to witness, that our animal soul is 'the lost daughter, the Kingdom of Heaven on Earth'.

One could certainly join a society for practical magic, and worship the Black Goddess overtly. One should find a very good one; Yeats belonged to a good one for more than thirty years, and still his final initiation was under the auspices of his newly-married wife. Another poet, Ted Hughes, entered into hermetic exercises of clairvoyant visualisation, probably in the system of Franz Bardon, which explicitly counsels one to feel and establish the electromagnetic polarities in oneself and one's partner, and to breathe through the skin, that perceptual organ of the unconscious mind, surrounding oneself with meditated colours of crackling electricity.

One might take this in a different direction, and study bio-feedback, and the conscious alteration of normally unperceived physiological events, such as skin resistance. If one increases skin resistance by relaxation, this can be signalled by a small instrument that gives out a tone. Then one can guide oneself into deeper and deeper relaxation and thus open oneself to synaesthesias and uncommon experiences of all sorts. There is biofeedback by guided imagery, and sensitivity training also.

One could join the Witches, who know what 'raising power' means, and do so raise unseen but actual power in their circles, and one might then be inducted into sky clad astral journeys by the touch of a gifted practitioner or High Priestess, for their religion is of the Moon; that is to say, into waking dreams.

One might practice Yoga, and by breathing open all the Nadis, or fine nerves of the soul.

One might very well go into analysis, and if it is a Jungian analysis, practice the work of the imagination, called by Jungians 'active imagination' which is identical to the creative process of the artist.

Or one might become what everyone in their soul is, an artist, and learn to read in the magic mirror of one's chosen medium the great Chiffernschrift or runic script of nature, 'that marvellous secret writing that one finds everywhere, upon wings, egg-shells, in clouds, in snow, crystals and the structures of stones . . .' under the direction of a Master such it was my own good fortune to meet in whom one sees 'a singular light burns in his glances when the great runic text lies before us and he stares into our eyes to see whether within us also has risen the constellation which will make the figure visible and comprehensible'. That is the constellation risen in the body of Night, the black goddess, that is only dark to those who will not see. And in the enhancement of one's vision one might enter into the worship of the incarnate Goddess directly by Yeats's means 'All, all the gyres and cubes and midnight things/Are but a new expression of her body/ And now my utmost mystery is out . . .'; and in the sexual trance, particularly at the magic and alchemical time of menstruation, when the neglected powers arise, allow to unravel some of the knots and mysteries of one's own nature and origin, amid the invisible yet perceived radiant cloud of the sexual conjunction, among the pheromones and radiances of that time which lovers know and the lords of this world deny; of the great schooling of the womb experience, in which we proceed from protozoon to mammal and human in a mere nine months, a feat that took many millions of years on the evolutionary scale, in this timeless world; and in the blood of that time read the mysteries of birth and of the death of one's surrogate and sustenance through that evolutionary feat, the providing Grail of the Placenta, like a brother and a Lord who dies to bring you to life and breath. And to know the simple mystery of being there, incarnate, present in the universe, for the presence or play of the lingam in the yoni is only one special case of the human being's presence and play in the living and nurturing world; and perhaps in this divine beyond the agonies of Oedipus how to live in sinless intercourse with one's second mother, Gaia, the world, reading her code as it unfolds in those inner depths which are the outer ones as well. And, above all, as all men and women are truly poets within — think of the wonderful uncalculated poetry of dreams and spontaneous fantasy that feeds on all that is unconscious in us, in the process of becoming conscious, — believe the poets, whose conscience is language and speculation. Believe in poetry, and where it comes from:

> She laughs aloud and bares her teeth again, and cries:
> Now that I am all black and running in my richness
> And knowing it a little I have learnt
> It is quite wrong to be all white always;
> And knowing it a little, I shall take great care
> To keep a little black about me somewhere . . .
> Drenched in the mud pure white rejoiced,
> From this collision were new colours born
> And in their slithering passage to the sea
> The shrugged-up riches of deep darkness sang.

# 15. Why the Bomb is Real but not True

Somehow it would be a relief if Einstein turned out to be wrong, since his physics seems to have created a world in which the atomic bomb not only exists, but in which his ideas and authority appear to make it easier to use that bomb.

What I mean by this I can only sketch, and it would he better for a professional physicist to describe these ideas. I hope the reader will forgive any gross errors I make here. But as I understand the matter, there seems to be not only a connection but also a feedback between a certain monstrous cosmic detachment there is in Relativity, which is held to describe the ground of our universe, and modern behaviour. Relativity has not only given us the bomb but its mechanistic aspects are no improvement on other cold-blooded systems of thought which bring despair into the world. Without Einstein's work, the bomb would not have seemed possible, and so would not have been looked for; and he himself got caught up in the terrible accident of the weapon's creation, and recommended its first use to Truman.

Should one blame Einstein? It is such a curiously-named theory: 'Relativity'. As Bertrand Russell remarked of it, the theory is 'wholly concerned *to exclude what is relative* and arrive at a statement of physical laws that shall in no way depend on the circumstances of the observer' (my italics). Einstein was not able to obtain a unified field theory which *related* human beings to the universe or each other. In David Bohm's words, the theory 'still retains the essential features of a mechanistic order, for the fundamental entities . . . are assumed to be connected with each other only through external relationships . . . relativity theory requires strict causality (or determinism) . . .'[1] So it appears that Einstein's basic work should be called 'Irrelativity', and like other mechanistic theories it is a recipe for alienation.

To the honest scientist, professing truth at all costs, this shouldn't matter, if the theory can predict experimental results which verify it. But does it? Because the physical universe seems to correspond to certain of its predictions, including the prediction that the atom can be split to release enormous power, that in itself means no more than that the theory uses a *selection of the data.* Our atomic age has seen that this selection has only negative significance to the human situation, the human data. Einstein wrote: 'Perception of this world by thought, leaving out everything subjective, became partly consciously, partly unconsciously, my supreme aim.' Another direction of mind might very well not have brought such encouragement to the generals.

Other selections of scientific data are verifiable too, and may be full of the energy of subjective, human meaning, as well as the energy of the objective universe, rather than the detachment and vacuousness of the thought-experiments of relativistic travels through the cosmic vacuum at the speed of light.

For instance, there is the fact that the sun, a star (which it is customary to describe as working like an enormous H-bomb), gives out its light by passing hydrogen nuclei along a chain of processes. It is also true that the reactions called 'photosynthesis' in the green leaves of plants are precisely comparable to this chain reaction, but on a slower timescale. Photosynthesis in the plants, then, receives this light on the cooled sun-matter we call the earth, and turns it into human life via the whole food-chain.[2] This image from science is one worth dwelling on, and its consideration might bring better consequences than those of 'Irrelativity'. It is as though the sunlight creates the receptacle that catches and seeks to understand it. Or, to take a more homely image, it is like a baby smiling at the nipple full of milk that has created the tender folds of flesh it smiles with. And Mother smiles back.

Accepting and contemplating this image, subjectively and objectively, seeing and wondering, can lead us to know that we are part of the continuum that begins with starlight; and issues now in our attempt to feel the meaning of that starlight, here, on this page woven of star-substance. We have no reason, except Irrelativity, which is sometimes called schizoid thinking, for standing outside this complex implicated interrelationship of everything we know.

I'm implying that the theories or mental images of human geniuses may, to our sorrow, cause working scientists who follow them to over-select data, and thus to create inventions that correspond to and perpetuate that theory or image or alienation. Because Einstein, 'partly consciously, partly unconsciously', showed that the bomb was possible, and because Einstein did not wish (according to the quotation I have given above) to turn his mathematics so far as for them to be relative to human existence, lo and behold, we have a bomb and a near-intolerable state of world. Perhaps, as Anthony Storr has suggested, Relativity was a reflection of a particular kind of failure in Einstein's personal psychology. If so, then it is a mental disorder that has spread like a virus.

Perhaps it follows that if we have a beneficent image in physics, which inspires our scientists to make discoveries of another kind, then we shall have a different world. If we have a human image, and not a mechanistic one, then we stand a better chance of living in an integrated human world; if we have a magical image (such as the amateur one I have offered about the starlight, which is pure Kabalah) then perhaps we shall have a magical world. Images, paradigms, are like tuning devices. With the right 'subjective' image to guide us, we can tune our circuits to resonate with a new, but still objectively-verifiable universe.

I have been very much impressed, particularly as a poet, from the first time I heard about it some ten years ago, with the physics built on quantum theory of David Bohm who worked with Einstein. Broadly speaking, he does indicate just such a beneficent image in physics. He proposes, and it fits the facts better than Relativity alone does, a universe of infinite *implicated* relationships, which could be called a holo-movement, and that the world we experience is like a writing, signature, or holograph of this holo-movement. A holograph is a picture which, if you take only one small piece of it, from that piece you can nevertheless still project the entire picture. This means that the image of the whole is present in every part of the holograph.

> That is to say, the form and structure of the entire object may be said to be *enfolded* within each region of the photographic record. When one shines light on any region, this form and structure are then unfolded, to give a recognisable image of the whole object once again. We proposed that a new notion of order is involved [in this image] which we called the *implicate order* . . . In terms of the implicate

order one may say that everything is enfolded into everything. This contrasts with the *explicate order* now dominant in physics in which things are *unfolded* in the sense that each thing lies only in its own particular region . . . and outside the regions belonging to other things . . . our basic proposal was then that *what is* is the holo-movement.[3]

In our ordinary world, manifested under the control of dominant images, we do not usually see how each entity is implicated with every other entity. The Buddhist Sutra which describes this would be taken by most scientists as a 'subjective fantasy': 'In the heaven of Indra there is said to be a network of jewels so arranged that if you look in one you see all the others reflected in it.' But with this fresh image proposed in quantum physics, scientists are looking for experimental verification, and finding it. For example, Alain Aspect at the Institut d'Optique Théorique et Appliquée seems to have demonstrated what is called technically instantaneous 'action-at-a-distance'. This appears to mean that if distant particles somehow 'know' or instantaneously resonate to what is happening to each other, then some signals can travel faster than the speed of light, which Relativity says cannot be so. So in the important case of 'action-at-a-distance', which Einstein found 'ghostly and absurd', too subjective and mystical, he appears to have been wrong.

The work has gone further than this. We have been speaking so far about the apparently outward world of theoretical physics, which for years has been taking on a more and more 'mental' aspect, open to the layman such as myself in such books as Fritjof Capra's *Tao of Physics* (Wildwood House, 1975), or the older and much more powerful *Symphony of Life* by Donald Hatch Andrews (Unity Books, 1966). In a recent book, *The Holographic Paradigm* (ed. Ken Wilber; Shambhala, 1982) Bohm in interviews speaks most powerfully about these matters, and amusingly about the jumps of dislocated thought scientists make to avoid integrations beyond the fractured physics they have inherited.

However, as I've suggested, Bohm's image of the universe as an implicated order of interacting fields and vibrations gives us permission to seek out new matters, which implicate in their holo-movement the whole human being. In atomised physics and nuclear strategy, the human being is merely a megakill number. Human beings and their subjectivity are not relevant to military science or to ordinary physical science: in this the scientists bear equal responsibility with the generals. In science, as in war, subjectivity is closed off. But what if this subjectivity, the inner world, is also seen as part of the implicate order, and as arising from it?

Here the neurosurgeon Karl Pribram has found a great deal of evidence that the human brain works as a holograph too, resonating to the universe as a tuned circuit resonates to radio waves. This must mean that subjective experience (as opposed to observations or measurements obtained from external instruments) is a mode of knowledge too, or can be. In Bohm's words again: 'In the implicate order we have to say that mind enfolds matter in general and therefore the body in particular. Similarly the body enfolds not only the mind but also in some sense the entire material universe',[4] and 'In the old physics, matter (which was the only reality) was completely mechanical, leaving no room for mind. But if, according to the new physics, everything is enfolded in everything else, then there is no real separation of domains.'[5] Or, as William Blake had it: 'If the doors of perception were cleansed, then everything would appear as it is, infinite', and 'Every man and every woman is a Star.'

Unfortunately, even though the bomb arises from a partial truth and a crudely mechanised physics, no concept, however magical or complete, will automatically switch off that mechanism once it starts ticking. But if we are lucky, and work aright, the deep and shared subjectivity of right feeling can make that bomb's use inconceivable, in a world of verified wonders. We are all working scientists, who follow, with our life-experiments, the images that the geniuses of our culture give us to work with: '*Weber:* Life is then a continuum; everything is alive? *Bohm:* Everything is alive."

**Notes**

I    David Bohm, *Wholeness and the Implicate Order* (Routledge & Kegan Paul, 1980) pp. 174, 176.

2 George Wald, 'Stars and Living Organisms: a Metabolic Connexion', Penguin Science Survey 1968.

3 Bohm, *Wholeness, pp.* 177-8.

4 ibid., p. 209.

5 *The Holographic Paradigm p.* 194.

6 ibid., p. 195.

# 16. Mesmer's Vision:
# The Shamanic Heart of the Romantic Movement


A way of describing the cultural passage from matriarchy to patriarchy, as represented in the Oedipus story, is in Charles Davy's words, as a transition from a participating mode of consciousness to the onlooker mode. I.A. Richards in *Science and Poetry* (1926) said that 'the central dominant change may be described as the *Neutralisation of Nature*'. Davy enlarges on this. He says that we are today more or less under the influence of the onlooker-consciousness, which I describe as the Oedipal stand-offishness, but even so 'we do not experience nature as neutral, but as hostile or friendly, cheerful or melancholy, turbulent or calm. These are some of nature's 'moods', and in our *experience* of them there is nothing to suggest that we have put them there.'[1] We can in fact, he says, on most occasions distinguish nature's moods from our own, except in very depressed and/or very open states. The romantic position is that nature's moods are not pathetic fallacy or projection, but true unconscious perception of outside forces that act upon our mind-bodies. I shall hope to show how science supports this common human experience, providing that we do not use scientific paradigms that have evolved to justify industrialisation and consumerism; that is, providing we do not obey science's morbid streak

N. O. Brown tells us that Freud believed that maturity was signalled by the individual having renounced the 'pleasure principle' and 'having adjusted himself to reality, he seeks his object in the outer world.' The Romantic contention is that such a renunciation is not maturity, that the feeling of enthusiastic pleasure is a stimulus to the imagination which is not egoistic, and that maturity evolves by relating inner to outer, and conscious to unconscious. Again Brown questions what a non-morbid science would look like: 'It would presumably be erotic . . . its aim would not be mastery over the world but union with nature. And its means would not be economising but erotic exuberance. And finally, it would be based on the whole body and not just a part . . .'[2] That is, it would involve all the senses, and not maintain the tyranny of the eye. Ernst Lehrs points out how science has withdrawn its field of sense-perception. He quotes Eddington, who says in his *Philosophy of the Physical World* that scientific knowledge of the universe could not only have been reached by visual sensation alone, but by the simplest form of visual sensation, colourless and non-stereoscopic. That is, to the seeing of a one-eyed, colour blind man. 'Out of everything that the world brings to the totality of our senses, there remains nothing more than mere movements . . . The picture of the world is a purely Kinematic one . . . all the qualities brought to us by our senses, such as colour, tone, warmth, density and even electricity and magnetism, are reduced to mere movement-changes.'[3]

N. O. Brown agrees: 'The mentality which was able to reduce nature to "a dull affair, soundless, scentless, colourless: merely the hurrying of material endlessly, meaninglessly" — Whitehead's description — is lethal . . .' Thus modern science confirms Ferenczi's aphorism: 'Pure intelligence is thus a product of dying, or at least of becoming mentally insensitive. and is therefore in principle madness.'[4] Freud's diagnosis is thus supported: Oedipus is mad.

This madness of the one-eyed, colour-blind school teacher of science can expunge in an individual the direct childhood experience of the romantic imagination, the memory of erotic exuberance and the experience of a natural non-morbid intellectual process. Goethe demanded the abilities of a child[5] in his science of 'exact sensorial fantasy' which unites *Sensualismus* and *Spiritualismus, volupté* and *connaissance.*

We can perhaps see in the experience of another great man of the present age how a potential visionary feels himself robbed of the potentialities of belief by what is called 'objective science'. The Nobel prize-winning novelist William Golding describes his West Country boyhood in a short autobiographical passage in his 1983 Nobel Lecture.[6] He speaks of his discovering and engaging himself in a 'magic place' among rocks on the seashore. 'I early became acquainted with the wonderful interplay of earth, moon and sun, and enjoying them at the same time as I was assured that *scientifically you could not have action at a distance.*' (My italics). There was a particular moon-phase — this must have been at either full or new moon — when the tide was lowest and revealed to him 'a small recess which I remember as a cavern.' There was plenty of life all around on the seashore, yet the life revealed here was special 'by an influence from the sky... this last recess before the even more mysterious deep sea had strange inhabitants which I found nowhere else.' He felt in watching the creatures there, not merely sympathy or empathy, but 'passionate recognition of a living thing in all its secrecy and strangeness.' They were as real as he was, and 'It was as if the centre of our universe was there *for my eyes to reach at like hands, to seize on by sight* . . . a discovery, a meeting, more than interest or pleasure. They were life, we together were delight itself . . .' (My italics).

Golding carried away the memory of this experience (in which the senses joined hands and the visible became visionary) like a private interior pleasure to his home far away from the sea. In sleepless and fearful nights when the supernatural seemed to plague him, he 'would work out the phase of the moon, returning in thought to the slither and clamber among the weeds of the rocks.' In dreams or reverie there were times when he actually seemed to visit, and 'I found myself before the cavern watching the moon-dazzle as the water sank . . .' The effect of this daydream was beneficial, for he was comforted by 'the magical beauty of our common world.'

Alas, when he went back, something had cleaned the recess of all life. It was no longer magical, it seemed no more than an empty socket, it was ironically clean. Golding wonders whether this sterilisation of this boyhood vision was a natural process or 'Was it sewage or chemicals more deadly that killed my childhood's bit of magic and mystery? I cannot tell and it does not matter.' But it does matter. He speaks of it as an environment problem, of pollution impoverishing the planet; this is true, and the cause then would be the carelessness and aggression of 'morbid science'. It reads also like a process of growing up in that scientifically assured world which at that time denied the influence of the moon and sky on living creatures and their perceptions, and for the cause of this we look to the same source.

William Golding went on to create his other magical worlds in literature, but to many they are haunted by the irony of disbelief. What is a magic if it can be destroyed, and one can rely no longer on the eyes touching like hands seeing like eyes, since it is not part of the scientific world picture as it is presented to children of educable age that they should do so? If there is no 'action at a distance' and no external reality to these visions, how can one grow up except in a state of irony and regret? Golding became a Nobel laureate because he stated for a majority consensus a dilemma which exists in the world as we have made it. Here, science working two ways, by polluting both the external and the internal environment, cancelled the romantic vision of a young child who, despite the comfort of the vision that worked on him internally to allow him to marvel at the miracles of the commonplace, 'was assured' that what he felt could not be true.

We have no great romantic inheritance in England, and it is arguable that this came about because the industrial revolution flourished early here, and science developed in obedience to it. When the ordinary person thinks of our great romantic precursors, it is to remember them as flawed. There is no total romantic achievement like Goethe's, both scientific and poetic, echoing down the English decades. Blake, we say, was mad; Shelley politically naive; Wordsworth celebrated only his fading vision; Byron was a poseur, and Coleridge — potentially the great theorist of a romantic revolution socially, politically and psychologically — a magnificent ruin haunted by the ghosts of enthralling conversations. As Harold Bloom puts it: 'the program of Romanticism . . . demands something more than a natural man to carry it through. Enlarged and more numerous senses are necessary, an enormous virtue of Romantic poetry clearly being that it not only demands such expansion but begins to make it possible, or at least attempts to do so . . .' Bloom though, then complains: 'The man prophesied by the Romantics is a central man, and though his major poems perhaps have been written, he has not as yet fleshed out his prophesy, nor proved the final form of his love.'[7] This is because it was for Science to 'flesh out his prophesy', and it has, in its 'morbid' aspect, failed us all.

It was exactly this search for the fleshing-out of science that drew Coleridge as a young man to Germany. His interest was in animal magnetism, natural magnetism, hypnotism and galvanism.

It was then the current romantic position that electricity was the spark of life itself. One remembers that in Mary Shelley's *Frankenstein*, lightning was the creature's father. For the great

German Romantic Novalis the galvanic current was 'a higher consciousness of Nature — of the soul of Nature.' It was an 'inner light' and the use and understanding of electricity, which pervaded the universe, would bring back the Golden Age. Schelling, the romantic nature-philosopher, identified the principle of life with an ethereal and electrical fluid. 'How,' he asks, 'is it possible to explain why animals take fright when the atmosphere is charged with electricity, or why experiments with animal electricity meet with greater success during thunderstorms, without assuming the existence of an invisible fluid that permeates both the organic world and inorganic matter and fuses them into one living whole?'[8] This universal fluid to him was the soul of nature and the creative ether. Life was seen by the German Romantic 'as a sort of cosmic circuit in which individual organisms interrupt the current and intensify it . . .'[9]

The Romantic physician and philosopher G. H. Schubert asserted that the solar plexus was the organ of intuitive knowledge. It appeared that people in the mesmeric trance were sometimes able to see without eyes, even to read books held over the solar plexus. This organ to Schubert was the link between the universal ether and the individual. It invested humans with a synaesthetic sixth sense able to transcend space and time, analogous with the instincts of animals. Tatar says, 'This new mode of perception, mediated by the ethereal fluids in which eighteenth century scientists bathed the universe, allowed man to establish communication with the entire world.' To Anton Mesmer, this fluid transmitted the therapeutic influence of the planets. It was in continuum with the healing powers of the universe, and was the same animal magnetism which flowed from accumulator tubs in his therapeutic salons from person to person, from magnetiser to subject, curing, it seemed, many ills in its wake. As Tatar remarks: 'Mesmerism does not, however, serve only the special needs of the medical world and the occult community. For German poets the trance took on the character of a mental state charged with revelation. Though deprived of sight, mesmerist mediums seemed to experience a moment of enlightenment; they were endowed with a higher vision — with insight in its literal and figurative meaning. The venerable theme of blindness and insight (as expressed in the works of Sophocles,

Shakespeare and Goethe) and the time-honoured motif of darkness and illumination in mystical thought supported the sacred character of such visions.'[10]

A modern romantic-Gnostic poet, Reverdy, describes the insight vividly: 'One no longer perceives a thing in isolation, but in its relations with other things, and these relations between things, among themselves are as well as with us, form the web, at once highly tenuous and solid, of an immense, profound and fragrant reality!' Nerval puts it as follows: 'How, I wondered, have I been able to exist for so long outside of Nature, without identifying with her? All things live, all things act, all things correspond: the magnetic rays which emanate from me or others travel without hindrance across the infinite main of created things, the world is embraced by a transparent network'.[11] Here too is the romantic nature-philosopher Schleiermacher: 'You lie directly in the bosom of the finite world, in that moment you are its soul. Through one part of your nature you feel, as your own, all its powers and its endless life. In that moment it is your body; you pervade, as your own, its muscles and members, and your thinking and forecasting set its inmost nerves in motion.'[12]

Dorothy Emmet says, '. . . the heart of Coleridge's philosophical interest lay in trying to understand the powers he found operating in his own mind, especially in creative work. Then he tried to see these powers as co-natural . . . with powers of life and growth in nature . . . seeing the same powers at work in the mind and in nature beyond the mind . . .'[13] The mesmeric fluid, with its entrancement and apparently enhanced powers and perception, seemed to meet the bill. Blumenbach, one of the foremost physiologists in Europe, was lecturing on the subject in Göttingen. In this breeding-ground of romantic ideas, Coleridge might reasonably have expected to find a complete theoretical justification for his own poetic vision of nature, and become strengthened in it thereby. If the magnetic fluid was the directly experienced continuum between man and nature, and there really was, as his friend Wordsworth had declared, a ground of being — 'something far more deeply interfused,/Whose dwelling is the light of setting suns . . .' and when one felt in touch with 'nature's moods' (as in William Golding's moon-phased meditation on the rock pool) one was perceiving a universal movement, like an intelligible spirit, and not merely projecting a physiological sense of well- or ill-being. 'The sudden charm, which accidents of light and shade, which moonlight or sunset diffused over a known and familiar landscape', was a pleasant experience, but if it implied also the involvement of a subtle physical force, then it was both scientific and poetic knowledge together.

Unfortunately, when Coleridge arrived, he found that Blumenbach was now a total sceptic in all matters concerning hypnotism. John Beer remarks, 'After the German visit, certainly, the atmosphere which one associates with some of Coleridge's previous poetry does not recur with its old power. The effect is not totally disastrous, but there is an absence of the former 'entrancement' which does not seem to have been directly willed by the poet himself.' The magnetic sympathies that were so much a part of the poet's life evidently had no objective basis in fact, according to the age.

Much later on, when Coleridge had already invested heavily in theoretical conjecture that omitted the evidence of hypnotism and direct communication of human with nature, Blumenbach recanted, and affirmed his belief in hypnotic phenomena. Coleridge's interest was re-awakened and he wrote an addition to his *The Eolian Harp*:

O! the one life within us and abroad,
Which meets all motion and becomes its soul,
A light in sound, a sound-like power in light,
Rhythm in all thought, and joyance every where . . .

but it is arguable that the magnetic fire in crucial years had been quenched. John Beer paints a picture of the contrast between the Coleridge who walked and talked with Keats in 1819 and his earlier self in creative companionship with Wordsworth in 1797. 'Instead of a bright-eyed eager young man, from whom such ideas issued in continuous bursts, he was listening to a stately, rather sad figure, walking at his alderman-after-dinner plate. Yet still from the darkling depths of that consciousness there proceeded a flow of ideas which struck home to the imagination.'[14] That conversation undoubtedly had important consequences in the poetry of Keats, but if the fire of romantic revolution was out, it was a result of the morbid side of science, for Blumenbach had refused even to explore the field.

Perhaps if we go to its hale and healthy side, science may at last make amends — if we side-step its concealed motivation and jealousies which I have suggested are malevolently unconscious. That is to say, with Novalis, that the process of renewal begins *when the spirit of poetry solves the riddle of the sphinx.*

## References
1 Davy (1965) p106
2 Brown (1959) pp208, 210
3 Lehrs (1958) pp34-5
4 Brown (1959) pp276-7
5 Lehrs (1958) pp135,154
6 Golding (1984)
7 Bloom (1970)
8 Tatar (1978) pp68-9
9 Blackall (1983) p145
10 Tatar *ibid* pp13 and 77
11 Cardinal (1981) pp 161-2
12 Reardon(1985) pp4-5
13 Beer (1974) p167
14 Beer (1977) pp221, 281

## Bibliography
Davy, Charles, 1965. *Words in the Mind,* London. Chatto and Windus, 1965
Brown, Norman O., 1959. *Life Against Death,* London, Sphere Books, 1968
Lehrs, Ernst, 1958, *Man or Matter,* London, Faber and Faber. 1958
Golding, William, 1984, *Nobel Lecture.* Leamington Spa. Nobel Lecture, 1984
Bloom, Harold (Ed.), 1970, *Romanticism and Consciousness,* New York, W W Norton, 1970
Tatar, Maria M., 1978, *Spellbound,* Princeton University Press, 1978
Blackall, Eric A., 1983, *The Novels of the German Romantics,* Ithaca and London, Cornell University Press, 1983
Cardinal, Roger, 1981. *Figures of Reality,* London, Crom Helm, 1981

Reardon, Bernard M.G., 1985, *Religion in the Age of Romanticism*, Cambridge University Press, 1985

Beer, John, 1974, *Coleridge's Variety*, London Macmillan, 1974

Beer, John, 1977, *Coleridge's Poetic Intelligence*. London. Macmillan, 1977

## 17. Pagan Survivals

### 1. May Day at Padstow

May Day at Padstow is a fertility rite that signals and arouses the energies of summer fertility both in the earth and in human beings.

It may seem foolish to recount this, but the first time I saw the Oss dying and coming to life again I was amazed to find that I was crying. Tears were spurting from my eyes like a child. And this was happening to the person I was with as well. I realised that what was going on at that festival was something that had never happened for me as a boy in church where they tell you it should. If I talk about it as a holy experience, everyone will dismiss it as religiose. But if I talk about it as a *whole* experience, in which the four sides of myself . . . thought, feeling, sensation and intuition . . . were imaginatively participating . . . well, these are the most important experiences in people's lives.

Padstow is joyous. It's a celebration of the beginning of summer, and you suddenly feel those energies present. The shadow of the energies is there, of course, in the darkness of the Oss's mask, and in his death. But he rises again.

In times past we are told that the dancer inside the Oss used to carry a tar-brush. As he danced he would catch young women, dressed in white, and take them under the Oss to mark them with the tar-brush. This would be a sign of their fertility. Today the dancer occasionally takes women under the Oss, but I don't think he carries a tar-brush.

Rumours and accounts have it that in former times everyone would go up to the woods on May Day Eve to collect their cowslips and green boughs and they would make love together. And nobody ever knew who the fathers were to any children that resulted. I don't know whether any of this is true, but it's what I've been told happened.

*How did the Padstow Festival originate?*

Nobody knows. One of the things I noticed about the great mask and the music is that they look and sound African, and indeed there have been traders from Africa to this Cornish coast for millenniums past. The Phoenicians came here 4,000 years ago. Perhaps the form of the festival came from Africa, but who can tell?

Before the Civil War all England had its hobby horses and Cornwall was a thriving centre of this kind of thing. There used to be a great abbey church in Penryn, near Falmouth, called Glasney, and at the time of the Dissolution of the Monasteries it was savagely razed to the ground. The terms of the indictment spoke of 'pagan practices and Obby Osses'.

*Implying that the Church would also have objected to Padstow?*

Yes. They might well have called it Satanism or witchcraft. But Padstow survived all this. It's not a Victorian revival as some of these things are.

*What was the essence of this experience for you?*

Everyone has the kind of experience when trivial everyday life deepens and seems more solid and important. Sometimes this comes with ecstatic or religious intensity, and sometimes as mere contentment. And these are the most highly sought-after experiences. Half of one's life may be lived in a state of anxiety and shallowing tension, but the experience of Padstow tunes us in to more complete levels of experience. It gave me a deep feeling of energy, harmony and contentment. A most extraordinary recognition of something I'd wanted for a long time which came on me quite unawares.

*Can you describe the experience?*

There's no sense of time or evolution there. Nor does there need to be. There is energy everywhere: the energy of opposites. Life and death are simultaneously present as the Oss dances, dies, resurrects, dances . . . and past and future are simultaneously present as we celebrate crossing the threshold from spring to summer. I felt the energy of achieved renewal and it was familiar because it is the kind of state of psyche from which we began.

Padstow is like a waking dream, when everything that is necessary is simultaneously present.

Dreams have a sequence of exposition rather than a temporal sequence, in that the dreamer will alter time according to the dream's purpose. But the deepest kind of dreams have no time at all. They're simply time turned into space. And they go below the various levels of personal history, like yesterday or childhood; into a realm where you meet with imagery that is not personal at all, but universal.

Now, this is also the nature of ritual: one has come into the dream time where all important matters are simultaneously and eternally present. At Padstow all the important things that we need to know are present: the dream is very deep and very still because the ritual has been so much the same for so many years.

*Do you value dream time more than the time of waking life?*

No. We're creatures of both worlds, aren't we? To live wholly we have to give each world access to the other. The old legends in Cornwall say that the gods need us as much as we need the gods. As though we bring that other world into manifestation for some purpose.

*This other world that you are talking about it sounds as though you see it as something more than my or your own personal unconscious.*

Yes. Another word for it is the Implicate Order.

*What is the Implicate Order?*

I think that the experiences of timelessness, or the simultaneous present, that we have in dreams (or at festivals, in poetry, or art) are a close reflection of that reality which quantum mechanics is beginning to envisage for us as an objective reality.

The physicist David Bohm has suggested a picture of reality of the universe in which every particle, energy and entity, is simultaneously implicated with every other one. There is a space/time continuum without past or future, where everything is present at once. Although this vision has not been accepted by all physicists, it has been the subjective experience through the ages of those we call mystics.

The simultaneity of this underlying structural reality, the Implicate Order, unfolds in our day to day experience into the 'common-sense' sequential time that we normally experience in the Explicate Order.

*So you're suggesting that a festival like Padstow gives us access from this 'explicate' world to a greater reality beyond?*

Yes, the Oss opens a door to that other world where all time is simultaneously present. It's a symbol reaching into the Implicate Order.

## 2. Effigy Burning

The Lewes Festival in November is near the start of the old Celtic year, which begins in darkness. It's close to Hallowe'en and All Souls' Eve, and it seems like a procession of the ghosts of the past. It's as though the dead are coming back as we enter the night of winter, because everyone is dressed up as figures of the past, including ghosts.

But the bonfires show that even though the sun is going, we have the ability to make fire and keep ourselves warm.

*It seemed as if the dressing-up was giving us successive layers of British history, which were falling all over the place in a very incoherent, dreamlike association, like a kind of collective unconscious of Britishness.*

Yes. And you go down through similar strata in dreaming, from the personal to the collective, but Lewes is still very confused, still wondering about itself, still evolving. Unlike Padstow which, as we've said, was a very deep, still dream, Lewes seemed like a kind of half-way house where there is both time and non-time.

*What did you think about the underlying violence at Lewes? The blowing up and burning of effigies?*

Perhaps it's better to burn effigies than actual people. It's as though the festival gives people a chance to purify themselves by getting rid of their anger.

*Don't you feel there's a difference between burning effigies of living politicians, like Michael Foot and Neil Kinnock, and burning effigies of dead people, whether it's Guy Fawkes or the Pope?*

I didn't much care for the blowing up of Foot and Kinnock. This seems to be doing nothing but raising anger, raising up spirits against the living.

But the burning of the sixteenth-century Pope seemed more powerful. It was more like conversation. If you burn effigies of dead people, you're bringing them back for what they can give you, then you send them away again. That is, in psychological terms, you are conversing with a part of yourself that is not conscious in order to relate to it.

Everybody likes to believe that they are pure and shining white and they don't want to be nasty to anyone. This attitude of course casts a very dark shadow in front of you. If you pretend that the shadow doesn't exist and that you're incapable of horrible acts, these capacities are still in you but they're going to work unconsciously. But if you relate to your bestiality, if you converse with your shadow and know the horror within you, then it is less likely to go out of control. If you know your dark side you have a fair chance of being human.

Burning the Pope at Lewes perhaps is a way of conversing with our shadow. The basis of the Christian religion is similar. We bring back our God every year to be killed again. God is crucified and this is the worst thing that can possibly be done. Yet he resurrects and we are forgiven. Likewise, the Oss is brought back year after year to dance, die and resurrect.

Now, if the hatred is personal, like the burning of Foot and Kinnock, there may be no 'resurrection'. But if the images are ritualised, as they are with Jesus, Guy Fawkes and the sixteenth-century Pope, the whole thing is seen as trans-personal, and the energies that are released in us are healthy.

*Is there some resistance to outsiders coming to festivals?*

I'm sure there is at Padstow, and should he. These things can be so easily de-natured, spoilt and lost.

*And if we're pointing a camera at them . . .*

I can't speak for them, but they might feel that you were trying to steal the soul of the Oss.

*Do you think we would be?*

You might be doing yourselves a disfavour by putting the experience just into a camera. You might be too concerned with your filming to participate.

## 3. Men, Menstruation and the Moon

*Why has the moon been associated with women in so many cultures?*

The moon measures out in the heavens four phases of seven days each which make a lunar month. This regularity can be observed by anyone who looks up at the sky and it must have been one of mankind's first timekeepers. What must also have been observed from earliest times is the connection of this measure with human fertility; the lunar cycle and a woman's average menstrual cycle are both twenty-eight days long. In fact early moon calendars have been found with intervals marked with menstrual blood, which was the sign of fertility.

The moon isn't the only thing in nature that we respond to. We respond to the sun and the seasons, day and night. We have many inner clocks, but one of these in women does seem to be a moon clock. This connection has been much disputed, but it seems likely that the womb responds to the moon as it changes the earth's electro-magnetic field in its monthly orbit of approach and retreat. This is the weather of the universe.

In ancient times this would have seemed magical: not only did women give birth to children, but they had this connection with the moon in the skies. They became like a walking moon on earth.

*Do you see this as magical?*

Yes. A woman carries round in herself this extraordinary power that men don't have: the capacity to have children. This is the first and original magic: without it there would be no people, and, for us, no world.

This power of childbearing is signalled by menstruation. The relationship of menstruation to conception and childbearing is traditionally this: a woman produces an egg; if it's fertilised it can grow into a complete human being; if it is not, it can release the energy that would have made the human being into the woman's body for her own use.

This is the traditional view and it seems to be close to the truth.

What has happened in our culture is that the exquisite sensitivity and charging of the body that occurs at the menstrual time has been shut away from the woman herself.

*And men have done the shutting away?*

Yes. By ignoring it, treating it as an illness, as madness, or as the 'curse'.

*Why?*

Throughout recorded history men have been jealous of any power, and women are born with this power. Anything full of power in this way is dangerous, which is why men have made it taboo.

We find the menstrual taboo buried in fairy tales, and in some it gets very beautiful and direct treatment. One of the clearest is 'The Sleeping Beauty'.

You will remember that twelve fairies were invited by the king to the christening of his daughter, the princess. But there was also a thirteenth, the wicked fairy, who was not invited. So she put a 'curse' on the child: that on her tenth birthday the princess would prick her finger on a distaff and bleed. And everyone in the castle would fall asleep for a hundred years.

So to avoid the curse the king ordered all the spinning wheels in the land to be destroyed.

But on her tenth birthday the princess entered a secret chamber in the castle where she discovered an old woman spinning. And of course she pricked her finger, which bled. Everyone fell asleep for a hundred years while a high wall of thorns grew up around the castle. Then a magical prince cut his way through the thorns and woke the princess with a kiss.

Bruno Bettleheim, in his *Uses of Enchantment*, shows how menstruation is the female, or fairy's 'curse'; and it is plain that had the king not tried to keep the princess from puberty, the bleeding would have been no curse at all. He was denying her her rite of passage. Why thirteen fairies? Because the solar, father's year, is divided into twelve months, while the woman's year of experience is divided into thirteen periods, since twenty-eight days is the traditional length of the menstrual cycle. To forget this, to forget the thirteenth fairy, is to bring on a curse. Bettleheim believes that:

> The story of Sleeping Beauty impresses on every child that a traumatic event, such as a girl's bleeding at the beginning of puberty, and later, in first intercourse, does have the happiest consequences. The story implants the idea that such events must be taken very seriously, but that one need not be afraid of them. The 'curse' is a blessing in disguise.

A rite of passage is a way of travelling from one condition of life to another without losing consciousness.

Festivals are rites of passage that initiate us through thresholds of the year: from spring to summer at Padstow, or summer to winter at Lewes. But there are also rites of passage for the initiation of a person into a new stage life. For example, in some cultures, the young woman who starts to menstruate is initiated into her new capacity to become a mother, if she is to bear children, or a shaman or magician if she is not. Unfortunately our society has no such initiations, or rites of passage, for either men or women, we enter new stages of life with no image of our capacities, save those provided for us by the mass media.

Similarly, there is no sense of threshold, no understanding of what a person may experience symbolically in a ritual for them to enter the menopause.

*What are the consequences for us of having no rites of passage?*

There will always be an interior initiation. A person approaching a crisis or threshold in their life will have dreams which symbolically reveal possibilities and ideas for conduct. If there is no ritual there will still be these experiences spontaneously in dreams. I believe it's necessary to encourage and amplify these dreams, to converse with them. If we study our dreams we provide these rites of passage for ourselves.

*What about women who don't experience menstruation positively?*

A lot of women don't, and perhaps this is the result of the shutting away, as it becomes painful instead. We don't yet know. It's only just now, when women are beginning to share their experience in this neglected quarter, at the real answers are emerging. One of these is that menstruation is a time of positive resource rather than an illness.

*What do you think men can learn from menstruation?*

The menstrual cycle is a 'feeling' thing, but men don't see this because we live in a masculine non-feeling culture. Feelings are left to the women to exercise.

Yet the most important thing for anybody to understand is that what happens inside another person is a reality, however different it may be from your own reality.

The events of the menstrual cycle are among the foremost things that happen to people. In a household where a woman has a powerful menstrual cycle, there's a bodily, sexual and mental rhythm set up between the two poles of ovulation and menstruation.

I believe that men can gain great enhancement in their relationships with themselves and with women by acknowledging and attending to this rhythm instead of ignoring it. By seeing what actually happens.

*What is your own experience here?*

Penelope, whom I live with, no longer suffers from menstrual distress. In the premenstrual time she now becomes full of an extraordinary imaginative and sexual energy. She experiences upsurges of energy which do not distress her any more. And she uses these creatively.

*But how does this affect you?*

I have these cycles of dreams which come to a creative resolution actually at the period. During the premenstrual week I have very strong inchoate creative impulses which are rehearsed in my dreams. I can start a piece of creative work, say a play or some psychological work, at the beginning of the month, and the solution will come with Penelope's period. Our daughter Zoë also has these dreams which I can describe as a lability of feeling in the premenstrual week.

*Don't you think that many women would object to being defined simply by their childbearing capacities?*

Yes. And it's something that the world's great religions have done. But I am not saying this. All I am saying is that the womb is an extremely powerful and magical organ and it's foolish to ignore these capacities. A woman's womb gives her two sides: ovulation, when she has the possibility of being the person who conceives a child, and menstruation, when she can be her own self, using her energy for imaginative and creative tasks, or withdrawing to the quietness of contemplation (a special 'sacred' time which in our culture there is no provision for).

This dialectic runs through interior life. It is the pattern for our humanity, yet it's something which the male culture has lost.

*What about men who don't have intimate relationships with women? Do gay men somehow bypass the menstrual taboo and all its problems?*

Every man has a relationship with at least one woman and that's his mother. A man can find perhaps that something cyclical in his nature has been established in him in childhood. Something which comes and goes in his energy which resembles the menstrual rhythm, and is perhaps picked up from his mother's attitude to her menstruation. Now if his mother, as is all too frequent, hated herself because she had periods which she'd been taught were dirty, nasty and taboo, then this hatred and suspicion would be passed on to the boy and the man.

There is something which psychology has hardly touched yet which we might call the 'menstrual trauma' in men. When his mother has her periods she may be full of emotions that are strongly loving and energetic but which have no form of expression because of the taboo of menstruation not being allowed for in the family. For the boy, who is representative of masculine culture, this is a great puzzle: he is both feared and rejected as representative of the culture that taboos menstruation, but he is loved and desired as the child in the flux of emotions at this powerful 'feeling' time. This contradiction is the menstrual trauma which boys pass through but don't understand. It becomes something about one's childhood history which is concealed.

My mother suffered most terribly from her periods. I remember how the whole house would be charged with an awful anger and I didn't know why this was. Why was my father alienated? Why did my mother knock things over and swear, saying, 'Hell's Bells and Buckets of Blood!' She had these energies in her anger but she treated her period as if it were a mad, awful thing not to be spoken about. It was something about her that she didn't like but which was important to her. And she didn't like it because she'd been brought up not to like it. I would ask why she felt like that and she'd say, 'It's a woman's time of the month.' But what was the meaning of this special vehemence she was filled with?

And then, when she calmed from her rages, she would tell the most marvellous stories, which I now think came from her dreams. And this has been found by women who have made studies of menstruation: that it's a special time for the imagination, for discovering images which are important and lifegiving.

*Do you think you've missed something in not being a woman?*

I think so, yes. The direct experience of growing a person inside yourself must be extraordinary, and a man can only have a shadow of this. This is moon envy! Yes, I think that if I could have a child I would.

*You seem to be suggesting that men can only get access to certain of life's fundamental energies and resources in a secondary fashion, as it were, through the mediation and example of women. Isn't there a danger of confining women to the traditionally feminine through a kind of idealisation? While at the same time men become some kind of inferior beings?*

Yes and no. Men and women are all faced with the problem of gender roles. When we're children it's as if we are both sexes, but as we move towards puberty, we divide, becoming a man or a woman.

But that doesn't mean to say the rest is lost. It goes underground and becomes an unconscious counter-sexual figure. For the woman there is a male dream person in her, which Jungians call her animus. And for the man, a female dream person, his anima. So the same person is both masculine and feminine, and needs to find the balance.

Many men have a strong feminine moon side, and they can discover this when they see that their dreaming patterns are influenced by the moon. But many men do not, and to get this magical capacity they have to learn from women.

The experience of women is that they return again and again to this life necessity which is required of them by their wombs. And menstruation is such a strong thing that it's too much for many women to deal with, especially when they are given no image in our culture to deal with it. Whereas women seem to be more able to transmit life's energies, men are more like a reflecting mirror to existence.

*Do you think that men experience time in a more linear way through not experiencing the menstrual cycle?*

Yes. Men tend to think as the sun thinks, in solar time. The sun doesn't change or alter its shape. It simply rises, goes across the heavens, and sets. The intellectual masculine culture is a solar culture in that it thinks only in the light. But the moon ebbs and flows. It is both light and darkness. In letting the dark in it's an alternative to the culture we have.

Men's time seems to be in straight lines, directed towards an object or a project. The great example is the Christian example, which I think is the man's view: the whole world started with Genesis; we had original sin in the Garden of Eden, from which point we go straight through to the Last Judgment where everything is settled.

Whereas for women, time is more a spiral, a re-circling. I was very impressed by the image of the spider's web that the women put on the wire at Greenham Common. The spider is something which people are afraid of, an image of catching and devouring, but the Greenham women have made this image of a web which is not just straight lines, but the covering of a view.

Thought moves in time, and the way we think embodies how we think about time. The Greenham women say we will go from this point to that point, seeing what is important, going here, going there, and then we will knit it together in a spiral. It is an interaction, a hologram.

There was also a slogan on the wire at Greenham which read: 'Warfare is disguised Menstruation', and it seems to be the case that the cultures that wage war most strongly are those which have the strongest taboos against menstruation. Our culture, which is the most bellicose in history, has either a very violent language of slang words against menstruation, or complete silence. On the other hand, there are cultures which honour women more, and which don't have such strong sexual and menstrual taboos. And these tend to be more peaceful and less likely to wage war.

## 18. Am I a Pagan?

## Interview with *Pagan Voice*

P.V.: Background — how did you become interested in the esoteric etc. — would you call yourself a Pagan now?

P.R.: The esoteric found me. My mother seemed to tell me that she had at least attended a magical circle. She appeared ashamed of this, and said she didn't like it. She was very fond of the words 'Sphinx' and 'atavism'. At that time she was trying to get pregnant with me, and took lovers to open her womb, since it was not responding to my male parent's desire for a child. There was a sinister male lover she told me about who seemed to be a magician. She would have experienced rather than studied for this circle, and might have attended for a fertility ritual only. There was certainly a group in Richmond near where she lived in 1931. Alternatively if she was already pregnant she may have attended a group that specialised in waking the child, rather than the egg in the womb, to awareness. This could also have been done by ritual intercourse with the magician lover. At any rate there was something done around that time that made her both ashamed and exhilarated and had to do with magickal adventures. Many mothers talk to their child in the womb waking, or visit it in dreams, like going to one's own alchemical laboratory or temple within the womb. I think she visited me then, as many mothers do, with or without benefit of magick.

In the house in Kingston I was very aware of her female rhythms. She became transformed just before her period into something wild with staring eyes and startling hair, a virago, swearing bloodily. Then, when the period arrived, her bedroom was taboo and darkened with the curtains drawn, and there was a wonderful smell on the landing of ripe plums.

I inherited from her a desire to run wild in nature. I was a Wild Man, joining myself with water and earth and trees. I remember inching out of the house in the small hours so as not to wake my parents, to lie on the earth or in the water under the stars. The penalties for being caught would have been terrible in this middle-class household just post-war, would have included being diagnosed as schizophrenic (which actually happened to me later), but I couldn't help myself. These were profound erotic experiences.

Then, much later, during the end of my first marriage, I met a great Pagan or heretic disguised as an analytical psychologist anthropologist and pupil of Jung called John Layard. He was my god-father, and showed me the meaning of my wilder side, and dreams. My godmother was a Wise Woman accidentally encountered. She gave me sex, and was bleeding. In her cunt I saw a vision of her womb, as an amphora with handles, a loving-cup, or the Horned God. This image appeared as a logo on the cover of the first edition of *The Wise Wound* and had been a guide to me in writing my parts of the book. This Wise Woman, *Fravishi* or 'Spirit of the Way' (I think she said she was a Sufi) told me that I must read two special books: one was Dion Fortune's *Mystical Qabala* and the other Bakan's *Freud and the Jewish Mystical Tradition*. She was right — both of these books prepared me for what was coming. This vision during intercourse was what Barbara Walker calls a *horasis* and I wrote about this in *The Black Goddess*. I had also experienced *horasis* the first time I made love to a woman: a profound stillness came into my head and into that stillness my first poem. You will be able to judge from this whether I am a pagan or not.

P.V.: What/who inspires/has inspired you?

P.R.: Let me quote Robert Kelly: 'The frustration and shame in alchemy comes, as in all else, with the sense that one's sentience is not matched because one is not sentient enough . . .' In sexual alchemy one approaches an adequate sentience, and the horasis has a lunar-feminine rhythm. Levels are breached. It streams. If I am a Pagan, I may be a Pelagian, as I do not believe in a Fall. The Fall, so far as I can see, was the concealing of the bountiful women's mysteries (linked to the menstrual cycle) from the whole world and the women themselves by the patriarchate. Certain thoughts inspire me, such as 'What is here, is elsewhere. What is not here, is nowhere' and 'Matter is visible spirit, spirit invisible matter.' Are these Pagan beliefs? In which case I share them. I believe also in the strictly literal sense that we became human when Black Mother Eve breached the levels and learnt the mysteries of the Rainbow Serpent. True humanity began in some exquisite apprehension of an inner time — the fertility cycle — which was or became identical with the moon's time. We suggested this in *The Wise Wound* but now the social anthropologist Chris Knight has confirmed that in the strictest scientific terms it is actually true. His book called *Blood Relations* shows how *actual* paganism is.

We came to write *The Wise Wound* because Penelope Shuttle was experiencing near-suicidal PMS. We analysed her dreams and found that the whole cycle told the story of a descent and return, and with the help of the dream images of this she was able to travel the menstrual-ovulation thresholds with insight rather than menstrual distress. We did not look up any menstrual psychology books so as not to prejudice the exploration. I then asked the College Librarian for books on menstrual psychology. There must be a lot of information, we reasoned, as 50% of the world menstruates. But it turned out, astonishingly, that there were no such books. So we had to write our own, as a thank-offering.

There was a Labour Government in when it was first published; the left-wing literati were very open to ideas then. It was satisfying and extraordinarily gratifying to us that our ideas were accepted both by the literati and by people practicing traditional forms of magic, or who were in the Craft. People practiced in the fertility rituals of ovulation seemed to find further areas behind these opening up, into the mysteries of menstruation, which seemed to have been partially lost or neglected due to the taboo. The gateholder here may be the Goddess Sekhmet, patroness of Day 21, angry for her unconceived children, who consents to transform and transmit altered energies with the blood of the period. If this is so, then she offers a rite of passage at the time of turmoil when the egg is dying yet the fertility hormones are running high, and the womb not yet sending out its alternative menstrual energies (ovulating is an ovarian event, menstruation a womb event — which is perhaps why I saw a womb-shape in my Fravishi's organ of touch-vision). Our book reflected an existing Current which has strengthened since the first publication in 1978.

P.V.: How do you see the poetic process as a mechanism of self-discovery? What about the work of Robert Graves in this respect?

P.R.: The poetic process also breaches the levels. I use the right-brain, left-brain model, though recent research shows that women have a greater spread than men do of nerve-fibres through the brain that connect the hemispheres. If you think of composing the music of a song and at the same time trying to find the words you have a picture of right and left brains co-operating, and from this a wholeness arrives which is both the subject of the poem and what the poem does to the reader. Poems which do not produce the magical state are useless and so are readers who resist this magical state. George Whalley says 'In Poetic, sight can be converted into sound and texture and even scent; single words can assume physical shape, contour, fibre; groups of words may take on meanings not implied by their grammatical relations; savour, aroma, cachet may be conveyed in texture and rhythm.' This is magical experience.

Robert Graves is first rate. His book shows the whole world of trees alive, and naming itself. This was our foundation. His White Goddess was the fertility goddess of the full moon. He spoke of her presiding over the One Theme — the death and rebirth of the poet. We became interested in her complementary, the Black Goddess. We saw this in terms of everyday contemporary life which was yet magical. It is the woman's psyche which descends and returns altered in the monthly cycle. A male partner can with her help follow and participate in this rhythm in daily and dream-life, rediscovering the archetypes at first hand, using, if they wish, magickal techniques.

We ourselves have practised this method of resonating male/female for many years. Call it (alchemically) the Double Pelican. I worked as a psychotherapist and for two decades have been gathering information and imparting it as far as possible to people like ourselves who had been brought up out of touch with this basic human magical rhythm. Many of my clients who went through the menstrual month with their eyes open to their dreams found a new life, as I did.

The political implications are enormous. The images of

the dreams are the images of the ancient woman cultures, recovered in the individual person. It means that people can act in accordance with them and in continuum with nature, which inspires and modulates the female rhythms. Through these images and ritual acts imparted by a full knowledge of the menstrual cycle, knowledge and sympathy with the earth and all its doings is known feelingly. Inner and outer merge and exchange. Once this unity has been experienced directly, it is impossible not to be Green. The basis of knowledge is understood to be female, and political action follows.

P.V.: How do you see 'the gods', 'the god(dess)' etc.?

P.R.: The Gods: the Moon, the Rainbow Snake, the Black Goddess, the White Goddess, their images are recreated in the dream-state and other states of unity. The images are the visual aspect of something that is happening at once to all the senses, as in the poetic state. I believe we are meant to dream them afresh. Blake says 'The ancient Poets animated all sensible objects with Gods or Geniuses, calling them by the names and adorning them with the properties of woods, rivers, mountains, lakes, cities, nations, and whatever their enlarged and numerous senses could perceive . . .' And Kelly again: 'Our intelligence is dumb before the divine intelligences that sweep through the atmosphere of this planet and our minds, like hurricanes and electrical storms'.

P.V.: Tell us more about weather sensitivity. We hear about SAD but are there more positive features of this human sense?

P.R.: I had a client who had a thunder-phobia. There was nothing in her life so far as we could see together, that would account for that. So I phoned round to the half-dozen main medical institutions — College of Psychiatrists, British Medical Association, etc. — to ask whether anybody in England was treating weather-sensitivity, as they were in Israel. Apparently nobody was. In another country there would have been treatment. Shortly after, my client died. In another age she would have been a sybil, knowing the weathers, able to predict the quality of the seasons and guide the planting and reaping of crops. 33 per cent of people have this weather-sensitivity to a clinical extent. Now the doctors have named a 'cloud syndrome' and treat it with a drug. Anybody reading this who has 'cloud syndrome' please consult a physician who is a homoeopath. One might seek to extend one's weather-sensitivity and articulate it by using the I Ching, which is a weather-oracle, and whose principles are Thunder, Mountain, Lake, Wind, Fire, Water, Sky and Earth.

I see this work on *The Wise Wound* and *The Black Goddess* (which described 'cloud syndrome' years ago) now joining a current with other people's work, and the ideas there as they flow together gaining greater currency. I would like the whole of Britain to become an enormous Moon-College with all the women dreaming their menstrual cycles into knowledge and action. I would like the ideas tested, and if they pass the tests, used. I want some physicist interested in 'psychic' phenomena to test my idea of a 'pheromone maser' (*Black Goddess*) as the physical basis of mediumship, the aura and intuitive knowledge of the cosmos. Riding the menstrual rhythms we hope to continue to testify through our poems, plays and stories, all of which have these themes as their foundations. For instance, there is my Radio 3 play ['From a View to a Haunt'] which shows the All-Ghost of the world entering the world first as haunts, then as the Padstow 'ObbyOss', one of the great pagan survivals. It is a new kind of ghost-story, with the Goddess taking new and irresistible forms among the folk we call mad.

Printed in the United Kingdom
by Lightning Source UK Ltd.
113577UKS00001B/304-345